The Uprooted Vine

The Uprooted Vine

(*Snehalata ba Palita*, 1892)

by

SWARNAKUMARI DEBI

Translated from Bengali by

RAJUL SOGANI AND INDIRA GUPTA

OXFORD

UNIVERSITY PRESS

OXFORD
UNIVERSITY PRESS

YMCA Library Building, Jai Singh Road, New Delhi 110 001

Oxford University Press is a department of the University of Oxford. It furthers the
University's objective of excellence in research, scholarship, and education
by publishing worldwide in

Oxford   New York
Auckland   Bangkok   Buenos Aires   Cape Town   Chennai
Dar es Salaam   Delhi   Hong Kong   Istanbul   Karachi   Kolkata
Kuala Lumpur   Madrid   Melbourne   Mexico City   Mumbai   Nairobi
São Paulo   Shanghai   Taipei   Tokyo   Toronto

Oxford is a registered trademark of Oxford University Press
in the UK and in certain other countries

Published in India
by Oxford University Press, New Delhi

© Oxford University Press 2004

ISBN 0 19 566502 3

Typeset in Minin in 10.5/12.7
by Excellent Laser Typesetters, Pitampura, Delhi 110 034
Printed at Pauls Press, New Delhi 110 020
Published by Manzar Khan, Oxford University Press
YMCA Library Building, Jai Singh Road, New Delhi 110 001

CONTENTS

INTRODUCTION

*S*warnakumari Debi (1855[1]–1932), the fourth daughter of Maha-rishi Debendranath Tagore and the elder sister of Rabindranath Tagore was a writer of great talent who made her mark as one of the earliest women writers in Bengal. Though a few women had attempted to write poetry and novels before her, their works lacked the maturity evident in her writings. She was born at a time when, under the impact of Western education, a wave of modernity was sweeping over Bengal, and her family was at the forefront of this new awakening. Swarnakumari Debi received her early education at home and began to show literary promise by composing verses and writing stories at a very young age. On 17 November 1867, at the age of thirteen she was married to Janakinath Ghoshal, a gentleman of refined tastes and liberal views. He was a deputy magistrate who became a prominent member of the Indian National Congress. They had a happy conjugal life and Janakinath encouraged Swarnakumari Debi to develop her intellectual and literary powers and take an active interest in the social and political movements of the time. Even after her marriage she remained in close touch with her paternal family, staying for long periods in the house at Jorasanko and taking part in their intellectual and cultural activities. Her brother Jyotindranath Tagore, an ardent theatre-lover, encouraged her to write plays to be enacted in their home on different occasions. She participated in these activities with enthusiasm and wrote tragedies, comedies, musicals, and interludes for the family theatre. She was the most prolific writer in the Tagore household after Rabindranath.

Her first historical novel *Deep Nirban* was published anonymously in 1877.[2] It was reviewed favourably in several journals and the discovery that the author was a woman created a sensation. *Deep Nirban* was followed by many other works.[3] Her novel *Phuler Mala* was translated into English as *The Fatal Garland* and published in *The Modern Review* in 1910. Her own English translation of *Kahake* was published in England as *An Unfinished Song* by T. Werner Laurie.[4] It was reviewed favourably in several British journals as an authentic picture of Indian life and went into a second edition in 1914.[5] A collection of fourteen of her short stories was also translated into English and the play *Dibya Kamal* was translated into German as *Princess Kalyani*.

Swarnakumari Debi had a keen interest in music and compiled several collections of songs, many of which she herself composed. She was also one of the earliest writers of children's literature in Bengali and wrote many books for their education and entertainment. In 1877 the Tagores launched a literary journal called *Bharati* which was initially edited by Dwijendranath Tagore. The work was passed on to Swarnakumari Debi in 1884 and she edited the journal with the assistance of her two daughters, Hiranmoyi Debi and Sarala Debi for eighteen years, from 1884 to 1895 and again from 1908 to 1915. After the death of her husband she withdrew herself from her editorial responsibilities, handing over the charge to Rabindranath Tagore. During her long association with *Bharati* she shaped the literary and cultural tastes of an entire generation of men and women. She wrote fiction, memoirs, travelogues, and essays on a wide variety of subjects, ranging from history, contemporary life, and women's emancipation to astronomy and natural sciences, in which she took a special interest, unusual for a woman of her generation. Her prose writings provide the best indication of her intellectual powers and her clear, independent thinking.

Swarnakumari Debi was associated with the political and social movements of her times. She attended the annual sessions of the Indian National Congress in 1889 and 1890 and made the acquaintance of outstanding women like Pandita Ramabai and Ramabai Ranade. She played an active role in modernizing the lifestyle of women in her family and community, bringing them out of seclusion and expanding their horizons. She started Sakhi Samiti, an association of upper-class, educated women like herself with the avowed intention of promoting goodwill among them and helping widows and destitute women. The Samiti wished to educate these women so that they could earn their livelihood by teaching girls who were still confined within their homes. In this regard Swarnakumari Debi wanted to go further than contemporary male social reformers and advocates of widow remarriage for she believed that education and financial independence were more essential for such women than marriage. Though Sakhi Samiti did not achieve much success in this project, it served its purpose as a meeting ground for women of respectable families who could come together to exchange ideas and organize cultural activities. They staged plays and held craft fairs in which the women could exhibit their talents and get recognition from others. It was a unique forum for Bengali women who had just started emerging from the seclusion of their homes to take part in larger, social activities.

Swarnakumari Debi's novels occupy an important place in the history of women's writing in India and also serve as valuable documents of the social history of nineteenth-century Bengal. They present a vivid account of life within the inner apartments of middle-class homes, the daily round of household activities, the preoccupation with rituals and festivities, the power struggles among women and also between the men and women in the family, the games and gossip sessions which provided a break in the monotony of daily life. As a member of the progressive Brahmo sect she was critical of the conventions that kept women confined to rituals and narrow, selfish concerns, particularly in the Hindu community, but she pointed out that it was women's financial and emotional dependence on men that made them weak and vulnerable and came in the way of realizing their full human potential.

The Uprooted Vine is the English translation of her Bengali social novel *Snehalata* (1892), which was brought out serially in *Bharati* between 1889 and 1891. The title was later changed to *Snehalata ba Palita* (Snehalata, or the Foster-child) when another novel by Kusum Kumari Debi with the same title appeared in 1890. In *The Uprooted Vine*, Swarnakumari Debi took up the cause of the victims of the Hindu patriarchal system, the daughters, daughters-in-law, widows, and poor dependents in the joint family who were deprived of their rights, exploited as domestic drudges, and marginalized to the extent of being denied shelter and maintenance. The protagonist Snehalata, an orphan and child widow, is driven to suicide by the callous behaviour of her own and her husband's family. Another widow, Jiban's mother, is turned out of the joint family to prevent her from claiming a share of the family property. Snehalata's sister-in-law, Kamala, dies prematurely, a victim of injustice and neglect. These women are united by a strong bond of sympathy as fellow sufferers under patriarchal oppression and represent feminine solidarity against familial tyranny.

Notwithstanding her deep sympathy for women, Swarnakumari Debi also uncovered their complicity in upholding patriarchy and exploiting it to oppress other women, weaker than themselves. In *The Uprooted Vine*, Jagat Babu' s wife and daughter are often harsh and unfair to Snehalata because they are jealous of her and see her as a threat to their power over their menfolk. They use her as a convenience, as an unpaid worker who can be cast out whenever it suits them. Snehalata's aunt-in-law, Jethima, though, herself a child-less widow, wields great power in the joint family as the heir of her husband. A harsh and domineering woman, she tyrannizes over other women in the family, for she has influential relatives to protect her interests and Kunja Babu, the head of the family, fears her and finds it convenient to treat her as an ally. She is the embodiment of patriarchal power in a female form, inimical to all those who hold a subordinate place in the family hierarchy.

Swarnakumari Debi derived her literary inspiration from Bankim Chandra Chattopadhyaya (1834–1892) and Ramesh Chandra Dutt (1848–1909) and her social novels form a bridge between Bankim Chandra and Rabindranath. She shared with Bankim Chandra a keen interest in history, an ironic vision which enabled her to expose the gap between ideals and practice or between expectations and conse-quences, an ear for racy, colloquial speech and the ability to present an argument with force and clarity. The influence of Bankim Chandra is evident in the style and structure of *The Uprooted Vine*, which closely parallels in several respects Bankimchandra's novel *Vishavriksha* (The Poison Tree, 1872), the story of a child widow, Kundanandini, whose love for Nagendranath leads to tragic consequences and her own suicide. In the sub-plot of *Vishavriksha*, another widow, Hira, is seduced and abandoned by her lover and punished for her trans-gression by losing her sanity and her place in society. Bankim Chandra was a patriarchal moralist who frowned on sexuality and independent enterprise in widows, but Swarnakumari Debi's novel subverted patriarchy in several ways, in the structure of the narrative, the delineation of characters, and in the discussions on gender relations and the status of women. In her reworking of the theme of *Vishavriksha*, she deliberately overlooked the story of Hira which demonstrates the disastrous consequences of feminine ambition. Though her protagonist Snehalata resembles Kundanandini in her meekness, her vulnerability and her tragic destiny, she is projected not as a *vishavriksha*, a poison tree who is a threat to society but as a *snehalata*, a tender creeper who ought to be cherished and not uprooted and cast away. Her death is not perceived as a retribution for transgression but as a consequence of the callousness of the social system.

Swaranakumari Debi exposes the hypocrisy and weakness of the men who love Snehalata but are unable to protect her and provide her with justice. Her guardian Jagat Babu loves her more than his own children and it is his ardent wish to keep her always with him and shield her from any pain or sorrow but he is a weak man, a procrastinator who cannot put his good intentions into practice in the face of opposition from his family. He is gullible enough to believe his wife that Snehalata has left their house voluntarily to settle down with her in-laws and even his son Charu who shows him a half-written letter by Snehalata as proof that she was trying to seduce him. When she commits suicide he convinces himself that her education was responsible for her tragedy. Charu, who professed to love her, forgets her as soon as he is married again and betrays her without any hesitation when he hears that his father wants to make Snehalata an heir to his property. Kishori, her brother-in-law is an unscrupulous villain who makes her his captive as he lusts after her person and her property but does not hesitate to turn her out of the house when he finds that he has nothing to gain from her. Jiban, her husband's cousin, adores her, but as a married man, struggling perpetually to meet the demands of his family, he cannot save her from the ultimate tragedy.

The Uprooted Vine presents a vivid picture of middle-class life in Bengal in the last quarter of the nineteenth century. The first part of the novel shows the impact of modernity on two generations of educated men, the change in their thinking, their effort to live according to the new ideals and their success or failure in that effort. The older generation is represented by Jagat Babu, a doctor by profession, whose efforts to adopt a modern way of life are described in some detail. As a schoolboy he gives up his conventional Hindu beliefs when he comes into contact with members of the Brahmo Samaj but his parents do not permit him to adopt the new faith. He wants to marry a widow and establish himself as a progressive individual but is forced to abandon the idea due to family pressures. After his marriage his main preoccupation, like that of many others in his generation, is the education of the women in his family, but his wife resists his efforts to teach her and thwarts every attempt to modernize the household, discipline his children, and give the orphaned Snehalata a fair deal in life. For all his good intentions Jagat Babu fails to put his ideals into practice and gradually comes round to believing that it is no use trying to change the system and it is better for women to remain ignorant and resign themselves to their unhappy lot.

The younger generation represented by Jiban, Charu, Nabin, and their friends is fired by the spirit of nationalism and social reform. They want to abolish those conventions and practices which hamper the progress of society, and to lift the country out of its abject political and economic state by promoting scientific education, indigenous industry, and national consciousness. However, their grandiose plans fail to materialize due to their immaturity, lack of resources and planning, and the absence of a strong leadership. Their secret club is merely a debating society which disintegrates without achieving any of their higher aims. Swarnakumari Debi treats with gentle irony the conflict between their patriotism and the pride in their culture and tradition and the desire to emulate the ideals propagated by their Western education. Ultimately Jiban has to forego his political activities and academic ambition to take up a low-paid job and marry against his wishes. Nabin, the fierce nationalist, migrates to England; Charu, the sensitive poet, settles down to a life of ease; and Kishori lives off the property left to him by his father, spending his time in reckless dissipation.

Jiban is by far the most sympathetic character in this group. He is gentle, studious, and committed to his ideals, but like Jagat Babu he lacks assertiveness and is unable to exercise any influence over his family and friends. Though Swarnakumari Debi treats him with the same irony which she reserves for the other characters in the novel, she makes him articulate some of her deeply felt beliefs about the status and rights of women.

The second part of the novel focuses on the problems of child widows, a recurrent theme in Indian social novels of the nineteenth and early twentieth centuries in the wake of social reform movement that sought to ameliorate the condition of women who were marginalized and victimized by society on account of their widowhood. Rammohun Roy (1772–1833) sought to abolish through legislation the practice of sati or the burning of widows on the pyres of their deceased husbands. Ishwarchandra Vidyasagar (1820–1891) campaigned for the remarriage of young widows, arguing that there was scriptural sanction for it. His landmark essay 'The Marriage of Hindu Widows' (1855) initiated a nationwide debate on the subject, and though widow remarriage was not generally accepted by uppercaste Hindu society, the controversy drew attention to the miserable condition of widows who were denied the right to lead a normal life, deprived of economic security, treated as inauspicious, and often exploited sexually even within the family. Most of the social novels written during the second half of the nineteenth century and the first quarter of the twentieth century form a part of the discourse on the condition of women in general and widows in particular. In *The Uprooted Vine*, Charu becomes concerned about Snehalata's lonely existence as a widow and tries to convince her about the need for a second marriage, using the arguments generally put forward by male social reformers. Snehalata finds these arguments disturbing because her faith and her upbringing have conditioned her to accept her situation and she is inclined to put other people's interests above her own. She knows that Jagat Babu's image in society would be seriously jeopardized if Charu married her. Hence, in spite of her love for Charu she is prepared to leave the house and stake her entire future security rather than opt for second marriage.

Swarnakumari Debi's answer to the problems of women like Snehalata is not remarriage, but more education and financial independence, an equal right in parental property rather than helpless dependence on selfish relatives. It is to be noted that Debendranath Thakur did not support widow remarriage and in Rabindranath's novel *Chokher Bali* (1902) which was written a decade after *Snehalata ba Palita*, the widow Binodini rejects Bihari's proposal of marriage and withdraws herself to Kashi, ostensibly renouncing worldly pleasures for spiritual ones, an option favoured by most Indian novelists. Contemporary readers may object to the fact that Swarnakumari Debi does not allow her protagonist to find a way out of her situation, to rise against her oppressors or express her anger in a positive manner. As it was written in the nineteenth century, it was not possible for her to do so without offending the sensibilities of her readers. Through her irony and authorial commentary, she protests against the unjust social system obliquely. Snehalata's suicide is an outcry against the treatment she has received from Jagat Babu's family and Charu, her beloved friend for whose sake she went into voluntary exile. The vindication of Snehalata and women like her comes from Jiban in Chapters 55 and 57 in which he argues about their moral superiority over men and makes a strong plea for their right to live with dignity and self-respect. It is in passages like these, and not in the depiction of conventional romantic scenes that the genius of Swarnakumari Debi is properly revealed.[6]

We hope the translation, which we have tried to keep as close as possible to the original, will interest our readers as an early example of women's fiction in an Indian language, which is significant not only for its thematic but also its ideological content.

Delhi   RAJUL SOGANI
March 2002   INDIRA GUPTA

The Uprooted Vine
(*Snehalata ba Palita*, 1892)

DEDICATION

Dear Milan,[7]
To gain happiness, sorrow forever strives,
Tears struggle to hide themselves in smiles,
Darkness wants to dissolve itself in light
Separation longs to be set ablaze to unite.[8]
Ah, vain is this fretfulness, false this fear
The further one seems to be, the more one draws near.
I search all around, I wonder and repine
To whom shall I offer this *Sneha*[9] of mine!
I bring it to you, dear friend,
  Pray, don't turn it down.
You may cast it aside later
  When I am not around.

PART ONE

1

*J*agatchandra Gangopadhyay is a prosperous gentleman. His father left a fortune for him and he has himself enhanced it considerably as a successful doctor. The front part of Jagat Babu's house gives sufficient indication of his wealth, but the inner apartment, which is the domain of his wife, does not give any hint of the presence of the goddess Lakshmi. The rooms in the inner apartment are small, as they generally are in any ordinary Bengali household and their décor is simple.

Let us now enter Jagat Babu's bedroom, the largest one in the house. There is a bed on one side with a sofa next to it. Facing them are two cupboards, a big and a small one, with various things heaped on top of them. In the centre of the room stands Jagat Babu's writing table. To the right is his wife's clotheshorse, next to which hangs a switch of false hair from an iron hook. On the other side is a folk painting of Krishna and Radha. There are a few more paintings on the wall and some pictures too, amongst which are two old and faded photographs of Jagat Babu and his first wife. Just below these photographs are two recesses in the wall. One of them is empty but has abundant water and oil stains. One doesn't need to be a scholar to guess that the lamp is placed here at night. There is an idol of Lakshmi in the other recess and in the left-hand corner of the room beside it there are two iron safes, covered with designs in oil and vermilion. Their flaming red colour attracts the eye at once and the mistress of the house derives great satisfaction by looking at them frequently. The duplicate keys of the smaller safe are in the possession of Jagat Babu and his wife and the key of the big safe he keeps himself.

There is also a mat which adorns the floor at present, but unlike the rest of the things, it does not occupy a permanent place there. Depending on the requirements of the inmates, it is sometimes spread out on the floor or rolled up to embellish a corner of the room. Constantly shifted from one place to another, it does not enjoy a comfortable existence. This is apparent from its frayed and shabby condition. If Jagat Babu had his way, this mat would have been relieved of its function a long time ago. He wished to have a seating arrangement on the floor with a carpet and counterpane, but things did not work out according to his wishes. His wife, known as the Mistress, who bullied him no end, was totally opposed to the idea. She declared that all this style was best suited to the women of the modern generation, and she would have none of it.

Jagat Babu had remarked, 'Why, you are not a grandmother, my dear. You also belong to the present age.'

After that Jagat Babu's wife did not speak to him for a whole week, and when he tried to placate her, she burst into such a flood of tears that Jagat Babu was nearly drowned. With great difficulty he saved himself and resolved there and then that he would never broach the subject again.

Right now the mat adorned the floor not by itself but by the presence of the four ladies who were seated on it, engaged in a game of cards. Jagat Babu's wife had a set of trumps in her hand. She gestured to her partner to move trumps. The partner acted accordingly. One of the opponents exclaimed, 'Bou[10] has given a signal to her partner. I won't let her play trumps.'

Jagat Babu's wife shook her plump body which occupied most of the space on the mat and, flashing her nosering strung with pearls, protested, 'Nonsense, I never did such a thing.'

Tagar, her eight-year-old daughter, was sitting next to her. She had been fiddling with the cards from time to time and as such had been told to leave the room. So she was sulking, and this was her chance to take revenge. She said, 'Of course, Mother, you did it just now.'

This enraged the mother and she said angrily, 'Get out of here, you hussy.'

'I will not go,' the child retorted.

The mother said, 'Have you ever seen such a cussed girl?'

Tagar was not scared of her mother. Although she scolded her frequently and even thrashed her at times, she made up immediately afterwards and indulged her so much that the child, uninitiated in the sense of right and wrong, continued to follow her own wayward impulses. These occasional outbursts of temper, apart from giving the mother an emotional release, did not benefit the child at all; rather they caused her great harm for she did not take her mother seriously, and became more and more unruly. So when her mother called her a hussy, she pertly retorted, 'Calling me a hussy? You are a hussy yourself!' Saying this she quickly moved away from her mother for she knew that it was not wise to be too close to her just then. Here the mother was clearly in the wrong, as she had set a bad example for the daughter, but she was incapable of realizing it. Tagar could see that while her mother had her way by screaming and shouting, she could not do so herself and the unfairness of it all troubled her far more than any physical violence.

Tagar thought that by moving out of the reach of her mother she was safe but she was mistaken. Anger made the Mistress agile despite her weight. Throwing down her cards on the mat she sprang on Tagar and began to shower blows on her. Tagar started yelling at the top of her voice. Thakurjhee[11] from the Old House got up to intervene and pulled Tagar away from the mother. The girl freed herself, stretched out on the floor and began to howl, whilst Thakurjhee tried to pacify her. Immediately the Mistress came forward, patted her on the back and said, 'Stop it now, child, don't cry.' This made Tagar howl even more loudly. The mother said, 'Good girl, stop crying now. I'll give you some money.' Tagar had no faith in her mother. She promptly said, 'Give it to me now. I'll buy something to eat.' The mother said, 'Let the sweet seller come. I'll give you the money then.' The girl said, 'No, give it to me now.' The Mistress took out two coins from the cupboard and gave them to Tagar who calmed down and settled herself on the bed. The ladies returned to their places on the mat and resumed their game.

Thakurjhee shuffled the cards. The Mistress cut and announced with a smile, 'The King of Spades! Thakurjhee is not destined to get a red one, even in a game.'

Jiban's mother was a friend of the Mistress and received a stipend from Jagat Babu for her son's education. So she never let go of a chance to speak on her behalf. She said, 'It is really a misfortune for a red (fair) person not to have a red partner.'

Thakurjhee said, 'If I were black myself, I would surely get a red one. This is how the world is. Topsy turvy.' She had turned the joke on the Mistress since Jagat Babu was fair and she was dark.

The Mistress in the meanwhile moved a trump and said, 'My dear, the Babu is quite enamoured of me whether I be fair or dark. Besides, your brother is no Englishman either. Your turn, sister.'

The Mistress forgot that even though a gentleman may not be an Englishman and his wife may be an angel from heaven, in the eyes of a sister, the brother's wife is never good enough for him. Thakurjhee played her card. The Mistress's cousin by marriage, the fourth member of the party, spoke up, 'Didi, you are right. This lady is much too proud of her brother. Come on, pick up your cards.'

Thakurjhee said to the Mistress, 'And you are too proud of yourself.'

Jiban's mother rose to her defence. 'And why should she not be proud? How many people have you seen with such an imposing personality? Oh, why did you play a ten, now they'll get it.'

Thakurjhee continued, 'I say it would be better for you to be a little less imposing. Really, sister, you have put on too much weight.'

The cousin said, 'No, it's not that. Actually Didi is becoming bald, so she has lost her looks.'

Jiban's mother added, 'And she has become darker too.'

The Mistress agreed, 'Yes, Ma was saying, "My Tara's complexion is not the same." Didn't she say that, Tagar?'

Thakurjhee said, 'But my dear, your complexion has always been like this. Of course, I don't know how it was when you were a child.'

Tagar, who was playing with her coins on the bed, said, 'Didn't granny say that Ma had become thin? Ma, when will granny bring me my doll?'

Thakurjhee burst out laughing. 'Get a little more plump, then, sister. This nosering does not suit your thin face.'

Jiban's mother protested, 'No, if she cannot carry off this nosering who can, I would like to know.'

The Mistress did not say anything. She just smiled with satisfaction and lowering her eyes, glanced at her nosering. Although she was not more than thirty or thirty-two, she did not like to be called a modern woman and her ways were quite old-fashioned. As such, if anyone complimented her on the quantity of vermilion in her hair and the size of the nosering, she felt really flattered. The sight of modern girls wearing just a hint of vermilion, no ring in their noses, and tight-fitting jackets infuriated her. She did not mind sending her daughter to attend religious festivals in an English frock and a bonnet, but she lost her temper if Jagat Babu suggested that the girl could wear a jacket with her sari, for she jumped to the conclusion that Jagat Babu was taking his revenge on her by making her daughter a memsahib. There were frequent clashes between them over such trifles, but, needless to say, the Mistress always won.

Jiban's mother noticed that her comment had pleased the Mistress. She continued, 'The pearl nosering looks so pretty against your lips, red with betel.'

Whereupon Thakurjhee remarked, 'Sister, you have finished up all the betel yourself it seems. There is nothing left for us.'

The Mistress called out to her daughter, 'O Tagar, go and fetch some betel for us, please.'

The child replied, 'I won't go.'

The Mistress frowned, 'You are being naughty again, I see.'

The child said, 'You order me about all the time. Why don't you ask Konedidi[12] to do it?'

The Mistress said, 'Yes, that is right. Where is she? Is she going to play the whole time? Call her, Tagar!'

Tagar did not object to that. She got up and yelled for the girl who answered back saying she was coming. When she entered the room, Tagar said, 'Where were you all this while? Ma has run out of betel.' Normally, in this situation the Mistress' voice would have been louder than Tagar's but in the presence of the visitors she said in a softer tone, 'Are you going to play all day long, child? You know there are visitors in the house. You should have been around. Go, bring some betel for us.'

The girl brought some betel leaves on a plate. The Mistress told her to arrange for their snacks. Tagar shouted, 'Didi, get me a glass of water first.' The girl brought water for her and when she finished drinking, took the glass away. In the meanwhile the Mistress had won a great victory in the game of cards. She offered the booty in jest to the male relatives of her opponents and then got up to serve the snacks to their better halves. Just then, Shyama, the matchmaker entered the room.

2

Shyama, the matchmaker, was a Kayastha by caste. Although she had adopted a Brahmin's profession, she had maintained the dignity of her calling. Her well-preserved body, long strides, and measured speech indicated that she was a person of importance. It was not easy to tell whether her husband was alive or whether she was a widow. She had no vermilion in her hair but she wore heavy gold bangles and a sari with a broad, red border. Entering the room with a haughty air, she settled down near the mat and enquired, why she had been sent for.

Women, everywhere, love the subject of marriage. In our country they like nothing better. At this moment the women were being taken to the other room for snacks. One of them had stood up. The Mistress was holding the hand of another who had declined the offer and was urging her to observe the proper code of a guest. All this came to a halt as soon as the matchmaker entered the room. The lady who had got up promptly sat down again. The Mistress also abandoned her gesture of hospitality, let go of the hands of her kinswoman and settling down on the mat, said endearingly to the matchmaker, 'You haven't come this way for a long time.'

The matchmaker said, 'I come only when there is work to do. Why, I came a few months ago, but the Master gets angry at the mention of any proposal. Keep your daughter with you if you don't want to get her married. It is none of my business. Why have you called me again? Is the Master willing now?'

'Forget about the Master. One can't follow his whims regarding everything.'

Looking in the direction of Tagar, the matchmaker asked, 'Is this the girl?'

The Mistress replied, 'O, no, no, not this one right now. It is the other one, the one who has been brought up in this house. Let her marriage be arranged first, what do you say? Is it right to get one's own daughter married before someone else's?'

Jiban's mother remarked, 'She is very particular about doing the right thing.'

The matchmaker said, 'So you are not getting her married to your son?'

'To my son?' retorted the Mistress, 'Am I so base as to marry my son to a girl who has devoured her own parents?'

Thakurjhee protested, 'But your mother-in-law was very keen about it. She used to call her "the bride".'

The cousin agreed, 'I believe Jagat Babu has also set his heart on it.'

The Mistress frowned. 'What can I do about that? But I am not going to get her married to my son.'

The matchmaker said, 'So, it's her marriage that has to be arranged first? Say, what dowry will you give her? She is an orphan, you will not get a match for nothing.'

The Mistress's sari had slipped off her head. Covering the bald patch on her scalp with her left hand, she said, 'My dear, I have fed and clothed someone else's daughter, and now I have to get her married too. I cannot shower everything on her. We also have our own children to think of.'

It may be pointed out here that the girl being referred to had come to live in Jagat Babu's house only two years ago. The matchmaker said, 'In that case you won't get a boy from a good family. Will the Master consent to that?'

'Who wants a royal family for her?' said the Mistress. 'An ordinary household will do. And it is not as though we will not give her anything at all. We'll give some cash and jewellery too.'

Certainly, this would not be done if the Mistress had her way. She was well aware that on this issue Jagat Babu would not listen to her. She continued, 'But I won't be able to give her what I would give to my own daughter.'

The matchmaker said, 'Of course there will be no problem in the case of your daughter. The moment you broach the subject you'll get two hundred suitors.'

Thakurjhee spoke up, 'Why, that girl is not bad looking either. All you can say is that she has no money. Had I a son, I would have certainly agreed to a match.' Jiban's mother also wanted that girl as a daughter-in-law but did not express her desire openly thinking that the Mistress might not like it.

The matchmaker said, 'A fair or dark complexion does not matter these days. It is money that matters.'

The Mistress's cousin said, 'She is a fine girl.'

The Mistress said, 'She is not like our Tagar. It is not enough to have a pale skin. What do you say?'

The matchmaker said, 'Exactly. Your daughter's face is like Radha in a painting and she is nice and plump.'

We must confess that we would not have thought of this comparison but the matchmaker's statement was not too far-fetched either. Tagar did not have very big eyes but her small forehead, joint eyebrows, sharp nose, and rounded face would probably be accepted as a model by folk artists. Yet we would not consider it a suitable comparison for the simple reason that Radha in a folk painting does not have a lively expression; rather, she has a blank, placid look. But whatever flaw Tagar's face may have had, it was certainly not a lack of expression, rather her face had a fierce and harsh aspect. Had her hair been allowed to frame her face loosely, perhaps this harshness would have been softened a little, but due to her tight hairdo, the parting in her hair had widened and the childish face of the eight-year-old girl had already acquired a mature and severe look. But tastes differ. The Mistress liked no other hairstyle. She made Sneha do all the housework but did not allow her to do Tagar's hair because she could not tie it up tightly like her. Not that the Mistress had any desire to keep this unique art of tying the hair to herself. She had tried her best to impart this skill to Snehalata by making her sit by her side when she plaited Tagar's hair. But it seemed Snehalata would never learn it—she always tied the hair loosely. A big, strapping girl of ten, didn't she have the strength to do it? No, it was plain mischief on her part. She just wanted to dress Tagar in that unsightly manner and make her look fashionable. The Mistress had understood this very well but could you imagine a bigger fool than Jagat

Babu, because whenever Snehalata dressed Tagar's hair in that horrendous manner he actually praised it, driving the Mistress into a fury. Earlier she used to let Snehalata do up Tagar's hair now and then, but after this she never allowed Snehalata to touch her head. Even if she had a thousand things to attend to, she would drop everything and comb Tagar's hair herself. Tagar had also got used to having her hair tightly plaited and was not pleased unless her mother did it for her.

The matchmaker's appreciation of Tagar's looks made everyone turn in her direction. She smiled and hid her face behind her mother's back. On the arrival of the matchmaker she had once again resumed her place beside her mother. Presently Snehalata entered the room with a book in her hand and announced that the snacks had been laid out. The Mistress looked at her and remarked, 'See, how tall she has become! There is no flesh on her body, she is just growing taller. day by day like a palm tree.' As though this was also her fault and she could have become plumper instead of taller if she had so desired! Everyone looked at Snehalata. What a difference there was between the two girls! Snehalata was truly sylph-like, slightly tall for her age, which made her look rather pretty. She was well proportioned, delicate and graceful in every limb. If their features were analysed, critics would probably declare Tagar's to be more perfect, because Snehalata's nose was not as sharp as Tagar's, nor her eyebrows as black; her forehead was slightly larger and her thick, black curly hair fell carelessly on it. There was a sad expression in her eyes, she seemed to be more mature than her years and her smooth, pale complexion added to the loveliness of her face. Just as a dust-laden jasmine flower does not attract the eye immediately, but when it does, its quiet beauty melts the heart, so was everyone moved by Snehalata's beauty. The matchmaker said, 'The girl is beautiful. You will get a match all right, my dear.'

Since the matchmaker addressed Snehalata directly, she felt embarrassed and tried to leave the room. Suddenly Tagar rushed towards her, and pounced on her hand like a kite exclaiming, 'Didi, you have taken my book.' Snehalata clung to her book and said crossly, 'No, Tagar, this is my book,' and freeing herself, tried to slip away. Tagar ran after her, crying. The Mistress said angrily, 'Look at her, she is making the girl cry. Give it to her. Her book has been missing for some time. I just wonder where the books disappear everyday. Give it to her, I tell you!'

Snehalata replied, 'No, Mashima,[13] it is my book. Tagar will tear it up right away. See, my name is written on it.' As soon as she lowered the book to show her name, Tagar grabbed it. Its cover got half torn in the scuffle. Afraid that the other half would also get torn, Snehalata let go of it. Tagar seized the book and rushed to her mother. Snehalata's eyes filled with tears of helpless rage. She cried out, 'Mashima, why should Tagar take my book away?'

Thakurjhee said, 'Tagar, my child, why did you take her book?'

The Mistress retorted, 'Her book? As though she has brought it from her father's house!'

Snehalata had no answer to this. Her tears overflowed.

Thakurjhee said, 'Sister, are you crazy? Why do you treat a child like this?'

The Mistress exclaimed, 'So much fuss about a book! What is the world coming to? As though they will all wear turbans and go to office.'

Snehalata said between sobs, 'Mashima, I have to learn my lesson just now. Meshomoshai[14] will hear me say it.'

The Mistress grumbled, 'The man has lost his wits. He ought to look for a groom for this grown-up girl, instead he is teaching her to read and write!'

At this point, Tagar's brother Charu entered the room. Seeing the commotion he asked what the matter was. Holding the book nervously Tagar drew close to her mother. Snehalata said, 'Tagar has taken my book.'

Tagar said, 'No, it is my book.'

Charu said, 'Well, let me see whose it is.' Despite Tagar's resistance and the mistress's pleading, he snatched the book from Tagar's hand, but as he handed it to Snehalata, his elbow knocked against the clock on the table which fell down and was broken. Everybody cried out in dismay. Tagar started crying and said, 'Serves you right! I'll tell Baba who has broken it.'

The boy replied, 'Then I'll also tell him that you have torn Sneha's book. And I won't give you toffees.'

Tagar said, 'Then give me a toffee.'

Charu took out some toffees from his pocket and gave them to the girls. Then he said, 'Ma, give me my food.'

Sneha said, 'Charu, I have laid out your food in the other room. Come, I'll serve it to you.' When they left the room, the Mistress remarked, 'See, how perverse she is? She made the little one cry, broke the clock, and made so much fuss about a book!'

Thakurjhee said, 'It seems she is quite interested in studies.'

The Mistress said, 'O, but she is not like our Tagar. There is no counting how many books I have got for her. I say to her, what is the use of reading so much. You don't have to take up a paid job, but she doesn't listen. It seems she is going to be another Lilavati.'[15]

Tagar asked, 'Ma, what shall I tell Baba when he asks?'

'About what?'

'About the clock.'

'Just tell him it broke by itself, otherwise he'll scold your Dada. Does one report such matters?'

Once again venting her anger on Snehalata, the Mistress took her guests to the next room.

3

Jagat Babu did not normally return home before sundown but today he returned early. After finishing her work, Snehalata was standing, as usual, in the veranda connecting the inner and the outer sections of the house, looking out of a window at the road he would come by. Seeing him from a distance, she was overjoyed. Since the death of Jagat Babu's mother he had been everything to Snehalata—her father, mother, family, and friend. Hence, he was more precious for her than for anyone else in the house. As soon as he came into the veranda, she took his hand enthusiastically and said, 'Meshomoshai, you have come quite early today. Why don't you come at this time everyday?'

Jagat Babu's right hand being engaged, he patted her cheek lightly with his left hand and said with a smile, 'That is what my Lata wants, but which scripture says that if I come early once, I have to do it everyday, Buri?'[16] Snehalata only smiled in reply and holding his hand, pulled him along.

At this moment Tagar also made her appearance in the veranda and seeing Jagat Babu caught hold of his other hand. Sandwiched between the two of them like the goddess Shashti,[17] Jagat Babu walked towards the inner apartment. Snehalata prattled happily, 'Meshomoshai, today I have prepared *mohanbhog*[18] for you myself.'

Tagar put in, 'Well, Konedidi, Hara's mother was standing by you.'

Snehalata was a little embarrassed. 'O yes, Hara's mother showed me how to make it, otherwise I would have taken it off the fire before it was done. But she did not stir it. You'll have to eat it all, Meshomoshai.'

Jagat Babu said, 'What will you give me if I do?'

'I'll give you some more mohanbhog and you'll have to eat it.'

'I'll have to eat that too?'

'Yes, and I'll give you a betel leaf after that.'

'But if I collapse after eating so much, how will you bring me back to life, Buri?'

Tagar said, 'No Baba, don't eat so much mohanbhog. Then you won't be able to eat any *luchis*.[19] Ma will be angry and you'll have to put up with her scolding.'

Jagat Babu said, 'Thanks for reminding me, Buri. I am willing to stomach anything but that.' Tagar laughed heartily at this remark but Snehalata's laughter died on her lips. She knew well how painful it was to be scolded and she did not find it amusing.

After a wash and a change, Jagat Babu came into the dining room and sat down to eat. Snehalata had laid out his food. When he was seated, she placed everything before him and sat near him. The Mistress was not present in the room. Tagar went into the veranda and shouted, 'Ma, come upstairs. Baba has arrived.'

Jagat Babu did not generally return early, so the Mistress was not prepared for it. When she came upstairs after changing her clothes, Jagat Babu had finished eating and was drinking water. But the Mistress noticed that two luchis and one-and-a-half *sandesh*[20] still remained on his plate. She glanced at the plate and then at Snehalata and said, 'I say, couldn't you have called me earlier? I can see that he hasn't eaten anything today.' She said to Jagat Babu, 'Please eat the *manohara sandesh*. My mother sent it.'

Jagat Babu knew that another bout of pleading would begin now, and if he did not cut it short, the Mistress would compel him to eat the two luchis and sandesh. Getting up promptly, he quipped, 'In this worthless world, only what comes from the in-law's house is precious. Don't I know that, Mistress? I have had a whole sandesh and yet you accuse me of neglect?'

This did not pacify the Mistress. Pulling her sari a little more over her forehead, she said, 'If you have eaten one, can't you eat two? You people have this bad habit of wasting food. As though it is all junk and can be thrown away and does not cost anything.'

Jagat Babu scratched his head and thought that one should also value one's health, but not daring to express his sentiments openly he slipped into the veranda. The attendant was waiting there for him with a jug of water and a towel. The Mistress had to abandon the hope of getting him back to eat, but she was not willing to give up the idea of redeeming the leftover. She turned to Tagar and said, 'Why should so much food be wasted? You sit down to eat.'

Unfortunately, Tagar was not hungry either. She had already eaten her share of luchis earlier. She turned down the suggestion, infuriating the Mistress. She was never comfortable about the way the girls' life was being ruined by Jagat Babu's example and his indulgence. Now this anxiety drove her to desperation and when she saw that Tagar was ready to walk away, disregarding her command, she caught hold of her hand and without mincing more words dragged her to Jagat Babu's seat. Ignoring her protests and excuses, she made a ball with the luchis and sandesh and thrust it into her mouth. Yielding either to such use of force or the taste of the sweet or compelled by both, Tagar finished the morsel like an obedient child and when her mother tried to feed her again she did not make any more fuss. Thus the Mistress was able to dispose of the two remaining luchis and the sandesh successfully and felt somewhat relieved; but she could not be fully reassured either, for she began to worry about the likely ill-effects of Tagar consuming all that leftover food. That wretched Snehalata was the cause of all this mischief. It made the Mistress boil with rage to think that she did not inform her of the Master's arrival on time.

Meanwhile, Jagat Babu had retired to the bedroom. Reclining on the sofa, he was smoking his hookah. Snehalata was sitting on a stool by his side, plucking his grey hair and chattering away to her heart's content. Jagat Babu had shut his eyes and was encouraging her to carry on by responding in monosyllables. After feeding Tagar, the Mistress came into the room and, sitting on the sofa near his feet, asked, 'I say, are you sleeping?' Jagat Babu replied, 'No.' Tagar, who had accompanied her mother added, 'Baba shuts his eyes and pretends to sleep.' The Mistress looked at Snehalata and said, 'Aren't you going to give out the provisions?' Snehalata replied that she had already done it. The Mistress said, 'Then don't you have any other work? Go and plait Tagar's hair.'

Snehalata was not a little surprised at this. Ordinarily, the Mistress would get irritated if she ever saw Snehalata handling Tagar's hair but what was she saying today? Right now she was not at all inclined to leave Jagat Babu's side. She said, 'Tagar will not get her hair done by me.'

The Mistress said, 'See, how obstinate she is! She is refusing to budge from here.' Jagat Babu understood that the Mistress had something to tell him and wanted to send the girls away. He said to Snehalata, 'Lata, you plait hair very well. Do it for Tagar today. Tagar, go to the other room, and get your hair done by Didi. Go, Sneha, take her along.'

Tagar didn't raise any further objections. Sneha went into the other room with her. Jagat Babu said to the Mistress, 'You could have told them to go plainly. Do they understand all this indirect talk? Is it right?' The Mistress retorted, 'No, whatever I say is not right. How can one be plainer? You only find fault with me.' Jagat Babu realized that any further discussion would only backfire, so he dropped the subject and said, 'What do you have to say, tell me.'

The Mistress said, 'I say, how long will you keep her unmarried? I cannot show my face to anyone now. The women from that house are saying all kinds of things. You don't have to listen to such talk.'

Jagat Babu said, 'She is just ten years old and there is already so much talk!'

The Mistress said, 'Is ten so young? And she looks like a sixteen-year-old wench already.'

Jagat Babu said, 'If you really want to get her married so soon we'll have to make the arrangements. However, I wanted Charu to grow up a little more.'

The Mistress's nostrils flared up along with her nosering. She said, 'See, let me tell you frankly—Charu won't marry her. If you insist on that, I'll hang myself.'

As long as Jagat Babu's mother was alive, the Mistress was not able to speak up. She knew that it would be futile to do so. But since her death, the Mistress had repeatedly said that Charu would not be married to Sneha. Let another groom be found for her. Jagat Babu did not think along that line. It was his wish to bring the Mistress round to his own point of view gradually. So there was frequent disagreement and exchange of hot words between them on the subject. Jagat Babu said, 'My dear, just think of it, will you ever get such a good girl anywhere?'

The Mistress replied, 'Good girl! I know how good she is. You would know it also if you had to run the house. Even that may be overlooked, but marrying a girl who has devoured her parents will not be auspicious for the boy. I will not allow it as long as I am alive.'

Jagat Babu said, 'Will your superstitious nature never change? This marriage should be arranged in order to disprove your conviction.'

The Mistress realized that she would have to change her tactics. She knew how to state things in a way that would touch him to the quick. She brought tears to her eyes and spoke in a nasal tone, 'See, you have taken me as a wife but you have never made me happy. Will you not even allow me to be happy with my son?'

Jagat Babu was silent. He got perplexed whenever she adopted this tone and was reduced to scratching his head. The Mistress knew that her tactics had worked. She continued, 'I am so unfortunate that none of my desires have been fulfilled. Should a person who hasn't received her husband's love ever hold any hope or expectation? Still, it is hard to accept it. I wanted to get a good match for Charu and enjoy some happiness but if you cannot endure it, go ahead and get him married to Sneha.' The Mistress had to pause here for Tagar came running and said, 'Ma, see how Didi has tied my hair. It is so loose. You do it again.' Saying this, she settled into her mother's lap, looked at her face and continued, 'Dada's marriage? With whom? With Didi?'

At that moment Snehalata also entered the room. Jagat Babu breathed a sigh of relief. At least for the time being he could have a respite from the onslaught of the Mistress. Rising quickly from the sofa he said to Tagar, 'Tagri, it is your test today. I hope you remember that. Bring your book to the veranda.'

Tagar said, 'Baba, my book is lost. Jadu hasn't brought one for me.'

Jagat Babu said, 'Should you lose your book everyday? It seems the mother and the daughter will have the same kind of education. Come, Sneha, let me see how much you have learnt.'

Sneha had come with her book. Jagat Babu took her hand and proceeded to the veranda. Then he suddenly stopped and said, 'Wait, let us take the clock with us. I have to go somewhere at seven sharp.' Saying this he came to the table and not finding the clock there, exclaimed, 'Where is the clock?'

The Mistress said, 'The clock? Bless me, what d'you call it, the tomcat came and dropped it. It broke into pieces. See, I have kept it on the top of the cupboard.' Jagat Babu could not believe this. He knew his wife very well. Examining the broken pieces he asked Tagar, 'Tell me who broke the clock?' Tagar looked at her mother and faltered, 'It broke by itself.' Jagat Babu asked Snehalata, 'Sneha, who broke the clock?' Snehalata turned pale. Her voice trembled, yet she managed to say, 'Charu.' Jagat Babu put the broken pieces on the table, and looking impatiently at his wife, said, 'You tell lies yourself and teach the kids to lie too?'

Charu came into the room at this moment. Jagat Babu questioned him angrily, 'Charu, who broke the clock?' A frightened Charu did not have the nerve to confess his fault. He said, 'Baba, I have come in just now.' Jagat Babu's patience was exhausted. Twisting the boy's ear, he said, 'Charu, you are lying. You don't have the courage to speak the truth after doing wrong!' Charu began to sob. Sneha and Tagar stood petrified. The Mistress started snivelling, and pulling Jagat Babu's hand away, shrieked, 'Oh my, you are beating such a big boy! What shall I do now? What wretched luck was I born with!' Jagat Babu let go of Charu's ear and muttered, 'Charu, I wanted to buy a watch for you. Now I won't. That is your punishment.'

Charu went away whimpering. Sneha and Tagar followed him. Jagat Babu's nature was such that immediately after taking a step in anger he felt contrite. The Mistress realized that this was the moment to get the upper hand over him. Whenever Jagat Babu over-reacted like this, the Mistress felt a secret satisfaction. She could manipulate him on such occasions as on no other and was always on the look out for them. Knowing this to be an opportune moment, she continued her whining, 'My dear, how have I wronged you? I have laid down my life for you, always. I have ruined my health for the sake of your household, and yet...'

The Mistress could not go on any further. The scene had suddenly taken a poignant turn. Her tears were flowing profusely. Jagat Babu was dumbfounded. He began to scratch his head in great perplexity and presented a far more pathetic spectacle than his weeping wife. At this juncture a servant appeared and announced, 'Master, somebody has brought a carriage for you. You will have to leave immediately.' What could be better news than this for Jagat Babu? The servant had really saved the situation for him. Without a moment's delay he made his departure from the house.

4

Charu stopped crying as soon as he was out of the room. He assumed the aspect of a stage actor with a stern and disdainful countenance. People feel great after a conquest; Charu began to imagine himself a hero like Napoleon after being reprimanded. Watching his bold attitude, his two companions were awe-struck and considered themselves the lowest of the low in comparison to him.

Having gone a little distance, Charu paused, turned and declared, 'Tagar, I think you reported me to Baba.' Tagar said, 'No, I did not. Didi did.' Charu looked at Snehalata with surprise and realized that she was the guilty one. Her pale face and sad expression confirmed his suspicion. He said, 'The clock fell in my attempt to give you the book and you betrayed me!' Snehalata demurred tearfully, 'But Meshomoshai asked me.' Tagar interjected, 'Baba asked me too but I didn't take Dada's name. I said that it broke by itself.' Sneha said, 'But that's a lie.' Tagar said, 'So what if it is a lie?'

Sneha said, 'But Meshomoshai has forbidden us to tell lies.'

Charu replied, 'But I was punished for it. Go away, I won't talk to you any more.' He moved off, looking very angry. Tagar followed him crying, 'Dada, Dada, Ma said that you will be married soon to Didi.' Charu turned around and declared, 'No, I won't marry her. She is naughty. You can tell her that.'

With these words he walked away. Snehalata's eyes filled with tears. She slowly passed into the inner garden and sat down on the stone platform of one of the *bakul* trees growing near the corner of the pond. She often sat here to practise her lessons. Today she sat by herself under the solitary tree and wept.

We pay little heed to the small joys and sorrows of little children but they often experience these emotions as keenly as we do. Since we do not understand this, our callous thoughtlessness often mars the proper flowering of their budding hearts. Though they grow up despite our negligence and lack of affection, they fail to attain the fragrance and beauty which would have delighted the world if they had been nurtured with care. In the absence of that they become blighted and grow up to be the cause of unhappiness to themselves and others and carry the permanent scars of the neglect all their lives.

When Charu went away in a huff, rejecting Snehalata's affection, she was devastated. How could Charu think that she deliberately got him into trouble? How could that be when she loved him so much? Could she ever think of doing him any harm? How could Charu imagine that? Snehalata brooded about it, cried her heart out, and gradually drifted into a state of oblivion. She felt that it would be good for her to die at that moment. Then Charu would realize that she did not get him scolded intentionally. He would certainly feel sorry for her then and would cry. Sneha had an intense desire to die, to make Charu cry. The thought never crossed her mind that if she died, Charu might not cry at all or even if he did cry, she would not be able to see him do so. Imagining her own death she continued to cry and felt utterly miserable. Sad memories of the past flashed before her mind and resting her head on a brick she lay down under the tree, weeping. Suddenly she heard the sound of footsteps. She got up with a start and looked all around. She imagined that if Charu came and saw her crying, he would not be angry with her any more. This thought gave her such relief that her tears dried up, but when she saw that Charu was not coming, her heart sank and her tears welled up again. Lost in reverie, she fell into a sleep. The rosy light of the setting sun fell on the shimmering surface of the pond. Birds chattered as they flew towards their nests. Shaken by a gentle breeze, the bakul flowers dropped from the branches on the sleeping girl. Sneha dreamt that it was raining. She got up and ran from the garden towards the house but when she entered it she discovered that it was not their house. Overcome with fear she tried to run away but suddenly all the doors closed shut and she found herself a captive. There was no way to escape. Her heart started beating wildly. All at once she saw that there was another girl in the room. She was so dark that it seemed that her body had been carved out of stone. Sneha gazed at her in bewilderment. Gradually her fear gave way to curiosity and she wondered whether the girl was real or a statue. She went up to her and stroked her, whereupon the girl burst out laughing and said, 'I know who you are. You live in Jagat Babu's house.'

Snehalata was astonished to hear these words. How could this stranger know so much about her? She felt as though she had entered the world of Arabian Nights. The sorceress, who could read her thoughts, smiled and said, 'Shall I tell you what Charu is to you?' This surprised Snehalata even more. It seemed the girl knew everything about her. She covered her face shyly and said, 'No, don't tell me.'

'Then what shall I tell you?'

Sneha asked, 'Is it really Arabian Nights? Tell me, honestly.' The sorceress replied, 'Of course it is Arabian Nights. Let me show you something'. With these words she walked towards the closed door and vanished out of sight. Suddenly an Englishman came near her and said, 'I haven't had anything to eat the whole day. Give me some money.' Sneha had one or two coins tied to the end of her sari. The man could have forcefully taken them from her but he seemed to have been sent by the sorceress to test her willingness to part with the money. Snehalata quickly untied the coins from her sari and offered them to him but he said, 'What shall I do with money? Give me that book of yours.'

Jagat Babu had lately bought this book for Snehalata and she did not want to give it to anybody on any account. She knew that if she did not give it to the Englishman, he would snatch it away, but she could not let go of her book. Just then she woke up and saw that it had become quite dark. She felt the presence of the sorceress near her in the darkness of the night. She quickly got up to go into the house. As soon as she entered it, one of the maidservants complained, 'We cannot cook because you haven't given us the oil.' Another servant said, 'There is no light. The Mistress's room is in darkness.' Over and above this din, the loud, angry words of the Mistress reached her ears. Overcome by dread, she forgot her sorrow, her pain, her dream, and everything else.

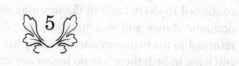

5

*D*r Jagatchandra Gangopadhyaya is just forty-two years old but his hair and beard have become so grey that he appears to be fifty. His face has a gentle and benign expression. He is neither too fat nor too thin, is fair, has a pleasant, smiling face, and impresses people at the very first encounter as a good man. However, these days the term 'good' is not always used in appreciation. A stupid man is also called a good fellow, hence it is necessary to explain that although Jagat Babu is a good man, he is not a fool. In his youth he was a brilliant student, now he is an established doctor. Yet in spite of his intelligence, he is an ingenuous person. He can participate in a scientific discussion but cannot enter into the minds of crooked people. You may call him a simpleton for that reason, but in our opinion this simplicity indicates his superior intellect. He understands Darwin's theory of evolution very well and knows the composition of the finest nerves in the human body, but he cannot conceive how people's outward behaviour can be so different from their inner feelings. He knows that this knowledge is very necessary for worldly dealings but he is such a novice in these matters that whenever he tries to put his meagre social skills into practice, his attempt meets with failure.

Jagat Babu has no idea how often the Mistress visits the Kali temple, the theatre, and other places on the pretext of going to see her parents. If he ever comes to know of it, his disapproval eventually ends up with his placating her on account of her tantrums. For instance, once Jagat Babu was invited to somebody's house for dinner, but the Mistress kept insisting on being taken to the theatre. With great difficulty he managed to dissuade her and was able to go.

As luck would have it, after the feast his friends took him to the theatre. He decided not to disclose this to the Mistress who would otherwise not spare him. It was quite late when he returned, and the Mistress, not in the habit of disturbing her own sleep in order to chat with him at night, turned over when he entered the bedroom and continued to sleep. Early in the morning she got up to attend to her domestic duties and was too busy to talk to him, but when she returned to the bedroom after finishing her work and saw Jagat Babu still lying in bed, there was no longer any impediment to her starting a conversation. 'It seems your morning starts in the afternoon,' she said. 'Now, doesn't that make you sick? And you make such a fuss when you have to take me to the theatre!'

Although Jagat Babu had not made sickness an excuse last night, he might have done so on some earlier occasion. He said, 'You know one gets delayed when one is invited out.'

In the meanwhile, Tagar had come in and got under the mosquito net with her father. She said, 'Baba, sing that song for me. I have forgotten it.'

Jagat Babu sang a few lines and then said, 'Let this be. I'll sing a new song for you. Listen. He began to hum:

'In the deep, dark bower
The soft flute plays sweetly,
Forgetting all shame and fear
Come, my dear friend, come.'

The Mistress said, 'This is a song from *Ashrumati*.' The Mistress had gone to see the play *Ashrumati* earlier, without informing Jagat Babu. He could have caught her at this moment, instead he got caught himself by his own remark, 'Yes, it was sung very well yesterday.'

The Mistress said, 'Indeed, so you went to see it yesterday.' Jagat Babu realized that the cat was out of the bag and began scratching his head. There was a great uproar. The Mistress left the room in a huff and afterwards sulked for a whole week. She cried and taunted Jagat Babu so much that the following Saturday he was compelled to take her to the theatre, putting some urgent work aside.

Once, Sukhibala, a poor woman, distantly related to Jagat Babu, approached the Mistress with a request for financial help for her daughter's marriage. A long time ago Sukhibala's grandfather was engaged in a lawsuit with Jagat Babu's father. Angered at being charged falsely, Jagat Babu's father cut off all connections with Sukhibala's family, even after winning the case. Although this happened long before Sukhibala was born or the Mistress was married to Jagat Babu, she remembered the story and instead of extending any concrete help to Sukhibala sent her away after giving her a piece of her mind. Sukhibala departed in tears and the Mistress congratulated herself on her laudable action. When Jagat Babu returned home she narrated the whole story to him with much complacency. Jagat Babu felt very upset by her behaviour and secretly dispatched five hundred rupees to Sukhibala to compensate for the uncharitable conduct of his wife.

Jagat Babu used to maintain a little diary in which he noted down these secret expenses. One day this diary accidentally fell out of his pocket on to the bed. Charu, who had come into the room, picked it up and began to read in English, 'Sukhi: five hundred.' Hearing Sukhibala's name, the Mistress was put out. 'What is that?' she demanded. Charu repeated, 'Sukhi, five hundred.'

'What does that mean?'

Charu explained it to her in Bengali. The Mistress understood at once. She remembered that the day she had narrated the incident about Sukhi to Jagat Babu, he had taken out five hundred rupees from the safe.

As soon as he returned home that day, she asked him, 'Has Sukhi been given five hundred rupees?'

Jagat Babu said, 'Who told you that?'

The Mistress retorted, 'Who told me? Can such things remain a secret? Only in my case you don't take out even a penny. I may be an outsider, but I am not your enemy, am I?'

Sometime back the Mistress had asked Jagat Babu for two hundred rupees to get some ornament as a present for her niece's wedding. Jagat Babu had given her a hundred rupees, saying that much expense had been incurred lately on a lawsuit and on the occasion of Charu's thread ceremony and so there was no need to give such an expensive present. The Mistress found this a good reason to taunt him. A flustered Jagat Babu tried to explain to her the difference between a present and a deed of charity but the reader can guess how far this argument was acceptable to the Mistress. She was deeply hurt by Jagat Babu's partiality and even after extracting five hundred rupees in place of two hundred for her niece's gift, she did not stop reproaching him.

So, although Jagat Babu was a good man, he was not strong-willed and he had to suffer more on account of that than for being good-natured. Like other weak-willed people, Jagat Babu was very scared of a confrontation, but in trying to avoid these conflicts, he got trapped into them. The more he gave in to his wife's tantrums, the more she was able to dominate him. Had he been more authoritative, this would not have happened. Anyway, for this reason he was thought to be an ideal husband by the ladies and a henpecked man by the gentleman. This proved to be an advantage for his wife and a disadvantage for him. Jagat Babu's wife was much esteemed in the society of women and enjoyed the highest place of honour at feasts and other social functions. The mothers of brides were never satisfied unless she presided over the marriage rituals and the rites related to the casting of a spell on the husband to keep him subjugated to his wife. Poor Jagat Babu, on the other hand, was referred to as a 'chicken-hearted baby', 'a good-for-nothing fellow'[21] and so on by his friends. Jagat Babu could endure these taunts and ridicule but was greatly distressed if any of his well-wishers tried to caution him seriously and counselled him about asserting his authority. This was so because he was fully aware of his weakness. He knew that if he remained firm on his decisions without being swayed by his wife's tantrums, her fits would also become less frequent. He did try to put his resolutions into practice. Whenever there was an argument with his wife, he initially remained firm on his resolve but, sadly, this unnatural firmness turned out to be the cause of his own defeat.

Jagat Babu's first child was born a weakling. The Mistress wanted to give him medicines to make him healthy and plump but Jagat Babu was against it as he knew that it might harm the child instead of benefiting him. In disappointment, the Mistress turned to indigenous remedies secretly. As a consequence the child's health deteriorated and even Jagat Babu had no other alternative but to take recourse to medicines. However, in spite of his best efforts the child's condition did not improve and he died a premature death. Jagat Babu was made to feel that it was due to his negligence and lack of proper medical treatment that the Mistress had to lose her son. He also blamed himself for the tragedy.

What other option did he have? He knew his weakness but lacked the strength to free himself of it. This was the nature he was born with and in this lay his individuality. Only God could rectify it, Jagat Babu could not do it himself. People failed to understand his problem. They thought that he ought to overcome his weakness as that seemed the most desirable course to take, but that didn't happen. Jagat Babu also craved for it but without success. Since childhood, whenever there was a conflict between his resolve and his weakness, it was the latter which triumphed.

6

*J*agat Babu's mother had great faith in orthodox religion. She spent most of her time in prayer and worship. Jagat Babu too was influenced by her faith. However, owing to the changing times and circumstances this faith could not sustain him steadily through life or hold permanent sway over his mind. In childhood, he was devoted to the family god, the shalgram shila.[22] Every morning and evening he used to accompany his mother to the temple, recite the same prayer as her, and when she prostrated in front of the idol, he also bowed in obeisance. At the age of seven Jagat was admitted to school and within a year his style of worship underwent a change. He stopped repeating his mother's prayers and when he bowed in front of the god he said to himself, 'God let me stand first today. Let the teacher not punish me in class. Let Manmatha be friends with me' and so on. He prayed in this manner up to the age of ten and then his style changed.

One day, seeing him crying in school, an older boy Bamacharan approached him and asked what the matter was. Jagat said, 'Debi snatched my pencil away and hit me.' When Bamacharan scolded Debi, he denied it and ran away, making faces at both of them.

Jagat cried angrily, 'I'll report the matter to Him.'

Bamacharan said, 'But how will you prove it to the teacher?'

The boy said, 'No, I'll report him to God.'

'Which God?' Bamacharan asked.

'Our *shalgram shila*. He will punish him.'

Bamacharan laughed and said, 'Shalgram is only a stone. Will He hear your words? You may as well complain to that pillar.'

Bamacharan's words shocked Jagat. That evening while attending the *aarati* at home he gazed fixedly at the idol. He felt that it was really a stone. That day he could not bow to it with the same devotion. Next day he said to his mother, 'Ma, shalgram is a stone. How does he hear what we say?'

His mother said, 'Fie, child, you shouldn't say that. He is God. He dwells in the stone.'

The boy asked, 'Does God dwell in every stone?'

His mother said, 'He is everywhere but we do not comprehend it. So, in order to accept our worship he appears in the shalgram.'

The boy did not quite understand the doctrine but the mother imagined that he did. He thought so himself and went away satisfied. But the next day he asked Bamacharan in school, 'If the stone is not God, then who is God?'

Bamacharan, who was a Brahmo, replied, 'God is Ishwar...' This did not enlighten Jagat very much. He asked again, 'What is Ishwar like?'

Bamacharan said, 'Ishwar is formless, conscious and full of bliss. He is the creator of this world. We cannot see Him with our plain eyes but we can grasp Him with the eyes of knowledge. If we worship material objects created by Him in His name, we dishonour Him. Only in meditating on Him lies our worldly and spiritual welfare.'

Bamacharan had tried to repeat, as faithfully as he could, what he had heard in the sermons at the Brahmo Samaj meetings, but Jagat could not comprehend such abstractions. It was easier for him to visualize the presence of god in the shalgram, but after this exchange even that became difficult. All that he could grasp was that God was formless and could not be seen. Gradually, as he grew up, his friendship with Bamacharan became stronger and through him he came to know a number of Brahmo boys. He started attending the Brahmo Samaj meetings regularly in their company. What he had found incomprehensible earlier, he now began to internalize as the ultimate truth.

At the age of sixteen Jagat Babu passed his Entrance examination. Full of youthful enthusiasm, he now decided to embrace the Brahmo faith. However, his resolve could not remain a secret. His parents came to know of it. His mother started crying and said, 'My child, have I brought you up in order to cast you off? What will happen to you if you leave us?' His father was furious and threatened to disown him if he became a Brahmo. He kept him confined at home until his marriage. After his marriage, when his father was satisfied that he had been subdued properly he was admitted to the medical college.

Jagat Babu could not openly embrace the Brahmo faith after this, but his heart was unchanged. In the first flush of youth he had experienced a great surge of religious fervour and enthusiasm. Besides, his attention had also been drawn towards the degenerated condition of society and he wanted to reform it. After his marriage, all these emotions and aspirations got channelled into one direction. He now devoted all his energy towards moulding his newly-wedded wife according to his own inclinations. At the time of his marriage, his bride was ten years old, but within three or four years she learnt to read and write and developed an interest in religion also. This made Jagat Babu very happy and he felt as though he had conquered the universe. He had been acutely disappointed when his father had prevented him from becoming a Brahmo. He had reproached himself severely for his weakness. Coerced into acting against his convictions, he had even contemplated suicide. He thought that it was meaningless for a coward like him to get converted to another faith openly. 'Would I ever be capable of fulfilling the highest obligations of a human being with a firm conviction?' he wondered. 'Rammohun Roy, Debendranath Thakur, Keshab Chandra Sen, these are the great people who have overcome hundreds of obstacles and dedicated their whole lives to establishing the truth. The world has been enlightened by their faith and will follow their example. I am an ordinary man who cannot resist authority. My religious convictions, whether overtly expressed or not, cannot be of any consequence to the world.' But again his mind was beset with doubts. 'What is this world?' he thought. 'It is made up of insignificant human beings. If a man turns his back on his duty, it is certainly a loss to the world and the progress of the world depends on his growth. It is true that at heart I am not an idol worshipper and believe in the true faith but being forced to repudiate it in my outward behaviour am I not harming my faith?'

Jagat Babu had no answer to this question. He was filled with self-pity which he interpreted as the compassion of God and felt absolved of guilt. He wondered whether everybody had the same commitment to duty or whether it could be looked upon differently by different people, depending on their nature and circumstances. The highest kind of duty lay in serving the world and keeping one's faith intact, but everybody was not capable of achieving such greatness. There were many people in this world who fulfilled their familial obligations quite efficiently but how many great men like Buddha or Jesus Christ were born in this world? It was difficult for ordinary people to perform great deeds. 'Had I given up my parents and my community to join the Brahmo faith,' he thought, 'I would have been able to serve neither God nor humanity. God has made me an ordinary man. I shall carry out His work by fulfilling my limited responsibilities. By obeying my parents and by educating my wife in her proper womanly duties, I shall satisfy God because this is what lies within my capacity. It is not possible for me to do more. In doing this if I fall short of fulfilling other duties, then God, who has created me as a weak man, will pardon me for my lapses.'

Rationalizing thus, Jagat Babu settled down happily to the life of a householder, but this peaceful phase did not last long. The year Jagat Babu reached twenty-one, finished his education and became a doctor, his beloved fifteen-year-old wife passed away after delivering a still-born child. This terrible blow shattered Jagat Babu's hopes and all his aspirations. Even his faith was shaken to the roots. For some time he drifted along as a rudderless person, in the depths of despair. So far he had not believed in the materialistic basis of the life sciences and had rejected the empirical evidence put forward by European scholars, but now he was unable to look beyond the boundaries of materialism, as though his eyes had been struck with blindness. One person's presence had made life appear wholesome and sacred—in her absence life seemed to be meaningless and without spirit. He could not feel the influence of the spirit in the world any more. He felt that ignorance, stagnation, and death were the only reality.

A few days after this another incident came to pass in his life. One of his patients, a widow, was related to his wife. She lived with her mother on whatever money she had inherited from her husband. Jagat Babu began to visit her regularly as her doctor and a friendship developed between them. Even after she was cured, he continued to see her. This caused a scandal and his friends began to disapprove of his conduct. He defended himself by saying that he was not in the wrong for he had every intention of marrying her.

He thought that the matter was settled but it proved to be otherwise. Everybody was greatly alarmed by his declaration and unanimously condemned his folly. The widow was treated with such malice that Jagat Babu's enthusiasm was dampened. He persisted in defending his stand. Eventually, he began to doubt whether he was taking the right course or not.

The truth was that Jagat Babu wanted to marry the widow not out of love but out of pity and the desire to rebel against social conventions. Thus, despite his promise of marriage to the widow, the opinion of his friends created a conflict in his mind. He did not have to face this dilemma for long, as the matter reached his father's ears. He quickly arranged a match for him and got him married within three or four days. Jagat Babu felt so ashamed that for some time he neither visited the widow's house nor made any enquiries about her. After a few months, while passing that way in his carriage, he noticed a lock on her door and realized that she had left the town with her mother. On further investigation, he was informed that the widow had committed suicide and her mother had left for Kashi, while some said that both of them had gone to Kashi. Jagat Babu was aghast. He realized what a dreadful thing he had done and his heart was filled with remorse. All his past errors paled in comparison with this perfidy. His earlier mistakes had been harmless ones, but now he had wrecked an innocent person's life. After holding out a promise of marriage to her he had let her down and caused her death. Had she become his wife, she would have been happy and stayed on the right path. He had killed her. This tragedy was brought about by his cowardice. He realized the horror of his loss of faith and its evil consequences. After this incident he recovered his lost faith. One tragedy had shattered his faith, another one restored it.

Although he had got married again, his wounded and remorseful heart had prevented him from attending to his domestic duties. He did not look at his wife for a whole year. Gradually, however, he regained his composure. He realized that it was unfair on his part to neglect his wife. He once again turned to his conjugal duties and tried to make his wife happy. The Mistress was married at the age of twelve. She was away at her father's place for a year and at thirteen she was accepted by her husband. Jagat Babu tried to educate her as he had educated his first wife, whom he still regarded as an ideal, but he failed to cast his second wife in that mould. He had also lost some of his earlier enthusiasm, and taught her merely out of a sense of duty. Besides, he had very little time to spare now. Before retiring to bed after the day's work he tried to teach her, but the Mistress was not interested enough to give up her sleep and concentrate on studies. While the husband lectured, the wife dozed. Eventually, Jagat Babu fixed up a time during the day when the Mistress and his sister Sumati would take lessons together from him. This schedule was followed for a few days which benefited Sumati but not the Mistress. She became more inattentive and disobedient day by day. If she was rebuked, she resorted to tears. At this stage she became pregnant. Her studies came to an end and she departed to her father's place. When she returned with her baby she was in seventh heaven. Was she to attend to her baby or listen to the sermons of her husband and learn her lessons? Seeing her attitude Jagat Babu lost heart and gave up his efforts. He could not succeed in moulding her according to his taste. However, bringing up his children properly still remained the cherished wish of his heart.

Later, he realized even that was not easy. When a husband and wife are not compatible, it is impossible to discipline children. When he insisted on their speaking the truth, his wife taught them to tell lies. When he told his daughter to study, the Mistress ridiculed and taunted him so much that he got discouraged. If he said anything to her, they ended up quarrelling. The Mistress sulked the whole day or departed to her parents' place with the children and did not return for a month. In the interval the children got totally out of hand. He gradually lost the enthusiasm to educate the children himself. He appointed tutors for them, that was all. Anyhow, the household functioned smoothly after that. Then his sister Sumati fell ill and came from her in-laws' house to stay with them. She was then twenty-eight years old but had no children. Her only sister-in-law had been married to a Kulin Brahmin and was kept at home by her father. She had been widowed after the birth of a daughter and died when the infant was only a few months old. Sumati was bringing up this orphaned child as her own and when she came to her father's house, she brought this child, Snehalata, with her. She died soon afterwards and left the little girl in the care of her mother and elder brother. Snehalata was eight years old at that time. Jagat Babu noticed that she had all the good qualities that he desired in his own children. She was diligent, honest, and affectionate. Jagat Babu began to love her as his own child and his mother simply adored her for her fine qualities. Jagat Babu's wife took good care of her initially and was even fond of her but when she realized that Jagat Babu adored her, and frequently expressed his disappointment that Tagar was not like her, she gradually developed a dislike for Snehalata. Snehalata became a cause of friction between them.

7

*T*hat night Jagat Babu returned home at eight and was surprised to see that the sitting room was still in darkness. When he questioned the servants they said that they could not fix up the lights because they were not given the oil. Jagat Babu realized that a new problem had arisen. Entering the inner apartments he discovered that there were no lights in his bedroom either. The Mistress was standing in the veranda and shouting. The truth was that the lights could have been lit had the Mistress so desired. Snehalata used to hand over the keys to her after finishing her work in the storeroom; but right now the Mistress wanted to prove to Jagat Babu how irresponsible Snehalata was. Had the lamps been lit this purpose wouldn't have been served. This was a rare opportunity to expose Snehalata, so the servants were not given the oil. Jagat Babu came into the room and asked why the house was in darkness.

The Mistress replied, 'This is the doing of your responsible, well-behaved daughter. Nobody knows where she is. She is not to be found. If it was Tagar I would not spare her, but I cannot say anything to Sneha!'

Jagat Babu said, 'Surely, she must be ill. Maybe she is in bed. Just go and see.'

As he came into the veranda to look for her, he saw her coming. Jagat Babu asked her, 'Where were you all this while?'

She said softly, 'I had fallen asleep.'

Jagat Babu's wife said, 'Call the doctor. Otherwise the girl will die of sickness. You have really spoilt her rotten. Go on, educate her to your heart's content. The fellow who marries her will be properly blessed.'

The girl quietly left for the storeroom. Jagat Babu said, 'My dear wife, why do you scold her so much for a little lapse? She is a child and has no parents. Don't you feel sorry for her?'

The Mistress replied, 'She has more than parents. Tell me which parents indulge a child so much?'

'You don't have to worry about that. Just speak to her nicely.'

'I cannot stand such pampering. I have to pull her up when she is in the wrong. If you can't tolerate it and if the girl is so sensitive— such a touch-me-not—why don't you get her married soon? That will end her suffering too.'

Tagar had just joined them. She said, 'Ma, Dada was saying he won't marry Konedidi. She is very naughty.'

Jagat Babu said, 'All right, if you cannot endure her, so be it.' Saying this, he prepared to leave.

The Mistress said, 'Where are you going? You must eat first.'

Jagat Babu said, 'I have work to do. I have no time to eat.'

The Mistress said, 'I beg you, you must eat before you go.'

At this moment Snehalata came and saw Jagat Babu leaving. She said, 'Meshomoshai, won't you have dinner?'

Jagat Babu snapped back angrily, 'No, I don't want it,' and went out.

Snehalata thought she was responsible for this situation. He didn't eat because he was angry with her. She felt very unhappy. To add to her woes, the Mistress started accusing her of making Jagat Babu go hungry and creating trouble in their household. Her sharp, shrewish tongue let forth a volley of savage words and her rasping voice, like a cracked flute, grew louder and louder and rose to a crescendo, piercing Snehalata's heart and the roof of the house at the same time.

8

*E*xasperated with his wife, Jagat Babu left his house on the pretext of work but actually he had nothing to do. He walked about for a while and then took the road leading to the Ahiritola bank of the Ganga.

It was a dark, moonless night. Only the stars shone in the sky and a few lights twinkled here and there. They brightened up a few spots, or cast a mild glow on others, while some places remained in total darkness. It was past nine o'clock. There were no carriages and only a few pedestrians on the road. Some fisherwomen were hurrying home with baskets on their heads. Some servants and maids, carrying hilsa fish were gossiping about their masters. A pot-bellied Marwari, wearing nagra shoes, passed by, singing raucously. Two schoolboys, returning home with their arms around each other's shoulders, followed him applauding. Jagat Babu passed them by and coming up to the riverbank, sat down. The place was still not deserted. Some sadhus, wearing loincloth and rudraksha beads, their bodies smeared with ash, were sitting there. Others were going down the steps, carrying water in brass vessels and chanting 'Jai Jai Harey Murarey'. Men and women were still bathing in the river. Some young men were sitting on the steps and humming softly. Their humming, mingled with the splashing of the water against the bank, sounded like the murmuring of bumble bees. Far away on the river, a Hindu boatman sang to the accompaniment of his ektara:

Take care, take care, O boatman of my mind
Your boat is sinking on the stormy river of life
O boatman, I cannot endure the waves

Tell me, who has taught you
The strange skill of rowing a boat?
Your helm cannot hold against the current
The ropes of your sails are snapping
Your broken boat is sinking.
Alas, what will you do?
How will you row me across?

Jagat Babu listened to the melancholy song intently, the words becoming indistinct as other sounds on the river grew louder. His mind returned to the turbulent thoughts that were agitating him. 'Why do I love her?' he said to himself. 'My touch is unwholesome. Why do I want to keep her close to me? The kiss of a poisonous insect can only give pain. Such a creature has no right to love anybody.'

The events of his past life came back to him. Every woman he had loved had been taken away from him. Like the pleasant morning, Snehalata too would vanish from his life one day. He would not see her any more when he returned home. His eyes grew moist. 'Let it come,' he murmured to himself. 'It will be better for Snehalata to leave me. I wanted to keep her with me always, as my own child, not entirely for selfish reasons. But would it make her happy? She is not very happy right now. If she were married to Charu she would have to face the animosity of the Mistress all her life. On top if it, if Charu does not love her it will be a great tragedy.'

So far Jagat Babu had believed that Charu loved Snehalata, and after they got married, being happy with her husband, she would be able to ignore other problems. But now he began to look at the situation in another light. What he heard from Tagar about Charu not wanting to marry Sneha, came as a rude shock for him. He knew that Charu was still immature and it was not easy to surmise how his feelings would develop towards Snehalata in future. They might be happy together if they were married but there was no certainty about it. The opposite might very well happen. In fact, it was more likely as it was natural for the son to adopt the attitude of the mother. The Mistress did not like Sneha and was always ready to find fault with her. In these circumstances how would Charu learn to love her? What is deeply impressed on one's mind in childhood is very difficult to overcome later with reasoning. Love and affection are matters of the heart and cannot be regulated with reasoning. Would it then be advisable to get Charu and Snehalata married? He reasoned that it would not be and decided to drive out the long-cherished desire from his heart, however painful it might be. Eventually, he felt that he had succeeded in his effort and had overcome his desire. He had uprooted Snehalata from his heart. She was no longer a part of his family. He imagined the future when she would not be present to receive him with a smile on his returning home. In her absence his life would become a wilderness. He tried to tell himself that it was all maya, an illusion, yet he could not break the spell of this attachment. Tears welled up as he ardently wished that Snehalata were his own child.

This thought had come to his mind several times but the harsh reality had not struck him in such a poignant manner. Today he realized that a great wall separated him from her. He cried out to God in agony but there was no response. He felt that the world was devoid of the spirit—there was no soul, no love or compassion. There was nothing beyond what was visible—everything was just mechanical, and lifeless. Jagat Babu shivered and shut his eyes. The song of the boatman echoed in his ears. He felt that his boat was really sinking in the absence of the helmsman. In his misery he began to sing a Brahmo prayer with a brimming heart:

> Take me across the boundless ocean of the world
> O guardian of the helpless ones,
> Come to my boat.
> You are my redeemer from sorrow and misfortune
> Remove the darkness of adversity
> Destroy my burden of sins.

He sang this over and over again, standing near the deserted riverside. A few sadhus looked curiously at him and passed by. A few stars in the sky looked down with compassion and disappeared. He continued singing, oblivious of his surroundings. Gradually, he regained his composure and his pain was soothed. He felt the touch of the divine and could see the coast beyond the ocean of life.

Returning home that night Jagat Babu told the Mistress that she could look for a groom for Snehalata and start the preparations for her marriage.

9

*F*our teenaged students were chatting in a secluded part of Beadon Garden in the evening, but as usual their conversation soon turned into a debate. Jiban was against child marriage. The other three were trying to argue with him and demolish his standpoint.

Hem said, 'Agreed that child marriage is not good for society. You are free to make speeches and write in the papers against it but I don't see why you should not get married yourself. What do you say, Kishori?'

Hem hero-worshipped Kishori. Kishori's opinion was like the gospel truth for him. In Hem's eyes, Kishori's failure to clear the examination the previous year was also a sign of his superior intelligence. Since Kishori said that very bright students could not endure examinations, Hem also expected to endorse his statement in the forthcoming Entrance examination.

Kishori said, 'I say, it's all *absurd nonsense hypocrisy.*[23] Actually, Jibanda has not found the girl of his choice. *Early marriage, female emancipation, social reformation*, all these grand notions are good for making an impression. I also air such views when the opportunity arises. The other day Reverend Smith was amazed to hear my *radical views*, but in case I get a rich and good-looking girl, I will not let go of her. Jibanda, we have had child marriage for centuries. Tell me, has our country gone to the dogs or has the world come to a standstill?

Jiban said, 'Yes, everything is going on somehow, but it would be better if things were different. Tell me, what do we have as a race to be proud of? Neither do we have strength of character nor dedication to a great cause. Even if great people are born in this country, they cannot survive long. Why is it so?'

Kishori replied, 'That is because of malaria and subjection to a foreign power. We had child marriage even in the past but there was no dearth of great people and they lived long.'

Jiban: 'Malaria is a recent phenomenon and it is not prevalent everywhere. As for our subjection to a foreign power, what is the cause of that?'

Kishori: 'It is the climate of Bengal.'

Jiban: 'It is the lack of education among Bengalis. Women are responsible for character-building. If our women were educated properly, if we knew how to give them their rightful status, our fate would not have been so tragic.'

Kishori: 'Oh, forget about women's education and giving them status. Were the writers of the scriptures less intelligent than you are? They say, "*Vishwasam naiva kartavyam, streeshu rajakuleshu cha*." One should not put one's trust in women or in royal families.'

Jiban: 'There are many things in the scriptures that we do not practise. Vidyasagar has shown that the scriptures support widow remarriage also. Then why do we have reservations about it?'

Kishori: 'Widow remarriage? What is that saying...*achar*...*achar.*'

Nabin: '*Aacharo vinayo vidya pratishtha tirthadarshanam.*'

Kishori: 'I know it...it just slipped out of my mind. After all we cannot give up our customs. The scriptures may support widow remarriage but our custom is different.'

Jiban: 'In the name of custom we are committing many offences. You will not find such *foolishness* in any other nation.'

Nabin: 'That is not true. You will find such *foolishness* everywhere. The British have persecuted so many people in the name of their religion. The fact is that people have such sentiments for their traditions that their reason ceases to function.'

Jiban: '*False sentiments!*'

Nabin: 'When human beings are *imperfect*, this is hardly surprising.'

Jiban: 'But whoever is content with such imperfection is not worthy of being called human.'

Nabin: 'Then the British aren't human either.'

Jiban: 'It is not as though the British are free from *false sentiments*, but the love of truth is so strong in them that they are able to overcome their prejudices. At least they are aware of them. But in our country, from primitive times up to the present age, we are driven by blind superstitions and the desire to imitate others. What kind of *justice* is this? Women and shudras—'

Nabin: 'You are applying modern *standards* to ancient societies. You cannot judge these matters by *absolute* standards. Maybe those rules were *absolutely* necessary in those conditions.'

Jiban: 'Fine, but times have changed and the conditions have also changed. Why do you want to remain blind to that? You are influenced by conventions and make the scriptures an excuse for them.'

Hem: 'Stop sermonizing now. How self-righteous you are! So now we have to discard the scriptures and follow you. Tell me Kishori, will you appear for the Entrance?'

Kishori: 'I am not sure. I am in *a juxtaposition*.'

Jiban: 'How is that?'

Kishori: 'Dada is busy with his studies. Baba cannot manage the affairs of the estate alone. I think some problem about the zamindari has arisen—*an equatorial mortgage*.'

Jiban and Nabin burst out laughing. Kishori paused for a moment and then said, 'What are you laughing at?'

Jiban: 'Nothing. Here, Mohanda is coming.'

Kishori: 'O yes, he is. I'll go now or he'll start lecturing. Come along, Hem.'

By the time Mohan arrived on the scene, Kishori and Hem had left the garden. Jiban said, 'Hello, Mohanda, what's the news? When did you arrive from Shibpur?'

Mohan replied, 'I am fine. I came yesterday and have to leave again tomorrow. Why were you laughing so much?'

Nabin said, 'Well, we were in *a juxtaposition* over your brother's *equatorial mortgage*.'

Mohan understood what the matter was. He said, 'That is the extent of his knowledge. He couldn't possibly go any further.'

Jiban said, 'He is intelligent enough. If only he had studied, he would have done well.'

'Baba and Jethima have spoilt him with their pampering, so no more studies for him.'

'Mohanda, you said that you would sign.'

'On the *early-marriage pledge?*'

'Yes.'

'On further consideration I have thought it better not to do it, because I know I will not be able to fulfil it.'

'You are nineteen. It is only a question of two years.'

'The way they are pestering me, it doesn't seem as though they'll leave me alone even for two months, let alone two years!'

Nabin interrupted, 'Jiban, you are going crazy about child marriage. Everything has its advantages and disadvantages. Considering the present conditions in our country, abolishing child marriage may not have good consequences and if it becomes necessary, it will be done in due course. You need not be so perturbed about it.'

'What is the necessity for any action then? Let us all sit quietly and let things take their own course. What is the need for education, or working for a livelihood? There is no necessity for anything at all.'

They drifted into a discussion on fatalism instead of child marriage and as usual it came to a premature end, before a resolution could be arrived at. They were about to launch into another debate when it started getting dark. Seeing the landscape bathed in moonlight they grew restless and began to miss their books. They preferred their little nooks lit-up by oil lamps to the moonlit scene outdoors and proceeded in the direction of home.

10

Jiban's unwillingness to get married made his mother very unhappy. Jiban was not a child. He was nineteen years old and he had passed a couple of examinations. Any other boy in his place would have got married a long time ago. His mother wanted him to get married like the others. She did not have a daughter. She would like to fulfil her longing for a daughter by getting a daughter-in-law, but Jiban refused to marry on any account. Offers from several well-established families had come and had been rejected. As Jiban grew up and got acquainted with the great minds of the West, the desire to do well in life got stronger in him and the conventions and customs of his society seemed a hindrance to his ambition. For a while he was very keen on going to England but realized that it was not right for him to think of it for he was still not financially independent. The monthly allowance given to him by his father's friend Jagat Babu as a favour was too meagre to sustain them. If Jagat Babu did not give them free shelter, or help them out in other ways, they would have had to face great hardships. In the circumstances, going to England was an impossible dream, and this realization increased Jiban's frustration. Tormented by his ambition in a vague and undefined manner, he tried to drown his frustration in his studies. He did not stop at regarding his studies as a means to enhance his future career, but derived the greatest pleasure in the company of books. If he ever came across an interesting book, he could not hold himself back from reading it, even at the cost of neglecting his course books.

Jiban was particularly interested in books on literature and science. He found both equally absorbing and discovered an underlying connection between these disciplines although they were independent of one another. He could clearly see the scientific truths underlying the liberal imagination of poetry and fiction. He entered the vast and complex world of human nature and acquired a deep understanding of the highest philosophy, realizing with amazement the ultimate meaning of creation through the constant clash between good and evil.

He derived much pleasure from being in close touch with great minds and ardently desired to emulate their ideals in his own life. He clearly saw the opening up of the wide portals of imagination even in the smallest truths of the natural sciences, and was fascinated by the profound beauty of infinite nature as revealed within the boundaries of science. He developed a great veneration for the vocation of a scientist and wished to adopt it himself. If he could go to Europe and associate with the scholars there, study science diligently and return to India after achieving success, would his country not benefit by his learning? After all, Huxley came from an ordinary background and became such a brilliant scientist through hard work. In his youthful enthusiasm and lack of experience he did not see any obstacles in realizing his hopes of success. It seemed to him that all he needed was the opportunity to go to Europe, the birthplace of Copernicus, Galileo, and Newton, where hundreds and thousands of great people were born. Europe was the land of his dreams, his El Dorado, and the more obstacles he encountered in the way of his going to England, the more he continued to dream of the future when he would become financially independent and go there.

At times his mother disturbed his pleasant dream by coaxing him to marry. Jiban knew well that once he was bound in the chains of marriage, his hopes for the future would be shattered. As such, his mother's pleading created an acute disgust for marriage in his mind which he expressed in his arguments and writings against the rituals of marriage. Furthermore, in order to counter his mother's pressure, he founded a society for the abolition of child marriage. Some of his well-meaning teachers were members of this society, though it was difficult to say how far they could promote its aims because they were all married and Jiban was the only bachelor among them. According to the rules of the society, when a young bachelor became a member, he had to take a pledge to remain unmarried at least till the age of twenty-one. Jiban wanted to raise the limit from twenty-one to twenty-five years but the proposal was not accepted. Anyway the pledge could not free Jiban from his mother's demands—she continued to throw tantrums and harass him.

Jiban was not a tough person; rather he was quite the opposite. He could not even mete out punishment to a culprit. One day, on entering his room, he caught his servant standing in front of the mirror and using his hairbrush. Jiban became nervous that the servant might be embarrassed to see him and quickly retreated from there like a thief. He never raised the subject with his servant and merely put away his brush inside the drawer.

One day, Jiban had gone with some of his friends to bathe in the Ganga. Kishori and Jiban, both strong young men, started a mock fight in the water. Suddenly, Kishori, in a seemingly casual manner, forced Jiban's head down in the water. When Jiban, with some difficulty, released himself from Kishori's grip and raised his head, he cut his lip against the stone steps and it began to bleed profusely. He was about to scold Kishori but Kishori forestalled him by saying, 'Dada, are you hurt? It was an accident.' Jiban immediately checked his outburst and instead of getting angry felt embarrassed. While the others disapproved of Kishori's rough behaviour, Jiban made light of it and tried to convince everybody that Kishori was innocent and that it was his own fault that he was hurt.

Jiban often behaved like this in order to free others of a slight discomfiture. It was a singular weakness of his character. However, he had no qualms about hurting his mother by not getting married. He could empathize with anyone who was in a situation which he himself would have found embarrassing, but he was blind in other respects. He could not understand why his mother felt unhappy about his remaining single. So when she said to him, 'Jiban, please get married. She is a very nice girl,' he lost his patience and again started lecturing to her about the evils of child marriage. His mother listened to him for a while and then said, 'Son, all of us were married off early. Didn't we grow up properly?'

Jiban said, 'If we did not have the custom of child marriage in this country, we would have been a great people.'

His mother replied, 'There are many great people among us

even now. Look son, you will get a lot of money. The girl is also pretty.'

Jiban's mother believed that since Jagat Babu loved Snehalata so much, he would marry her well and give her a good dowry despite his wife. This made Jiban angry for he hated the idea of accepting a dowry. He wanted to marry for love, not for money, and never wondered whether it was possible to do so in our society. Losing his temper, he said, 'I trust I shall be able to earn enough money to satisfy you. You don't need to become rich with your daughter-in-law's money.'

His mother said, 'Then marry without a dowry.'

Jiban replied, 'You say the same thing over and over again. You know that I will not get married before completing my studies. I am tied up for at least two years.' Then, in order to avoid further discussion, he said, 'Nabin will be coming any moment now. I am going out.'

Jiban's mother persisted, 'The girl is very pretty. Just take a look at her once.'

Jiban was tempted to ask her how pretty she was, for the love of beauty was one of Jiban's many weaknesses, but he did not have the courage to ask any questions. That would make his mother get out of hand. So he left without a word.

Jiban's mother was very unhappy. She thought that fate was against her. Otherwise why did she become a widow? Would her son be so disobedient if her husband were alive? After shedding a few tears she was struck with an idea. When Jiban came home at night, she said, 'Well, Jiban, if you don't get married, Mohan can. We should not let go of such a good girl.'

Mohan and Kishori were Jiban's cousins. Jiban and Mohan were born within the space of a few months when Jiban's father was alive and they were a part of the joint family. As Mohan's mother fell ill a few days after his birth, Jiban's mother nursed him and looked after him as her own son. Jiban dismissed her remark, saying, 'Ah, marriage has become an obsession with you, it seems. Do whatever you like. It is no concern of mine.'

Jiban's mother realized that it was no use discussing the matter with Jiban and decided to proceed with her own plans. The next day she approached Jagat Babu's wife with a proposal of marriage between Mohan and Snehalata. She said, 'Mohan is a fine boy. I have brought him up since childhood and know him well. He is much more obedient than my Jiban. Only my sister-in-law, Mohan's aunt, is a bit cross-grained, but that shouldn't matter to a girl if her husband is good.'

The Mistress was in a hurry to get Snehalata married. She happily gave her consent to the proposal and brought up the matter with her husband the same day, only concealing from him what she had heard about Mohan's quarrelsome aunt. Jagat Babu was Kunja Babu's family physician and was familiar with everybody in the house. He knew Mohan to be a good boy. Now he started meeting him and talking to him in order to know him better. Eventually satisfied that Snehalata would be happy as his wife he gave his consent to the marriage proposal. When Jiban's mother heard of this from the Mistress, she sent for Kishori. She hadn't gone to her brother-in-law's house ever since he had seized her property after the death of her husband and separated from them. He had also never called them over or made enquiries after their welfare. But she had not let that create a breach between herself and her nephews, Mohan and Kishori, whom she invited often and with whom she regularly kept in touch. Mohan's father was unaware of it. Otherwise he would not have let them go to see her. Mohan and Kishori could never take Jiban to their house because of their father.

Calling Kishori over, Jiban's mother placed the proposal for Mohan's marriage before him. She said, 'The girl is beautiful, they will give a good dowry, the family and all the rest are fine. Tell Didi not to let go of this chance. Jiban is not willing to get married now, otherwise I wanted to have that girl as a daughter-in-law myself.'

Kishori said, 'I understand that the girl is good and will bring a substantial dowry but how can you say anything about the family when she is an orphan.'

Jiban's mother retorted with some irritation, 'Why do you say she is an orphan? Jagat Babu is more than a parent to her and she has a maternal uncle too, a rich man's son. His wife is barren, that is why they have become a little withdrawn but they will accept the match with pleasure.'

Kishori took the proposal to his aunt without further ado. In the meanwhile, the matchmaker from Jagat Babu's house also approached them. The negotiations went on for some time. The boy's father demanded a number of ornaments, gifts, and cash. There was some bargaining from the girl's party. Eventually, a compromise was reached, both families visited each other, and the match was finalized. The wedding day was fixed for the fifteenth day of the coming *Phalgun*.[24]

11

Snehalata got married. Jagat Babu's brother-in-law, Snehalata's maternal uncle, gave her away. Jagat Babu only stood by her side and shed tears. That was all he had the right to do. The marriage rituals were completed the next morning and after the midday feast, preparations were made for sending off the newly-weds.

Everybody knows what a sad day it is for a Bengali family to bid farewell to a daughter after her marriage. Although Snehalata was not a daughter of the house, she had become like one. The Mistress forgot the animosity she had towards her for so long and only thought of her virtues, rather than her faults. When the bride and the bridegroom came and stood near the staircase, she wiped her eyes and said, 'Snehalata, my child, you are leaving us desolate.'

Snehalata had been crying the whole day. The loving words of the Mistress made her cry even more. The servants were weeping silently so far. Now they started murmuring their blessings for Snehalata's long and happy married life. Tagar put her arms around her, sobbing. Charu did not cry but wore a sad expression. Jagat Babu was heartbroken. He placed his hand on her head and said, 'My child, be happy in your husband's home. May the goddess Lakshmi be with you. Leave your sorrows here and cheer up your new home with your presence.'

Snehalata entered the palanquin amidst blessings and tears. She carried her gloom to her husband's home.

There was no band with the wedding party. There were only two carriages, and a few baton-wielding footmen and maidservants accompanying them. Two teams of musicians were waiting at the Darjipara crossing to welcome them. As soon as the carriages with the red banners came into view they struck their tunes. The groom's house was at the end of the lane where a crowd of people had gathered in the veranda, the courtyard, and the terrace. When the music reached their ears, they shouted, 'The bridegroom has come.' There was a flurry of excitement and activity even before the palanquin reached the end of the lane. The people on the terrace rushed down; those standing downstairs ran into the lane while others moved towards the inner apartment. The women got busy. They blew the conches and ululated together to welcome the bride.

The mistress of the house, Mohan's aunt, known as Jethima, was fasting. She was a frail, pale-skinned, sharp-nosed, long-necked, sharp-tempered, tonsured (she had just returned from a pilgrimage), sour-faced elderly woman. She cried out impatiently, 'Blow into the fire. The milk must boil over.'

Jiban's mother, who had a soft, golden complexion and a smiling, cheerful countenance enquired excitedly, 'Didi, who will carry the bride, you or I?'

Jethima was screaming, 'O, Mejo Bou, where is the puffed rice? The bride is coming.' The married women who were standing with all the things needed for the reception of the bride replied, 'We have everything. We are ready.'

Even in an orderly household, there is some confusion on such occasions. In the midst of all this turmoil, thrill, and excitement, the palanquin carrying the bride and the bridegroom was brought into the courtyard. The women of the house came out and, ignoring the presence of the outsiders, stood around the palanquin. Jiban's mother picked up the bride in her arms without waiting for the permission of Jethima, her elder sister-in-law, and told the bridegroom to follow her. Partially veiled women and maidservants dressed in red garments accompanied them on the path decorated with *alpana*, scattering puffed rice and cowries and sprinkling water on the couple. Jiban's mother crossed the outer courtyard and entered the inner hallway, where a small fire was burning in a makeshift stove on which a vessel of milk was placed. A woman was assiduously blowing into the flame. Jiban's mother came near it and told Snehalata to look in that direction. Accordingly, she turned her veiled face towards it. Whether she could see anything or not, the others could see clearly that the milk was not boiling over. Jiban's mother was dumbfounded with fear while the others looked meaningfully at one another, whispering that the bride was unlucky.

Jethima came forward at this moment and saw the disaster. She was not the one to remain quiet. 'O, Mejo Bou, what kind of a bride have you got for Mohan?' she exclaimed. 'The milk hasn't boiled over.'

In the meanwhile, due to the insistent effort of the woman at the stove, the milk suddenly boiled over. Everyone expressed their satisfaction. Jiban's mother was immensely relieved and said, 'See, Didi, it is boiling over.' Proceeding to a banana tree standing in the centre of the hallway, she made the bride stand on a low stool. The bridegroom stood on another low stool next to her. Their clothes got wet from a vessel of curd placed there, in which a live fish was writhing. Satisfied with this auspicious sign, a woman removed the vessel. Now the vermilion ceremony was to be performed. A woman placed the basket of vermilion on the bride's head, partially removing her veil. The bridegroom put vermilion in the parting of her hair with his ring. Then the ritual welcome of the bride and groom started, accompanied by ululation, blowing on the conches, music, and much noise. The couple was brought to the nuptial chamber and seated there. Young women joked with them and made them play games. When these feminine rituals were over, the father-in-law was called to the inner apartments to see the bride. Jethima stood with her present in her hand awaiting her turn after him. When Kunja Babu came into the room, Jiban's mother lifted the bride's veil and asked him, 'Well, Thakurpo,[25] how do you like the bride?'

Everybody knows that the bride has to keep her eyes closed for this ceremony but unfortunately Snehalata was not aware of this because she had never attended a wedding since her childhood. The Mistress did not like to take her to such functions. Nobody had even briefed her about it. Nobody could imagine that Snehalata was ignorant about such a common practice, so when Jiban's mother lifted her veil she did not close her eyes but looked shyly at her father-in-law. In these unfamiliar surroundings she longed to see a kind and friendly face, but before she could see him properly, someone exclaimed sharply, 'O dear, what a shameless girl! She is staring at her father-in-law.' Trembling with fear, Snehalata cast her eyes down. 'My dear, shut your eyes,' whispered Jiban's mother in her ears. Snehalata closed her eyes, tears trickling down her cheeks.

The father-in-law gave his present and went away. Then the elders, the friends, and finally the other invitees gave her their gifts and the bridegroom left the room. Now the women started scrutinizing her appearance and her ornaments. This went on for a long time. First of all they expressed their disapproval of her coiffure. This was the first time the Mistress had done Snehalata's hair. She had tied it tightly enough but it was not properly set in front and instead of a gold pin, a silver pin had been used.

Next, a woman commented on the pale complexion of the bride. Another one held her hand and said that it was soft but the fingers were too long and then proceeded to examine her feet. Yet another said, 'Bou, look up.' The bride continued to look down shyly. The woman said sharply, 'Why don't you listen? I said, look up.' Snehalata glanced up. Another woman directed her to look towards her and satisfied herself that she had a good expression and a calm nature.

The scrutiny was coming to an end when someone held Snehalata by the hand and made her stand up so that they might see her figure. 'She is too thin,' was the general verdict. Now they turned their attention to her jewellery. 'Only four thin bangles and a heavy one,' said one. 'That is next to nothing.'

A young woman lifted Snehalata's veil, examined her throat, and turned away smiling, not considering it worthwhile to comment on the single gold choker she was wearing. Was that any ornament?

Such talk went on for a while, when Jethima, who had until then been busy elsewhere came in and wanted to see the bride's ornaments. 'What cheap ornaments has the girl been given!' she commented. 'Why they bothered to give her even these, I don't understand.'

Everybody looked reproachfully at Jiban's mother who had negotiated the match. She tried to explain, 'Thakurpo has already taken the money for the ornaments. Still they were good enough to give a few to the girl.'

Jethima said crossly, 'What riches has Doctor Jagat showered on my Thakurpo? He may as well have not given anything at all. Why talk about it?'

Jiban's mother had taken the initiative to attend this wedding herself because she had not been invited by her brother-in-law. Jethima had just sent word through a maidservant, asking her to come, but it was Mohan's wedding and she had been the prime mover in the negotiations. So, in spite of their coldness, she had come with a present the day after the marriage. If she said anything, it would lead to a quarrel, which she did not want, so she kept quiet.

One of the women present said, 'Well, after all it was our own Mohan's marriage. Could he not have got a better girl?'

Everybody started discussing these matters in the presence of the newly arrived child-bride without showing the slightest consideration for her feelings. How she must have suffered!

Early in the evening, Jiban's mother took Sneha for a light repast. Needless to say she could hardly eat anything. By the time they returned to the room, many of the guests had left after the refreshments, while those who were staying in the house had gone to wash their clothes. Jiban's mother took leave of the bride, saying, 'I'll be off now, my child.'

In this harsh and unfamiliar household she was the only relative and friend who had talked to Snehalata with affection. Holding her hand and looking at her with tears in her eyes, Sneha said pitifully. 'Mashima, when will I go home? Please take me home.' Jiban's mother wiped her tears and said, 'Child. I am not your aunt any more. I am your aunt-in-law. And you should not speak about going home. Now you will have your *phulsajja* and *boubhat*.[26] Then you will visit your home with your husband. This is not the time to go there. I'll send your maid in here. She will come after washing the clothes.'

While Snehalata and Jiban's mother were talking alone in the room, Jethima passed through the adjoining veranda, draped in her wet towel, on her way to her room to pick up her rosary. She peeped in and enquired, 'What is the bride saying, Mejo Bou?'

'Oh, nothing,' Jiban's mother replied. 'She is missing her home and crying.'

Jethima said, 'Why should a big girl behave like this? It is not as though her father is crying for her over there!'

Thus expressing her concern for her summarily, she went off to her room. Snehalata began to sob. Jiban's mother could not check her own tears. She couldn't help thinking that if Sneha had been her daughter-in-law she would have protected her from such harshness. Why didn't Jiban agree to getting married? She wiped Sneha's tears and said, 'Don't cry my child and don't let that old woman upset you. This is her nature.'

12

This was Snehalata's first day at her in-laws' place. Most of the girls in Bengal would have a more or less similar memory of their first experience as a new bride. Separated from their families and surrounded by strangers, when their tender and sensitive hearts long for an affectionate glance or words of sympathy, they often face bitter criticism as a sign of welcome in their marital home.

Perhaps it does not occur to these critics that the tender young creature has human feelings like anybody else. They go on expressing their harsh judgements as though they are in the presence of a lifeless rock. Those who are engaged in disparaging the newcomer have been victims of a similar treatment but the memory of that experience does not arouse in them any compassion for the young bride. Those who have suffered and seen others suffer, take it as a matter of course and do not look upon it as cruelty.

The second day after the wedding was phulsajja. The women guests started arriving after two in the afternoon. Only the close relatives of Kunjalal Babu had been present the previous day but on this day all the near and distant relatives of Kunja Babu and Jethima, with the exception of Jiban's mother had been invited. Many of them attended the function but Jiban's mother did not come.

Once again the elderly women examined the bride and her dowry and then settled down to a gossip session. They discussed how the uncle of a certain young woman had covered her from head to toe with gold ornaments studded with gems and weighed her in silver; how someone's uncle had been duped by a rich daughter-in-law's family, and how the cousin of someone's sister-in-law had been lured by money to get a dark girl as a bride. Their talk mainly centred around this subject. In the other room, young girls, both married and unmarried, surrounded the bride and tried to make friends with her.

In such a situation the conversation tends to be one-sided. The bride is silent, the others ask her questions but continue to talk amongst themselves without waiting for her answer. Mostly they talk about their husbands—how their husbands tried to make them talk on the wedding night, how much it took someone to get over her shyness, how much someone was loved by her husband and how that love was expressed on various occasions and so on. The girls chattered on and began to deck Snehalata up.

They arranged her hair, applied red dye to her feet, put vermilion in her parting, sandal on her forehead and collyrium in her eyes. Their time was spent pleasantly while they waited eagerly for the arrival of the flowers and clothes for the phulsajja after which the bride would be adorned with flowers. A little after the lighting of the lamps in the evening, Jethima called them and announced that the wedding presents from the bride's house had arrived and should be put away carefully. They ran excitedly towards the front hall, leaving Snehalata alone in the room. Male and female attendants dressed in colourful clothes and bearing trays covered with coloured cloth entered like ants in a procession and put the trays down in the hall one by one. Everybody looked at the gifts with interest and praised them. Someone held up the clothes for the phulsajja for the gathering to see. They said, 'The Doctor is generous. He has given plentifully.'

But there are people in this world who cannot appreciate anything and find fault with whatever they see, however good it may be. Mohan's Jethima had a nature like that. Even if Jagat Babu had sent brocade for them, it would have failed to please her. She cast a sidelong glance at the clothes, wrinkled her long nose and commented, 'Benarasi sari for the girl, Dhakai dhoti for the boy—what is so special about that? Come girls, take away the flowers, sandal and clothes for the bride.'

The attendants from the bride's house were offended by Jethima's sour remark but did not have the courage to speak up. Gradually, the hall was cleared and the things were taken inside. The attendants departed. The bride and groom were adorned with flowers and brought to the nuptial room, lit-up with lamps and chandeliers, and seated on the divan. The dancers had not arrived yet. Young women made the bride and groom play games. There was ululation and sprinkling of attar and flowers. Gradually, the spirit of fun caught up with everybody. The old jokes associated with marriage—a part of every woman's memory of her own wedding—were repeated, creating a merry atmosphere. The teasing was initiated by an old lady who lifted Snehalata's veil and said to Mohan, 'Look at your bride. Will she convert you into a sheep?'

Jagaddhatri, the universal aunt of the neighbourhood couldn't resist the temptation of joining in the teasing. She put a sweet in Mohan's hand and asked him to feed it to the bride. Not seeing any reason to object, Mohan obeyed her and everyone burst into laughter. A young woman who was distantly related to Mohan as a sister-in-law twisted his ear from behind, then came forward and said, 'What a dumb bridegroom you are. Sing a song for us.'

Mohan said, 'I cannot sing.'

She said, 'You can at least take the bride in your lap. Go on, do it now.'

Everyone all around pressed him to lift her in his lap. When Mohan did not comply they pinched his nose and ears and disconcerted him thoroughly. A woman picked up Sneha and forcibly put her on his lap, to everyone's delight. The poor bridegroom was in a fix unable to decide whether he should put her down or continue to hold her on his lap. Even Kishori had never faced such a *juxtaposition*.[27] He was rescued from it by the sound of ankle bells. The dancers had arrived. The celebrations couldn't have been complete without this entertainment. Taking advantage of the commotion, Mohan quietly put Sneha down. The dancers entered and began dancing to the accompaniment of cymbals and drums. They sang:

> My gallant is after my heart
> His beauty soothes my eyes
> And lights up my world.

The singing and dancing went on till midnight. Then, as the bride and groom began to feel sleepy, the dancers were taken to another room. Now the guests could have their supper and go home or stay on to watch more dancing. In the meanwhile, preparations were made for the couple to retire. All the lamps except one were put out.

The women put flowers and perfume on the newly-weds. Three of them lifted the net around the bed while others blew conch shells and ululated. When the couple sat on the bed, one woman made Sneha lie down in a certain position while the others showered them with blossoms. After completing the ritual of the phulsajja and teasing the couple, they left the room, closing the door behind them.

In the silence of the room Snehalata could not hold back her tears any more. She wept as she lay in bed and suddenly sat up with a start when Mohan placed his hand on her shoulder and asked lovingly, 'Why are you crying?'

Sneha had come to believe that she would only receive the kind of harsh treatment in her in-laws' house as she had got up to this moment. Touched by his kind and sympathetic tone she cast a look of surprise at Mohan. The young woman had made her lie down facing Mohan but she could not see him properly through the veil. As she lifted her face, Mohan gently removed her veil and she was astonished to see his face glowing with compassion and love. A new hope welled up in her heart and she said, 'I want to go home.'

Mohan told her, 'I'll look after you. Won't you stay with me?'

She replied, 'No, I will go home.'

Mohan said, 'All right, I'll tell them to send you home.'

She asked, 'When?'

He said, 'After the boubhat', and wiped her tears. Seeing that she was perspiring, he took up a fan made of flowers which was lying on the bed and started fanning her slowly.

Suddenly, there was a sound of giggling. Mohan's sister-in-law emerged from the other side of the bed and said, 'I have heard everything. Thakurpo, you have already fallen so much in love! Fanning your bride in the month of Phalgun—how wonderful!'

The speaker did not realize that the presence of five boisterous women had raised the temperature of the room so much that even a spray of ice-cold water could not bring it down, leave alone the breeze of a fan.

Mohan was abashed by this teasing and Snehalata turned pale with fear lest she had committed an offence by speaking to her husband and would not be sent home as a punishment.

The sister-in-law departed after that but the interruption brought to an end the conversation between the couple for the night for fear of other eavesdroppers. Mohan did whisper a few words cautiously but Snehalata did not have the courage to respond. Then both of them fell asleep.

Early next morning Mohan left the room. All the young married girls who had come to attend the wedding settled down on Snehalata's bed, eager to know what exchange she had with her husband the previous night. As Sneha did not answer their questions some of them were offended and others called her stubborn. They overcame their present disappointment by talking about a certain nice girl who had narrated everything that happened on phulsajja night. Anyway, in spite of Snehalata's silence, what passed between the couple the previous night filtered out and even reached Jethima's ears. She expressed her outrage by placing her hands on her cheeks and exclaiming, 'O my, what a girl! She has already said so much in such a short while. She will cast a spell on the boy, you wait and see.'

E ventually, Snehalata's wish was fulfilled. Eight days after the marriage the couple went to visit Jagat Babu's house. Snehalata was delighted to return to her old, familiar surroundings and be with her relatives. It was as though she had come out of a closed, dark room into an open garden, flooded with moonlight in springtime and could breathe freely once again. Charu, Tagar, and the servants had gathered in the courtyard before her palanquin alighted there. Jagat Babu could not come because he was standing outside to receive Mohan. Standing in their midst Snehalata was speechless with happiness and embarrassment and shrank into herself like a sensitive creeper. The maids greeted her and said, 'O dear, you have become coy within such a short time. Hope you haven't forgotten us.'

Charu said, 'Sneha why are you standing here? Come to the garden.'

Tagar intervened and said, 'No, Didi has to go to Ma first.'

She led her by the hand and Charu followed them. Jagat Babu came to meet them before they could reach the veranda on the first floor.

That day was like a dream for Snehalata. Time passed swiftly as she laughed and played with Charu and Tagar, chatted with Jagat Babu, plucked flowers in the garden, and ran around on the terrace. In the evening when she heard that the palanquin was ready to take her back she was taken by surprise, for she felt as though she had just arrived there. Tearfully she told the Mistress, 'Mashima, I won't go today.'

Tagar also requested her mother to let her stay. The Mistress said gently, 'Child, you cannot stay on this occasion. I'll call you again another day.'

When Jagat Babu came to see her off, she clung to him. He said, 'I can't keep you back today. You go now. I'll send for you within a week.'

Snehalata could not say anything further. The entire day's happiness was washed away in her tears of farewell, and a gloom descended on her as she entered the palanquin.

Jagat Babu would call her after seven days but how was she to spend the intervening period? There was no young girl of her age in the house and she could not even take up a book to read. Jethima had created a scene when she saw a book in her hand the other day. As a bride she had no responsibility in the house and no liberty to go to the terrace or the garden. She was supposed to stay inside the room the whole day. She could just lie down or walk about in the room or veranda if she wished to. That was the extent of freedom she was allowed.

Jethima had sent away the maidservant who had accompanied Snehalata from Jagat Babu's house on the day of the phulsajja. 'Don't we have enough maidservants here that we have to get one from the bride's house?' she had said. Snehalata would have been happy to have her company. The maid in this house came to Sneha from time to time to make enquiries, to take her for a bath or a meal and laid out her clothes. Being a bride, Snehalata could not talk to her but in this lonely prison she was grateful to hear her voice.

If Mohan could be with her sometimes she would have been able to endure her captivity better. A young husband's friendship and sympathy is the only comfort for a child bride at this stage. His support helps her to adjust to the new household gradually. Forgetting her own parents and family she unhesitatingly accepts the husband's house as her own. But Mohan stayed in Shibpur. Earlier, he used to come home for weekends but as his exams were approaching, his father had forbidden him to come home. Once, he did arrive stealthily, thinking that he would stay the night and depart early in the morning without anybody's knowledge, but when he entered the inner apartment, Jethima was praying in the veranda and he had to pass by her to go into Snehalata's room. He was caught and thoroughly humiliated. To cap it all, he was made to return to school the same evening.

Notwithstanding all the restrictions in her in-laws' house, Snehalata was allowed a few pleasures. She was free to cry and Jethima did not stop her from playing with her dolls, though this pastime was a severely limited one. The dolls given to her as a part of her dowry were kept in her room. Sneha would often take them out of the box, arrange them in the room, try to play with them but this did not provide her with much diversion. In Jagat Babu's house she had enjoyed playing with her dolls in the little free time she got after doing her household duties and her studies. She loved to dress up her clay dolls, talked with them and felt a kind of affinity with them. Here too she sometimes sat with her dolls, tried to dress them up or play with them but nothing seemed to work. The dolls remained in her hands and she got lost in the memories of her home. She even missed the scolding of the Mistress which now seemed to her as an expression of maternal affection. She would rather have endured that scolding all her life than the loneliness of her in-laws' household.

Somehow that miserable week came to an end for Snehalata, and the maid, Hara's mother, came to fetch her. Snehalata's heart leapt up with joy, but Jethima objected, saying, 'The month of *Chaitra*[28] is approaching. If we send her now, we cannot call her back before a month. She is a big girl; why should she go home so often? She went there the other day with her husband. Let her get used to her own household now.'

The maid replied, 'Of course she will get used to it. When she grows up and becomes familiar with her husband, she will not want to come even if we call her. She is still a child, she feels homesick and keeps crying. Let a couple of years pass, she will be all right.'

Whatever likelihood Snehalata had of going home upto now, there was no question of it after this. Jethima said, 'After all she is not chained and beaten up here that she should cry so much. And why should a girl be indulged like this. Go and tell your master. She won't go.'

Standing near the door, Snehalata heard everything. When the maid entered the room with a fallen countenance, Snehalata was crying. Hara's mother wiped her own tears and cursed Snehalata's aunt-in-law heartily. Jethima did not consider it proper to allow the bride to stay in the company of the maid for long. In a few moments she also appeared in the room and blamed Snehalata's guardians for calling her again in such strong language that the maid was forced to beat a hasty retreat.

The next day, Jagat Babu himself met Kunja Babu and proposed taking Snehalata home. Kunja Babu did not object to it but pointed out the necessity of obtaining his sister-in-law's permission. Jagat Babu then approached the lady, obtained her consent after some coaxing and, fearing that any delay might cause some fresh hindrance, took Snehalata home the very same day.

Through the month of *Chaitra*, Snehalata stayed on at Jagat Babu's house. At the onset of *Baisakh*[29] a palanquin with bearers was sent from her in-laws' house to fetch her. Snehalata departed crying, as before. She made Jagat Babu promise that he would send for her soon but when Hara's mother came again after ten or twelve days and broached the matter before Jethima, the old lady flew into a rage. 'She spent the whole of Chaitra there and within a few days you have come to take her back again! If they are so fond of her, why did they marry the girl off at all? It is not our practice to send the bride home so frequently. If this does not please your master, let him eat a little more rice and cool off.'

Hara's mother went away. Hearing the report, Jagat Babu felt that he should have gone personally instead of sending the maid. The next day he met Mohan's aunt and put forward the request again. The lady could not turn down the doctor's request and was forced to give her consent. She said, 'All right, I'll send her tomorrow. But don't talk about taking her ever again.'

Jagat Babu went to see Sneha with this good news. The next day, he sent Charu and Tagar instead of the maid. Snehalata was ever so thrilled. Chattering with them she forgot that she was still in her in-laws' house. Charu pushed back her veil, and when she tried to pull it up, Tagar held her hands and there was much merriment. As they were having fun together, Charu noticed some pictures on her shelves. He picked them up and remarked, 'These are nice pictures. Where did you get them?' Tagar also ran towards them and asked, 'Has Jamaibabu[30] given you these?'

Snehalata said yes but immediately realized that she hadn't done the right thing. She had just begun to learn that one had to be coy while talking to one's husband or referring to him in front of others. She blushed with embarrassment. Tagar clapped her hands with delight and Charu laughed out aloud. Snehalata also joined in their laughter. In the midst of all this merriment she forgot to cover her head. Hearing the sound of their laughter, Jethima peeped from the veranda into the room, saw Jagat Babu's children and went away, grumbling to herself. A little later, when Charu and Tagar came to her and said that they had come to fetch Snehalata, she replied that it was not an auspicious day for sending the daughter-in-law. Charu protested, 'But you promised my father yesterday.'

Jethima quickened the movement of her prayer beads and said, 'I did not remember that today was Tuesday. The world will not come to an end if she does not go today. She can go some other day.'

Losing his temper, Charu said, 'Come, Tagar, let us go. We have been insulted.'

Just as Charu had felt mortified the day Jagat Babu had slapped him, he was greatly offended by this insult. He even forgot to say goodbye to Snehalata. Holding Tagar by the hand, he stalked noisily out of the house, and got into the carriage in a huff. At the end of the lane they met Mohan who stopped the carriage and heard the whole account from Charu. Trying to appease Charu, he said, 'Charu, Jethima is mad. She doesn't understand things. Don't be angry. I'll try to send Sneha later.'

Charu did not reply. Wearing a frown on his little face, he commanded the coachman sternly to drive home. The carriage started moving. Feeling thwarted, Mohan entered the house and sat down quietly in the outer room. When the lamps were lit, the bells for the evening prayer began to chime and conch shells were sounded, he slowly went to Sneha's room. He knew that Jethima would be in the prayer room at that time. He found Snehalata lying on the bed and crying. He sat down near her and asked her gently what the matter was.

Snehalata did not remember to be coy. She said, sobbing, 'I want to go home.' Mohan said, 'All right, I'll get round Jethima to send you there.' She continued to cry and said, 'Jethima will not listen to you. She won't let me go.'

Mohan said, 'Don't worry, I'll persuade her somehow.' He wiped her tears, fanned her, and reassured her that she would be sent home soon.

The next day, Mohan approached Jethima early in the morning before leaving for Shibpur. Jethima was cutting vegetables with a bonthi[31] for dinner. She said, 'Ah, Mohan, what brings you here?'

Mohan replied, 'I have come to see you, Jethima, shouldn't I?'

Jethima said, 'You don't come to see me these days. I have brought you up since you were a child and now you don't come anywhere near me.'

Mohan said, 'I come whenever there is any need.' Jethima's hand remained on the bonthi. She lifted her head and asked, 'What is the matter now?'

Mohan was suddenly at a loss for words. He said, 'I just wanted to see you. After all, you don't call me.'

Jethima said, 'How can I call you? Your father gets angry if he sees you at home even for a couple of hours. See, Kishori failed his exam and your father blamed me for it. Well, sit down on that box.'

Mohan said, 'Jethima, I am going to Shibpur. I'll come back in the evening tomorrow. There is a holiday.'

Mohan left, finding it impossible to broach the subject. He thought he would venture to do it the next day but, to his dismay, she was in a foul mood when he went to see her.

'Mohan,' she demanded, 'what kind of a girl have you got married to? I never see a smile on her face nor hear anything except that she wants to go home.'

Seizing the opportunity Mohan said, 'Why don't you send her off then?'

Jethima said, 'Ah, she doesn't know how to behave. She is a bride and she can't even keep her head covered. If she goes home every now and then she'll be thoroughly spoilt.'

The readers know that Jethima had seen her head uncovered the day before only for a moment. Mohan pleaded, 'She is so young and homesick. Is it wise not to send her when they come here to fetch her?'

Jethima growled, 'She is not a girl, she is a witch. She has cast a spell on you, that is why you came to see me yesterday.'

Mohan got angry. 'Yes, that is why I came to you. What is wrong with that?'

Jethima said, 'Ah, things have gone so far. Oh God, what shall I do!'

A heated exchange followed. She left the place in tears and announced to the servants and everyone else who came her way that Mohan had quarrelled with her on account of his wife. She told

Kishori the same thing when he returned home and sent for her brother-in-law from the outer apartment and reported the matter to him too. Kunja Babu heard her story and said, 'So his wife has turned him into a sheep. Now let him send her home if he wants to, we won't call her back again.' Mohan suffered in helpless rage at this high-handedness.

14

*M*ohan's effort to ease the situation for his wife backfired. Snehalata lost all hopes of going to Jagat Babu's house soon. Mohan was more upset by her misery than he was by his father's unfairness. Our country is well known for the oppression of brides but the misery of young husbands is no less acute. The fear of elders or social censure prevents them from openly protesting against the oppression of their wives but they suffer much in isolation and silence. Even in the midst of great misery, the wives derive comfort from the sympathy of their husbands but the husbands get no sympathy from any quarter for their hard lot. If they support their wives directly or indirectly they face the condemnation of the elders, if they don't, they face the reproach of the wife.

When the family situation is different—the husband is the breadearner and the wife the mistress of the house—she faces no problems, but even this arrangement is not satisfactory. The world submits to power; therefore, in this situation the husband's relations are dependent on and obliged to him and often he also abuses his power over them. If the wife misbehaves with them, the husband is blamed and if he tries to correct his wife, he is denounced by her. In either case he is considered a partisan. Having no control over his situation, the poor man is tossed about like a ball with no will of his own. His identity is determined by the manipulation of others.

In any case, the above discussion is not quite relevant here for although Mohan suffered on behalf of his wife, he did not have to face her reproaches. After the altercation with Jethima, when he retired into his bedroom at night, Snehalata had already cried herself to sleep and there was no exchange between them before his departure to Shibpur. He sat for a long time on the bed, gazing at the sad expression on her young face in sleep and finally lay down thinking of her tender, girlish countenance. He did not sleep well that night; his sleep was interrupted by terrible dreams. At last when he was fully awake, the night had ended but the moon had not set. The light of dawn, mingled with the pale moonlight, flooded the chamber and cast a silvery glow on Snehalata's sweet, innocent face, making it look ethereal. Mohan looked at her with anguish, then kissed her face lightly, breathed a long sigh, and went out with an aching heart. Throughout his journey he only remembered her sad, innocent face. It had made a deep impression on his mind and while he was away from home and amidst strangers, it was this image which floated up in front of his eyes until the day of his death.

In the meanwhile, Jagat Babu was deeply offended on hearing the whole account from Charu, but a girl's father doesn't have the right to be angry. Even if he is dealt an insulting blow, he has to swallow it. Jagat Babu went to see Kunja Babu again but did not argue with him. He said, 'Well sir, it was settled that you would send Sneha over. What made you change your mind?'

Kunja Babu said, 'It is a women's affair. I have no role in it. Please do not mind. *Jamai Shashthi*[32] is approaching. She could go then. The Mistress is very angry. Let some time pass.'

The reason Kunja Babu gave so much importance to his elder sister-in-law was because she had a claim on one-third of the family property. If she quarrelled and separated from the family, he would have to forego that portion forever. Jiban's mother had neither money nor family support. Hence, he could easily deprive her of her share, but in this case it was not possible to do so. This sister-in-law's relatives were very alert about her rights and often suggested that she should come and live with them but Kunja Babu had influenced her to such an extent that she could not leave his establishment. Jagat Babu knew well what power she wielded in Kunja Babu's household and that nothing could be done without her permission. He approached her again but she was adamant and did not consent to sending the bride home before Jamai Shashthi.

On reaching home, Jagat Babu had to face a harsh rebuke from his wife: Charu and Tagar had gone to fetch Sneha and were refused by the old lady. The Mistress could not swallow this insult as calmly as Jagat Babu. She was all too ready to send her maid to their house with a fitting rejoinder. At the most they would not send Sneha over again. How did that matter? Jagat Babu told her that there was no need to do that. He would go there himself, say what was proper, and bring Sneha along with him. But now Jagat Babu too had been humiliated and sent back alone. This angered the Mistress no end. Jagat Babu was caught in a dilemma and Snehalata's plight became worse. Charu and Tagar were forbidden to visit her again. Jagat Babu still continued to see her sometimes; the Mistress could not prevent him from doing that.

A fortnight later it was Jamai Shashthi. The previous day, Jagat Babu had gone to Kunja Babu's place to invite the young couple. On that morning his servants came with the *tatva*.[33] Jethima turned up her nose on seeing the gifts. As it is she was of a carping nature; added to that she had a prejudice against anything connected with Snehalata. She saw the mangoes and declared that they were not of the best variety from Bombay, and even without looking at the sweets claimed that they were of an inferior quality. Casting a sidelong glance at the clothes she commented that she had never seen such cheap stuff in her life. In this way she made disparaging remarks about every item and concluded by saying, 'Why have they sent presents with such indifference? We were not greedy for them, after all.'

Kamali, Jagat Babu's maid could not bear such treatment any longer. The Mistress had even hinted that given a chance she should say a thing or two to Snehalata's old aunt-in-law. She said, 'Oh dear, our master has cast pearls before swine.' This infuriated the old lady and she screamed, 'What is the hussy saying? Have they sent presents to insult us? Get out, you slut, and take your presents back with you.'

Kamali hadn't expected such a reaction and was stunned. The other servants also quaked with fear. Hara's mother said, 'O, please, don't take offence at this woman's remark. She is mad. The Mistress hadn't told her to be cheeky.' Jethima said, 'Of course, she must have. Can a maid show such effrontery without encouragement from her employer? She may be your mistress but what can she do to us? Get out at once, all of you.'

There was a great commotion. The maids stood petrified. Jethima rushed to the outer room, calling out to her brother-in-law who appeared nervously on the scene. Jethima said, 'I won't stay in this house any more. The bride's people come and insult us like this.' She cried and created such an uproar that Kunja Babu was convinced that Jagat Babu's wife had sent the servants on purpose to be disrespectful to them.

'Send back the presents,' he growled. 'I shall explain things to Jagat Babu myself.' He went to the outer room to dash off a letter to him. Jagat Babu's retinue returned with the presents, crestfallen. Jethima scolded and cursed Snehalata, who wept bitterly. 'This inauspicious creature is the cause of all this trouble. She has set our house on fire—this trash!'

'Then don't keep the trash in the house, send her away,' someone said from behind.

Jethima turned round and saw Mohan who had just come in. She was flabbergasted at his temerity in speaking on behalf of his wife. 'O God, take me away,' she cried. 'I have given the boy to a monster. Now he has no respect even for his aunt.' Striking her head wildly she once again rushed towards the outer room.

Meanwhile, Mohan went up to Snehalata and said, 'Come down with me. I have kept the palanquin waiting for you.' He had seen the palanquin bearers leaving when he came home and had stopped them. He did not know what was going on inside the house. He had been thinking of persuading Jethima to send Snehalata home but things took a different course. He now braced himself to take Sneha away against the will of the elders.

Had Snehalata known what Mohan would have to suffer after her departure, she might have been refrained from taking such a step, but Snehalata was a child. Her husband's words only held up a pleasurable dream before her eyes. She eagerly responded to his affectionate gesture and got into the palanquin with him without imagining the consequences.

Neither Kunja Babu nor Jethima saw Snehalata leaving, but when they came to know about it, they were enraged. Jethima started abusing Snehalata while Kunja Babu sent word to Mohan that he need not have any further expectations from him. He had been disowned for having disgraced the family.

Mohan related the whole account to Jagat Babu. A distressed Jagat Babu offered to pay for his education at Shibpur. Mohan felt hesitant to accept help from his father-in-law but as there was no way out, he agreed to take it as a loan. He said that it would take five years to qualify as an engineer from Shibpur but it could be done from Roorkee in half the time. Under the circumstances, he proposed to complete his studies at Roorkee which would enable him to become financially independent one-and-a-half years earlier. Jagat Babu accepted it as a sensible plan. Within a week Mohan left Calcutta for Roorkee.

15

*M*ohan defied his father and went away to Roorkee but Jiban's mother had to suffer the consequences. That Mohan did not incur any loss on account of his rejection or fall at his feet in submission made Kunja Babu furious with him and all his supporters. Jethima was equally angry but her anger was directed not so much at Mohan as at Snehalata and her people whom she considered the root of all this trouble.

Fortunately for Mohan and Snehalata, they were out of their sphere of control and so were not affected by their wrath. For that reason, however, those who were exposed to it had to suffer much more. A snake in fury does not see who is crossing its path: the lucky ones escape, the unlucky ones fall a prey to it. Unable to harm anyone else, the combined rage of Kunja Babu and Jethima was directed at poor Jiban's mother because she had negotiated the match between Mohan and Snehalata.

Jagadamba Debi, whom we know as Jethima, was the veritable goddess Durga in fury, ready to strike Mohan's allies, who had now become her enemies. She waved her arms and exercised her tongue relentlessly, cursing and abusing them. In this she was egged on by her attendants.

The next day was *Ekadashi*.[34] Jethima was fasting and so had ample leisure. She sat with her prayer beads and prayed heartily for her enemies' departure to heaven. But as this did not appease her rage, she called her favourite maid Khemankari and asked her to go to Jagat Babu's house and convey to them her opinion of the family. When Khemankari expressed her reluctance to go there and brave their ire, she ordered her to go to Jiban's mother and give her a sound tongue-lashing. Khemankari very willingly agreed to go on this mission, but before she could leave the house Jethima declared that she would go personally to Jiban's mother and asked her to fetch a palanquin. She was determined to confront that ungrateful wretch and have it out with her. Forgetting her hunger and fatigue she arrived at Jiban's place, vented the full force of her fury on his mother and finally returned home feeling a little relieved.

Jethima's revenge was limited to a verbal assault but Kunja Babu's vengeance was a more substantial one. When Jiban's servant approached him on the appointed day to fetch the monthly allowance from him, he was sent back empty-handed with the message that the allowance had been discontinued. The same evening Jiban returned home with the news of his success in the BA examination. He had already started planning about his future. He wanted to become a pleader which would require two years of waiting. However, his hopeful imagination had already made a leap across that interval. It was as if the present and the future had become one for him and he could visualize nothing but the fulfilment of his dreams. Full of youthful enthusiasm and self-confidence, how could he have any doubts about his success? At this moment he had already become an established pleader enjoying fame and wealth which was but a step in realizing his ultimate goal of going to England. He was experiencing the thrill of landing there.

He hurried home in great spirits, full of hope and pleasant fantasies. Calling out to his mother excitedly, he rushed upstairs into the veranda where she usually waited for him. But today she did not greet him affectionately with a smile. Her eyes were tearful, her expression was grave. Seeing her like this Jiban could not utter a single word of all that he was planning to say. He came near her and asked gently, 'Ma, what is the matter? Did Jethima come here again and quarrel with you?'

Jiban's mother replied, 'No, my boy, your uncle has stopped our monthly allowance. How will I pay the servants now or buy the groceries? We have already lost everything we had. I had preserved your father's watch and chain for you but today I had to send it to the pawnshop.'

Jiban was jolted out of his pleasant dreams in a moment. His mother wiped her eyes and continued, 'My son, I have suffered much in this life. I wanted to protect you from all that misery, but your uncle has dashed my hopes to the ground.' Jiban did not say a word. He just gazed at the sky in silence. Evening was approaching. The clouds had lost their colourful aspect. The sky was a dull blue. A flock of wild geese streaked across it soundlessly. A few kites flying high in the sky descended suddenly. Perhaps Jiban's hopes would also meet a similar fate. He sighed deeply and turned to his mother. The pale evening light falling on their faces made their expression even more gloomy.

Jiban pulled himself together and said, 'Ma, I have passed the examination and have been awarded a scholarship of thirty rupees per month. Can't we carry on with that?'

This news was like the proverbial straw for Jiban's mother who felt as though she was drowning in a sea of troubles. She thanked God with all her heart and hoped that He would not abandon them in this crisis. Jiban was relieved to see this change in his mother. When the first impact of the news abated, they started budgeting for the future. Jiban's mother said, 'We can manage our daily shopping with thirty rupees. I can dismiss the cook and the other servants and take on the housework myself. But you have to study for another couple of years and there are other expenses too.'

'Ma, don't worry,' Jiban reassured her. 'I shall work. I have passed the BA examination and should get a job easily.'

This saddened Jiban's mother who knew how keen her son was to study law. She said, 'How can you work along with your studies?'

'It is possible,' he replied.

'But it is not easy to get a job. You need a patron for that. My cousin has passed four examinations but for want of a patron he has only got a tutor's job for thirty rupees after searching hard for a long time. We don't have a patron either except for Jagat Babu. Only he can help us out.'

Jiban was an optimistic person. He wasn't discouraged by his mother's pessimism. He did not believe that he wouldn't be able to get a job if he tried for it. He said, 'All right. Let us approach Jagat Babu first. If that doesn't work, we shall try other sources.'

The next morning the mother and son went to Jagat Babu's house. Sitting on the tattered old mat in Jagat Babu's bedroom, Jiban's mother narrated her sorrowful tale to Jagat Babu's wife. There was no one to disturb them that day as Tagar was away at her uncle's house and Snehalata was in another room. Nowadays, she did not come to the Mistress' room unless it were necessary. On hearing the account the Mistress said, 'They are such unscrupulous people to have grabbed your property and turned their nephew out in the streets. God will never tolerate such injustice. I tell you, you will get back your wealth. They will be rightly punished, you wait and see.'

Jiban's mother wiped her tears and said, 'I don't wish them ill, sister. May Kishori and Mohan do well and may Kunjalal not suffer. All we want is what is due to us. I became a widow when Jiban was just a little boy. I did not want him to have a bad time, but God willed otherwise. That upsets me.'

The Mistress said, 'Don't cry. Everything will turn out all right for your son. He is such a good boy, so studious, he is sure to do well. I haven't seen him for a long time. He used to come often when he was a child. Why don't you bring him here any more?'

Jiban's mother replied, 'He has also come to see Jagat Babu in the outer apartment to find out if he can get a job. You are our only support, sister.'

The Mistress said, 'He will definitely get a job, I'll see to that. After all, you must not be reduced to poverty.'

Tears of gratitude welled up in the eyes of Jiban's mother. She had always received the Mistress' affection although she was not related to her by blood. Their fathers lived in the same locality so they had been friends since childhood and the Mistress had always maintained this friendship faithfully. It is true that the Mistress was indifferent towards Snehalata but she was not a heartless or uncharitable person. She readily extended her support to alleviate the suffering of those she regarded as her friends. However, her affection was not based on any principle of universal generosity. It was decidedly not spontaneously directed towards Jagat Babu's relations.

She was really happy to know that Jiban had come to their house. She expressed her eagerness to see him and sent Hara's mother to call him inside. A little later, footsteps were heard in the veranda. Snehalata, who was in another room, thought that Jagat Babu was coming and rushed out to welcome him. Seeing a stranger in his place, she gave him a surprised look and hastily withdrew to her room, overcome by embarrassment.

The Mistress was also surprised to see Jiban. He had not visited her for nearly ten years and instead of the boy she had expected to see, an unknown, handsome youth stood before her. He was tall, and had a pleasant, intelligent face, curly hair, large expressive eyes and well-formed nose and lips. His charming appearance spoke of his refined intellect. The Mistress looked at him with maternal appreciation and welcomed him warmly. Jiban touched her feet and sat down. The Mistress said to his mother, 'Your son has grown up now. Ah, he is really handsome! Why haven't you got him married?'

His mother replied, 'I have told him often enough but he doesn't listen to me. Now I think it is for the best, otherwise a girl from another family would have come to grief. Let him become independent now and find a bride for himself.'

Jiban began to feel uncomfortable at this turn of the conversation. Changing the subject he said, 'Mashima, where is Charu? I don't see him hereabouts.' This ploy proved to be successful. The Mistress told him that Charu had gone out somewhere and would return soon. Jiban's mother asked him whether Jagat Babu had told him anything about a job. Jiban replied, 'There is a vacancy for a teacher in the Metropolitan school. The salary is fifty rupees a month. Jagat Babu will take me to see Vidyasagar Mashai[35] just now. Let us see if anything comes of it.'

The Mistress said, 'Don't worry. Vidyasagar Mashai will never turn down my husband's request.'

Overwhelmed with gratitude, Jiban's mother blessed their household and wished for their prosperity. 'Sister, you are closer to me than any relative,' she said. After some time, when Jiban was called away by Jagat Babu, the Mistress said to his mother, 'What more can I say to you, sister, I feel as though Jiban is my own son and has always been dear to me. I must make him my son-in-law.'

Jiban's mother replied, 'I have no objection to that. It would be madness to refuse such a good offer. But my son is not prepared to get married now. He has joined some society mociety and taken a vow that he will not marry before he is twenty-one.'

The Mistress said, 'That is fine. Let two years pass. Tagar, God bless her, has just stepped into her ninth year. There is no hurry. We know each other well. Let us have an engagement now; the girl can be with us for a while longer.'

Jiban's mother had no reason to demur. Tagar was rather wilful but she was after all a child and would herself become sensible when she grew up. How could she refuse the Mistress who had done so much for them and Jiban could not possibly marry into a better family. Yet Jiban's mother hesitated to give her final word. She could not rely on Jiban; it would be disastrous if he refused to honour her commitment. 'Let me speak to my son,' she finally said. 'He is so wayward, he might say that he doesn't have the money to feed and clothe me, how would he support a girl from another family.'

'Why do you say that?' the Mistress reassured her. 'You have so much property. You just have to go to court to claim it and the matter will be settled in your favour.'

'But sister, one cannot fight a case without money.'

'Do you think there won't be money enough for that after the marriage? I'll fight the case in the interest of my daughter and son-in-law. He will be my own relative, after all.'

A new world, full of possibilities, unfolded itself before the eyes of Jiban's mother. She said, 'Sister, I am really keen on this marriage.'

The Mistress echoed her feelings, 'Everything will materialize; the marriage, the property and wealth. I'd like to see Kunja Babu's face then. You know, sister, you will build a three-storeyed mansion in the vacant plot adjacent to Kunja Babu's house. The old man and the old woman will die of jealousy.' The Mistress settled into a more comfortable position on the mat as though her ambition and her fantasy had been realized at that moment itself.

Jiban's mother said, 'It will happen if God wills it so. All I want is the happiness of my son and his wife.'

'You will get everything: son, daughter-in-law, grandchildren, wealth, and prosperity. Just be patient and wait for a while.'

The two women started making plans for Jiban's bright future, while poor Jiban, totally unaware of these prospects, began wandering from pillar to post for the sake of a petty job.

16

Jiban got the job for which Jagat Babu had taken him to see Vidyasagar. Who does not know the great man's compassion for the distressed and his love of the deserving? Seeing Jiban and hearing about his circumstances Vidyasagar promised to help him immediately. Jiban returned home successful, but he wasn't as happy as he had expected to be; his feelings were ambivalent. Although he was relieved of his previous anxiety regarding food and shelter, when he contemplated his future prospects, he was overcome by dejection. Was this going to be the end of his hopes and fantasies and was his ambition going to culminate in a petty job? However, this disappointment did not last long. He imagined that this was a temporary setback and he would be able to realize his cherished goal in future. He regained his confidence gradually and was content with his present success. True happiness lies not in the achievement of a purpose but in its anticipation.

Returning home, Jiban was happy to see his mother in a cheerful mood. She had just come back from Jagat Babu's house and was thinking of what had passed between her and Jagat Babu's wife. She was still excited about Jiban's future prosperity as though it was already a reality. The news of Jiban's appointment made her feel that it marked the beginning of a revival of their fortunes. Unable to restrain herself she said to him, 'My dear Jiban, don't refuse the offer this time.'

'Which offer?'

'Charu's mother is very keen on this alliance. She wants you to be her son-in-law. They have been so good to us.'

Hearing this, Jiban suddenly recalled Snehalata. Her flower-like figure, her tender, bewildered glance, her timid, hasty retreat flashed before his eyes and he was reminded of Tennyson's lines, 'Airy, fairy Lillian/Flitting fairy Lillian'. He said to himself, 'Yes, if I were to marry now, I wouldn't mind marrying her.' Aloud, he said to his mother, 'You know that I cannot get married now, so why do you talk about it?'

'I am not talking about the present,' she said. 'Charu's mother is willing to keep her daughter for another two years if you give your consent.'

Jiban said, 'I don't know what our plight will be in another two years. How can we take a decision about it at this moment?'

'I tell you, if you get married, our circumstances will improve. You cannot get a better patron. You won't have to worry about the court case. Your property and wealth will come back to you and you won't have to carry on with this ordinary job.'

'No, no,' Jiban protested. 'Don't give your word right away, expecting all this.'

'What shall I tell them, when they are so keen on it? Where would we have been without them, you tell me.'

Jiban said, 'That is true but they didn't help us thinking that I would marry their daughter. You just tell them that it is not possible now.'

They argued for a while. Finally, Jiban's mother declared, 'I tell you, my son, you won't have to work if you accept this proposal. Charu's mother has promised to fight our case in the court for us.'

Jiban laughed, 'Then you tell them that there is no need for the marriage. Let them pay the money for the court case. We shall be grateful to them and I shall pay back the loan later on.'

Jiban's mother lost her patience. 'I can't say that,' she said. 'You can say it yourself if you like. We should count ourselves lucky they have come up with this proposal.'

Jiban had seen Snehalata and thought her to be Jagat Babu's daughter. So he could not ignore his mother's suggestion altogether. He just laughed again and said, 'Why, Ma, doesn't your son have enough merit of his own that people might consider themselves fortunate to give their daughter in marriage to him.'

Jiban's mother forgot her ill-humour at once, and said, 'Oh, so that's why you are so proud! No, you must consent to this marriage, that's a good boy.'

Jiban did not submit to his mother's pressure but insisted that he would wait for two years before committing himself. His mother was satisfied with this because he had never discussed the subject so calmly earlier. Her mind was filled with a new hope. She thought that he was half-willing and she would be able to bring him round gradually. She did not press him any further, fearing an adverse reaction.

In the meanwhile the Mistress started preparing a dowry for her daughter. There was a silent agreement between the two mothers. No matter how much Jiban protested, they were certain that this marriage was going to take place.

17

*T*wo years have passed. Charu is a sixteen-year-old boy now but he does not consider himself a boy any longer. He recalls with amusement and embarrassment the Charu of the past who cried after being slapped by his father. In these two years Charu has become a dignified personage in his own estimation. It is natural because now he is a student of the Entrance class. Many boys older than him are his classmates and he interacts with several bright boys of the senior classes. Besides, he is also a member of a secret club, a coveted position which a number of students haven't been able to attain, whereas Charu has been appointed a member without any effort on his part. The sun's rays cannot remain hidden behind a cloud for long. Charu's talent has brought him into the limelight automatically.

Charu's claim to fame was established the day a fellow student pulled out a piece of paper from his pocket on which the following lines were scribbled:

> On a moonlit night
> Trembling with delight
> In a lonely wood
> Their faces glowed
> And the dark pupils of their eyes
> Gazed at each other

The boy read it out to the class and everybody burst out laughing. They asked him who the dark-eyed beauty was and where he had met her. Charu remained silent in the midst of their pointed enquiries, because the poem did not refer to any specific person but had sprung straight out of his fancy. He was disgusted by the lack of imagination in his classmates. While they continued to tease him and make fun of his poem, another young man appeared on the scene and asked what the matter was. They said, 'You know, our Charu Babu is a poet,' and read out the lines amidst derisive laughter and applause. The young man snatched the paper from the boy who held it and after reading it declared that it was a beautiful poem. Charu blushed with pleasure. Who wouldn't have felt flattered after being complimented by a clever and mature person like Kishori who had discontinued his studies for two years after failing in the Entrance examination but had again sought admission in Charu's class. Kishori's remark changed the attitude of the other boys. They also looked at Charu with appreciation. Since then Charu and Kishori became great friends. Charu could not rest content till he read out all his poetic compositions to him. Kishori was always well-disposed towards his admirers so he accepted Charu as a friend and it was he who made Charu a member of their secret club. Charu became their poet laureate.

It was Sunday. The members of the club were to meet in Jagat Babu's farm house in Chandan Nagar. It was about two o'clock in the afternoon. Two students were posted outside the closed door of a room on the ground floor. In spite of the trees all around and the covered portico in front, the heat of the August sun was scorching them. They remained rooted to their places but their minds were not at rest. They glanced impatiently in all directions and expressed their agitation in fairly strong language.

When it was past three the two men they were awaiting entered the premises. After a brief exchange the students blindfolded the newcomers and knocked on the door. When it was opened they took them by the hand and conducted them inside. Then the door was closed and everyone sang in chorus.

> From today our lives are bound in a single thread
> We shall abide by our vows in life and death.

The room reverberated with the sound of their singing. The blindfolded newcomers trembled with fear. They wondered what unknown snare they had walked into. Although they had been told that there was no cause for alarm, they felt certain they had been deluded into joining a group of revolutionaries.

When the singing ceased, the president picked up two daggers from the table with a lotus design on them and handed them to the newcomers, saying, 'This lotus is the symbol of the motherland and the daggers represent our struggle. Hold them up and swear.'

Everyone chanted in unison, 'Hold them up and swear.' The president said, 'Swear that from today you will dedicate your life to the welfare of the motherland and join our brotherhood.' Everyone chanted, 'Hold these up and swear.' The president continued, 'Even if you leave the club for some reason, you will keep its activities a secret and not betray our trust.'

Everyone repeated, 'You will maintain this trust in life and death.'

The newcomers did not quite understand what they heard or what they said. They only repeated everything in a trembling voice. Then their blindfolds were removed and one by one all the members embraced them and sang together.

> We shall lay down our lives for our motherland
> Witness these sacred swords and the God above
> Sing heartily of our victory
> Dharma is on our side and there is nothing to fear
> Thousands of lives bound in a single thread
> We shall abide by our vows in life and death .

This was Charu's composition. When everybody sang it together Charu felt that he was an equal of Shakespeare.

18

After the singing when everybody was seated once again, the new members got a chance to look around. They realized that there was no reason for the anxiety they had felt when they were blindfolded. The president sat at a table on which were placed a couple of incense burners, a few daggers, and some implements for writing. From time to time he engaged himself in throwing a pinch of incense in the burners. There were a number of chairs in the room of which only sixteen were occupied by the old members. They were neither strong men from the north nor Sikh rebels from Punjab. All of them were average Bengali students and even they had put their daggers aside on the table. Looking at them the newcomers felt relieved but were doubtful about the prospects of the nation's future.

Next, the president of the club, Jibanchandra Mukhopadhyaya stood up to deliver his speech. 'Brothers,' he began, 'we have joined ourselves in this sacred brotherhood and taken our solemn oath to promote the welfare and progress of the nation and enhance the glory of our race.

'What are the practical steps to achieve this goal? The answer is the spread of education and increase in the national wealth. It is said that Lakshmi, the goddess of wealth, and Saraswati, the goddess of learning, are hostile to each other, but our experience does not bear this out. Where there is knowledge, there is material prosperity and Lakshmi's bounty goes hand in hand with intellectual enlightenment. In spite of a number of schools and colleges having been opened in our country most of our people haven't received proper education because of poverty. The impoverished, unfortunate multitudes do not have the time to devote to learning. In general, the goal of our education is not to acquire knowledge but to earn money, but even that goal cannot be achieved with our half-baked education. Just look around and see how terrible is the struggle for survival in our country. The plight of our peasants and artisans is deplorable. College graduates, after putting in years of labour, get a degree which qualifies them to be employed for just thirty or forty rupees a month and even that is not available to hundreds of graduates because the government is unable to provide them with jobs. Both the educated and uneducated people are desperate but no one is aware of the measures that should be taken to improve the situation. The only practical way to increase the national wealth is the development of our trade and crafts. Countries like England have prospered because of the relative growth of their trade and industry. In the past we were also highly proficient in our crafts. Even before the coming of the British, India exported its handicrafts to different countries but now our crafts are nearly extinct. Far from exporting our wares to other countries we are now importing even essential goods from clothing to matchboxes. The more the West has advanced its scientific knowledge and technical skills, the more the ancient handicrafts of the East have lost their prestige. With the use of machinery, large-scale manufacture of goods is possible using less time and labour and these goods are cheaper too. We must also pay attention to proper scientific and technical education which will enable us to improve our crafts. The real aim of our club is to promote rational and scientific discussion as is prevalent in European countries.

'Our motherland is rich in agricultural and mineral resources. Is there any dearth of precious materials here? We have plenty of mines and raw materials for trade. The Europeans are digging out iron from our mines and sending our fine cotton abroad for the manufacture of textiles. For lack of awareness we are losing our wealth and precious raw materials to outsiders while our ignorant and starved population waits pathetically for the crumbs to fall in their begging bowls.

'The government does not hinder us from indulging in these activities. It says that it wants our crafts to develop. Hence, the only reason for our backwardness is our own inadequacy. If we determine to overcome it we shall achieve success sooner or later. What can we not accomplish with unity, determination, and joint effort? We have formed this secret club to promote this unity. The more close-knit the group is, the more efficiently it can work. Besides, we have to be careful so that our activity does not arouse the ridicule of cynics at the beginning itself and cause its untimely end. There is no other reason for this secrecy. We are neither rebels nor the opponents of the British. We are their followers. The British deserve our gratitude for opening our unseeing eyes through their education and example. We Indians have always been engrossed in thinking about life here-after. We consider the path of withdrawal as the best course. The British have explained the importance of worldly progress to this fatalistic and passive race. They have initiated us into patriotism, nationalism, solidarity, and enthusiasm for work which contribute to the building up of a race and have provided inspiration to us. So they deserve our thanks, not our animosity. We do frequently receive unfair treatment at their hands, but if we want progress we should direct our attention to our own shortcomings and make an effort to remove them instead of finding fault with them. It is universally acknowledged that might is right. Incompetence always invites con-tempt. Who will not take the offensive and derive pleasure from striking a blow when there is no fear of retaliation? Those who are capable always emerge victorious. If we want to put an end to their tyranny we must become competent ourselves. One does not acquire competence by merely being abusive. We must single-mindedly pursue our goal of unity, determination, and diligence.'

Jiban sat down amidst applause and cheering. Nabin stood up and when silence was restored, he began:

'It appears from the speech of our brother, the president, that a civilization based on the principle of "might is right" is a true civilization. I do not deny that it is the watchword of the Western civilization but a little thinking will convince us that genuine and great civilizations are far above this dictum. The greatness of our culture is self-evident. It shines uniformly like the sun's rays over the strong and the weak; its glory is based not on selfishness but on self-sacrifice, not on physical might but on justice.

'I do not deny that the British are a great race. But is it so because they have been able to oppress weak, helpless Indians or because they frown upon Indians—who are their equals in knowledge and intelligence—as natives and barbarians? This is not their greatness but their narrow-mindedness, their baseness. They are a great race in their self-denial and their liberal, humanitarian outlook. There are many great people among them who have laid down their lives for others, stood up for universal humanitarian ideals, and braved the bitter criticism and disapproval of bigoted people. They have proved through the example of their own actions, that "might is right" is not the fundamental principle of their civilization.

'It is true that merit deserves success but there is an essential difference between the merit of an animal and that of a human being. The essence of brute strength lies in destroying others and that of humanity lies in sacrificing oneself for the benefit of others. The cultivation of the latter is the goal of true civilization. No one can deny that. Wasn't India at the pinnacle of worldly prosperity once upon a time? But its downfall began the moment it accepted "might is right" in place of the rule of justice as its ideal. The roots of our civilization were weakened when Brahmins started misusing their power and instead of selfless service, self-interest became the sole purpose of their existence. Nevertheless, how is our wrecked civilization still able to hold up its head? It is because it is based on the firm foundation of justice and spirituality. Whatever is significant and worthwhile endures. That in spite of our fall we have survived and are once again trying to rise speaks of the strong foundation of our ancient civilization which has saved us from annihilation and maintained our distinctiveness. Therefore, it is only by directing our efforts to the restoration of the past glory of our race that we can arrive at our desired goal, because that is our exclusive heritage and we have the ability to establish our right to this tradition, handed down to us by our ancestors. It is a delusion to think that we can prosper by fighting shy of the effort to re-establish our past glory and by depending on the charity of others. In fact, it is an unhealthy practice to imitate foreign ways. While English education has benefited us in some respects, it has also caused us much harm. Bengalis have not been slack in imitating the English. We have become like the English in our speech, in our opinions, in our dress, in our sports and entertainment, yet to what extent have we been able to imbibe the English character? How can we do it? A green jackfruit cannot ripen properly. How can we become like the British? We do not have their grit, their proficiency in work, their amazing physical and mental prowess which enables them to grapple with adverse conditions tirelessly. How can we acquire the tremendous energy and drive of the Western civilization in the enervating climate of the tropics? In imitating them we are not really imbibing their greatness, their vigour and excellence, we are actually losing our hold on the best part of ourselves. We have even started looking down on our inherent racial virtues such as tolerance, forgiveness, modesty, and civility which could be an example for the Western world. This is because the British have no respect for these virtues. Although Christ preached that on being struck we should turn the other cheek, the British, with their pride in their brute strength do not practise it. They do not respect humility or fortitude, they take it as a sign of weakness and cowardice. They consider it dishonourable not to retaliate when they are insulted. We have also lost our honour and are vainly holding up the honour of others. Instead of condemning the use of brute force and regarding self-restraint as a sign of humanity, we are loudly advocating the policy of tit for tat. This does not promote our strength to strike, it only enhances our vanity and cowardice. So I say, let the aim of the club not merely be scientific discourse but also spiritual development and the preservation of our national identity.'

This time the applause and cheering was louder than ever. Kishori's excitement far surpassed that of others even after everybody had quietened down. Not able to contain himself, he burst out, 'Bravo, nationhood! We shall wear dhotis, sit on the floor, and not touch outcastes. We shall preserve our religion as true Hindus.'

Jiban interrupted him, saying, 'Cool down, Kishori, what you are suggesting will only enhance casteism, not nationalism. In fact, upholding the evil traditions of our community will not further the progress of the nation for which we must preserve the greatness of our national character. I believe brother Nabin has used the term nationalism in that sense. Therefore, it is incumbent on us to practise our spirituality and religiosity. There is no doubt about it. But if we try to strictly confine it to the observance of rituals and customs it won't yield desirable results. Adherence to rituals and the caste system has led to disastrous consequences in our country. The progress of the country is possible only if the abhorrent system which makes people look down upon their fellow humans as contemptible and untouchable is uprooted. Only by remaining indifferent to this narrow-minded and hateful system can we destroy it, hence the practices which encourage casteism cannot be acceptable to the members of this club.'

Jiban might have continued like this much longer, but he stopped because just then the clock struck five and the attention of the assembly was diverted. Kishori said, 'Time is up and we shall have to leave just now, but we haven't settled anything with our new members.'

The new members had been brought in by Kishori. It seemed they had developed the technique of producing glass through their experimentation, but had not been able to start their venture properly due to lack of funds. The aim of the club was to pursue the practice of science and increase the national wealth through industrial enterprise. As such, the members were happy to recruit these newcomers in their club. Nabin said, 'Gentlemen, can we see the soap which you have made? Since making glass is more expensive than making soap, the club would prefer to start with soap.'

One of the newcomers replied, 'We haven't been able to make soap because of shortage of money. Although we had made all the preparations we had to give up the idea.'

Jiban asked how much it would cost to start the venture on a small scale. The man replied, 'A manufacturing unit cannot be started for less than five hundred rupees.' The club members looked at each other. This was the crux of the problem. They were all schoolboys and came from middle-class homes. All they got was a meagre allowance for their daily tiffin. If the capital required came to about twenty rupees, each of them could have contributed two or three rupees towards it by doing without snacks for a month or so. They were willing to make such a sacrifice for the cause of the nation, but no one except perhaps Jiban, Kishori or Charu could contribute such a large amount. Jiban had a job, and Kishori and Charu had rich fathers. Everyone looked at them expectantly. Finally Nabin spoke up, 'Jiban Babu, if the amount is five hundred rupees you people should contribute. There is Kishori, there is Charu, you are working. I can sell off my clothes and contribute my pocket money.'

Jiban smiled. He had only his father's watch-chain to rely on but he could imagine how angry his mother would be at this proposal. Kishori asked Jiban, 'Dada, how much will you give?'

Jiban replied, 'Well, a hundred.'

Charu said, 'I shall also give a hundred. How much will Kishorida give?'

It wasn't as though Kishori had much money at his disposal; his allowance was meagre and his habits were extravagant. Kunja Babu gave him only five rupees a month as pocket money, and Kishori did not have the courage to ask him for more. Now and then he bullied Jethima into giving him a few rupees. Yet when Charu and Jiban agreed to give a hundred rupees each, he could not quote a lesser amount for fear of losing face before them. So he said without flinching, 'I shall also give a hundred, but what about the remaining two hundred?'

Nabin said, 'The rest of us can contribute another fifty. That makes it three hundred and fifty rupees. Brother Kartikchandra, please calculate once again and see if you can start the work within this amount. When a quantity of soap is ready, we can make a sale which will fetch money and the factory can carry on. One must make a beginning at least.'

The new member Kartikchandra made some calculations with the help of his brother Ganeshchandra and then declared, 'We can do with another fifty or so which we can raise ourselves and start the work.'

Everyone was happy. It was decided that they would bring their contributions the following Sunday.

19

$\mathcal{A}$s the train moved along, Nabin and Kishori, seated in a second-class compartment, looked out of the window, talking to each other. The number of members in the club was quite large, so everybody did not get a place in this compartment. It was past six o'clock. Dusk had fallen but the light in the western sky had cast an orange glow on the landscape outside. One could clearly distinguish stretches of uncultivated land, green fields, banana and jackfruit groves, lotus ponds, dilapidated houses, and new gardens next to them.

Nabin was humming to himself:

> The daylight is waning
> Yet the light of the heart sparkles in the eyes,
> There is no night or day in the realm of the mind
> Forever burns the light of love.

Kishori who was quietly looking out of the window suddenly spoke up. 'Nabinda, last night I saw in my dream the same kind of house as you see near that pond.'

Nabin stopped singing and exclaimed, 'Really?'

'Yes, I tell you, it was the very same house. What does that mean?'

'You may have seen that house last Sunday.'

'No, I am sure I never noticed that broken house earlier.'

'Maybe you didn't notice it, but there is no doubt you saw it. This is called *unconscious cerebration*.'

Kishori did not know what this phrase meant but he did not contradict Nabin for fear of exposing his ignorance. He said, 'That may be so, but what about my dream? I saw myself collecting a lot of money in that house. What does that mean?'

Nabin said, 'You must have gone to sleep thinking about money, what else? It is not a surprising thing.'

Kishori replied, 'I swear I didn't think of money when I went to sleep. I was so happy in my dream. I really felt bad when I woke up.'

'All right,' Nabin went on, 'tell me, somebody regularly has happy dreams but during the day he is unhappy while another person is happy during the day but has bad dreams at night. Which of them is more happy? This is a psychological riddle.'

'How do you say that? Then you have to consider the dream to be real. Why do you call it a dream? That is where your *fallacy* lies,' Kishori said, very proud of his profound statement.

Nabin continued, 'If that is what you say, our life itself is a kind of dream. You see all those houses there. You think they are real, don't you? But they are actually nothing but a conglomeration of our sensations. In simple language, they are just our ideas.'

'But if these objects are not real,' Kishori asked, 'how do they arouse those ideas in our minds?'

'Bravo!' Nabin exclaimed, 'Descartes also said the same thing in the reverse order. He said, "I think, therefore I am. That is sufficient proof of my existence."'

'And if I exist,' Kishori concluded, 'others exist too.'

A little later the train came to a halt and an Englishman entered the compartment. Seeing him, Nabin and Kishori stood up and said, 'Hello.' John Sahib, the missionary, greeted them affably and shook hands with them. Then they all sat down and started talking. John Sahib asked Kishori in Bengali, 'Have you read that book?'

It was John Sahib's belief that he could converse in Bengali like a native.

Kishori said, 'No sir, one is so busy studying for the examination, one doesn't get time to read other books.' The gentleman looked at Nabin. Nabin said, 'Yes, I have read it. Christ's teachings are really beautiful.'

The gentleman's heart filled up with hope. He said, 'Who except the Son of God can say such things? I hope God has instilled faith in you.'

Nabin replied, 'I don't believe that he is the Son of God, because we are all children of God.'

'Not like him. Jesus and God are the same. He is the incarnation of the Father.'

Nabin agreed, 'That is possible. God has many incarnations.'

Kishori added, 'Yes, our scriptures say the same thing.'

John Sahib said, 'Your scriptures are not true. They are false. Jesus is the only incarnation of God.'

Kishori objected, 'Sir, why should your scriptures be true and ours be false?'

'Our Bible contains the word of God and God's word cannot be false.'

'You may say that but why should we believe it? What is the proof?'

'How can it be false when different apostles have said the same thing? There is historical evidence to prove it.'

'There is historical evidence about the prophets too,' said Nabin. There is no reason to believe that the evidence in the case of Christ is acceptable but not in the case of others. Besides, whatever your historical evidence points to, scientific evidence questions the truth of the Bible. If you believe in the theory of evolution, then you cannot accept what the Bible says. Moreover, our Hindu cosmology is supported by science. Your scientists say that the human embryo passes through the same stages of evolution as human beings have passed through to assume their present form, the three important stages being the fish, the tortoise, and the boar. According to Hindu scriptures God has been incarnated in these and other forms and eventually in the human shape.'

'*Nonsense!*' said John Sahib.

'Even if you leave out "non", the sense that remains will be enough for our religion to survive. Genuine Hindus are those who reject the trivial part of the scriptures and accept the essence. But if one does not accept the fantastic part of your doctrine, one cannot be a Christian at all. Can one be a Christian if one does not have faith in the miracles of Christ?'

'*O Lord, save them!* I always pray for all of you.'

Kishori said, 'We are grateful to you for that, although we have no hope of being saved.'

'*O you of little faith!* Jesus said, "Have faith, with faith you can move mountains."'

Nabin remarked, 'Sir, may I point out that Christians preach one thing and practise another. What can we learn from them? Your religion says that you should give away your coat if someone robs you of your shirt, but you believe in taking an eye for an eye and a tooth for a tooth, and we poor things are scorned if we turn the other cheek after being slapped. This is your generosity and fellow feeling and this is why you call us niggers.'

John Sahib smiled and said, 'Christians don't do what you are saying.'

'Then Christians can be counted on one's fingers,' Kishori replied.

The argument could not continue further as the train came to a halt and everybody looked out of the window at the bustling crowd outside. John Sahib caught a glimpse of Jiban who was in the next compartment and got down to have a word with him. Just then an English couple approached the compartment but seeing Kishori and Nabin hesitated to enter. The lady looked askance at them and spoke to her husband who replied in a clearly audible voice, 'All the other coaches are full. If you don't get in here, you will have to sit in a ladies' coach.' They were speaking English. It seemed that the lady did not consent to her husband's suggestion and both of them moved off. Nabin said wryly, 'Where is John? He could have witnessed the famous broadmindedness of the British.'

Kishori said, 'How scornfully the woman looked at us, as though we were snakes or toads—and with her kind of looks too!'

Nabin said, 'I believe that if these English women did not come to our country, we would have carried on quite smoothly with the men. A number of them cannot mix with us because of their wives. Several Britishers look upon this country as their own and have worked selflessly for its welfare. They love Indians as their brothers, but I have never seen these English women doing anything sincerely for Indians or associating with them on an equal footing. They are so snobbish, supercilious, and touchy that they recoil at the very sight of a native.'

Kishori remarked, 'But I hear that European women like us very much. Our coppery skin seems more attractive to them than silver. A Frenchman told our neighbour's son that if he had a complexion like him, he would have become a great favourite with women.'

Nabin said, 'It seems one will have to make a trip to Europe once. The women who come to India do not show any preference like that in spite of our using so much of Pears soap.'

The train whistled. An Englishman boarded the compartment in a great hurry. As the train started moving, he sat down on the opposite bench and began reading a newspaper. After a while he put up his feet on Nabin's bench, perhaps without intending any offence, but Nabin misunderstood him. He retaliated by putting his own feet on the Englishman's bench. So far the man was concentrating on his newspaper; now he gave Nabin a sidelong glance and said, '*Will you shift to the other bench? There is plenty of room there.*'

Nabin replied, '*You can do it yourself if you like.*'

The Englishman got angry and said, '*You must.*'

Nabin said, '*Why must?*'

The Englishman stood up and shouted, '*How dare you?*' and began rolling up his shirt sleeves. Nabin was unruffled. He also stood up and started rolling up his sleeves. Kishori cried nervously, 'Don't, Nabinda, come over here. Don't start a quarrel. He'll surely beat us up.' However, the Englishman was taken aback by Nabin's boldness and could not make up his mind whether he should strike a blow or not. Kishori said to him, '*Beg your pardon, sir, don't mind him.*'

By then the Englishman had changed his mind and let his arm drop. The train had also arrived at a station. The missionary entered the compartment once again to take leave of Nabin and Kishori. Sensing some tension in the air he enquired what the matter was. Nabin smiled and said, 'We have just had a taste of your western courtesy,' and briefly narrated the incident. The priest said to the Englishman, '*This is shameful. You ought to apologize to the young gentleman.*' The man frowned and replied, '*I would rather apologize to a piece of stone than to a nigger,*' and demonstrating the highest ideal of courage and civility, angrily alighted from the train.

*K*ishori had gone for a walk in the evening. He returned home after dusk, stretched himself out on the sofa in his room, and shouted for his servant, but in these modern times no servant considers it necessary to respond till he is called over and over again. At last the man answered in his raucous East Bengal tone and entered the room with a coconut oil lamp in his hand, saying, 'Did you call?'

Kishori's temper had been rising in the meanwhile. He grimaced and mimicked the servant, 'Did you call? Where were you all this while—there has been no sign of you.'

The servant placed the lamp on the table and replied nonchalantly, 'I was bringing the lamp.'

Kishori sent him to bring his food from the house as he was not in a mood to go and eat inside. When the servant went out, he opened his desk and not finding what he was looking for, closed the lid noisily and sat down in his chair, looking disgusted. The servant entered again with a plate of luchis and a glass of water, and Kishori shouted at the top of his voice, 'Where is my perfume?' The servant put the food on the table and replied calmly, 'The shopkeeper is not willing to give it on credit. He says that you owe him sixty-five rupees, three annas and three paisas, and if you don't pay up within a couple of days he will inform the Master.'

'How do I owe him sixty-five rupees?' Kishori asked.

The servant replied, 'I have brought you several silk handkerchiefs and so many bottles of the same kind of eau de cologne. Why don't you see the account yourself?'

He brought out a scrap of paper from his waistband. Kishori

said, 'Let that be for now. I'll look at it later and I'll pay back the sixty-five rupees within two or three months. Just explain it nicely to the shopkeeper, understand!'

The servant said, 'I can tell him that but how will you manage your expenses for two months?'

Kishori replied, 'You don't worry about that. For the time being take these six annas and bring me a bottle of perfume. I need it now, I have to go out, do you understand?'

The servant took the money and went out, only to return a few minutes later and announced, 'Dadababu, Jibanbabu is coming.'

'Jibanda?' Kishori exclaimed. 'All right, you bring the eau de cologne and quietly put it in the desk, understand?'

Kishori came out on the veranda and was really surprised to see Jiban. Jiban hadn't crossed their threshold ever since Kunja Babu had turned them out of the house. Kishori said, 'Come, Jibanda, come into the room. What brings you here this evening?' They went into the room.

'I have some urgent business,' Jiban told Kishori. 'I have to go to the west by the nine o'clock train today itself. I have come to give you a hundred rupees as my contribution to the club which is to be given on Sunday.'

'How is it that you are going west, all of a sudden?' Kishori asked.

Jiban replied, 'I have no time to talk now. I have to leave immediately. I shall tell you everything when I return.' Jiban gave him the money and left immediately. The fact was that Mohan had been taken ill in Roorkee. Jagat Babu had received a telegram, giving him the news but it was not convenient for him to leave his work and go there. As the schools and colleges were closed for Puja, Jiban was free to undertake the journey. Jagat Babu had given the news to one more person besides Jiban. When Kunja Babu heard of Mohan's illness he was silent at first, and then told Jagat Babu, 'You are his guardian and you have received the news. You can make the necessary enquiries. What can I do?' After Jagat Babu's departure, Kunja Babu called his old estate manager and sent him to Roorkee, very anxious about Mohan's well-being. Jiban did not know this so he did not want to convey the news of Mohan's illness to Kishori and cause him any worry unnecessarily. A little after Jiban's departure the servant appeared with the bottle of eau de cologne and giving it to Kishori, said, 'Here, I have brought it. But there is a problem. The shopkeeper is a rascal. He is not willing to agree. He says that if he does not get the money by tomorrow he will definitely complain to the Master. I tried hard to bring him round but he wouldn't listen.'

Kishori put his hand in his pocket. 'The low-caste rascal,' he grumbled. 'Mind you, don't try to mollify him any more. Here is the money—you settle the account right away but remember to take a receipt from him.' Kishori gave him seven ten-rupee notes and said, 'You give him sixty-five rupees and keep the balance with you.'

'But it is sixty-five rupees, three annas, and three paisas.'

'Yes, I know.'

'I don't know, you may blame me later and ask for your three annas and three paisas. That is why I am telling you beforehand.'

The servant went away wondering how Kishori had come by so much money. Finding no other explanation he concluded that Kishori had squeezed it out of the old hag Jethima and was much tickled by the thought: 'She doesn't give anyone even two paisas willingly. That is the only way to get anything out of her. I should also make some money while I am working here, now that I have got him into the habit of drinking. As he gets older I'll get more. What else is the point of serving a rich man!'

The servant went out to gain his end and the Master went in search of Jethima to gain his end. The old lady was in the veranda, telling her beads. 'Is that Kishori?' she called out. 'Why don't you come inside to have your dinner these days?'

Kishori ignored her question and said, 'Jethima, give me something for Puja.'

Jethima replied, 'Why, only the other day you took away ten rupees from me. That is all I had. How can I give you anything more, my dear?'

'No Jethima, I am not going to listen to all that. The boys in college have asked me to give them a treat.'

'Why, your father gave you ten rupees the other day for the same purpose.'

Kishori grimaced, 'As though ten rupees are enough. After all I can't feed them *chire murki*[36] or such old-fashioned stuff. Baba does not understand these things.'

'Then approach your father. I am a poor woman. Where can I get the money from? Hare Krishna, Hare Krishna.'

'I won't listen to that. If you don't get up, I'll take your key.'

'Don't touch me,' Jethima shouted in alarm. 'Don't touch me—don't interrupt my prayers.'

Kishori threatened, 'Open your box or I'll touch you.'

Jethima sprang up and taking out her key with her left hand, pleaded with Kishori, 'Good boy, I don't have any money. You took away everything the other day.'

Kishori said, 'Telling a lie at the time of prayer! Let me see whether you have anything or not.'

He snatched the key away from her hand. Jethima screamed, 'I haven't seen such a plunderer in my life. Just you wait, I'll report you to Thakurpo. I cannot live here any more.' Ignoring her totally, Kishori opened the cupboard but realized that Jethima had become smarter and removed the money from its usual place. He continued to rummage into her clothes and finally came upon a box. Seeing it in his hand, Jethima started shrieking again, 'Good boy, don't take anything. I don't have any money. How will I manage my pocket expenses?'

Kishori opened the box in spite of her protests, but after all that effort he found only a single ten-rupee note in it. Showing great dissatisfaction, he pocketed the money and threw the box away. 'You have to worry about pocket expenses?' he sneered. 'You manage all the money for the daily shopping. Come on, this won't do. You'll have to give me something.'

By this time Jethima was really angry. She said, 'Take everything. Take whatever I have. I'll report you to Thakurpo just now.'

Kishori wasn't at all perturbed by her threat. No matter what she said, she loved him the most because of his unreasonable demands. He said, 'All right then, Baba will turn me out of the house like Dada.'

The pitch of the old lady's voice suddenly dropped an octave lower. She asked, 'Have you had any news of Mohan? Is he all right?'

Kishori replied, 'How will I get the news? Go and ask the doctor for it.'

Jethima said, 'But you are a friend of the doctor's son. Don't you hear anything from him?'

'As though I am going to ask him,' Kishori said. 'Is it necessary to tell them that Dada doesn't even write to us?' Saying this he dropped her key near her feet and made his escape. Jethima shouted, 'O Kishori, please give me back my money. My good boy, it is my pocket money.'

21

*K*ishori was worried. He had been confident that he would be able to replace Jiban's money by extracting the necessary amount from Jethima. He had been let down badly and was disappointed. The next day he raided Jethima again but with no success. She had sent away all the money except that ten-rupee note to her parents' house. In utter helplessness he told his servant Hari to somehow get him a loan from somebody or the other, urgently. Hari realized that this would be a troublesome business. He quickly decided on his course of action and said, 'All right Babu, I'll try to do my best.'

After his meal, the faithful Hari took his shawl and his umbrella and went out. The Babu thought that there couldn't be a more loyal servant than him. He spent the whole day waiting anxiously for his return, while the servant passed the time in the company of his relative and returned in the evening. Kishori asked him eagerly what he had accomplished. Hari replied, 'I can't tell you how many places I have been to. I am dying of thirst.'

'What about the money?'

'You can't imagine what rascals, what scoundrels these people are. They didn't give me a penny. Whatever I had is also finished and I am choking to death.' Kishori couldn't utter a word. His hopes were shattered. Seeing his crestfallen, pale countenance the servant began to feel sorry for him. He said, 'What do you need the money for? If you ask the Master for it, won't he give it to you?'

Kishori got angry, 'Get out of here. *The fellow is giving me advice!*' The servant shuffled off. Kishori opened the desk, took out the bottle of eau de cologne, drank the nectar and lay down on the sofa. A little later he heard the sound of footsteps, and lifting his head saw Kartik

Babu. He got up hastily and said, 'Oh, sir please sit down. What's the news?' Kartik Babu had been Kishori's tutor for sometime. He took a seat and said, 'I have come to find out where the meeting will be held.'

'It will be in the same farmhouse. There cannot be a more convenient venue.'

Kartik Babu said, 'But it is not convenient for us. We have to commute by train every time. You are rich folks, it is all right for you. *Rich people are nature's favourites.*[37] At present my office is closed, but when it opens I won't be able to go at all.'

'Do you have office on Sunday also?' Kishori asked.

Kartik Babu replied, 'I slog the whole week. On weekends I have to attend to my family. *Home, sweet home.*'

Kishori said, 'If you talk about sweetness, I think there is nothing as sweet as money.' At that moment he was experiencing the need for money intensely. Kartik Babu agreed with him. He said to himself, 'Why else have I joined your group? But there is no trusting you till I have the money in hand.' Pulling his chair closer, he murmured softly, 'Kishori Babu, I have some doubts in my mind. Can we trust all the members of the club?'

'Why do you ask?' Kishori asked. 'We think they are honest people.'

Kartik Babu said, 'I have a specific doubt—did you hear the news last night? They passed the Gagging Act in the Council so suddenly!'

'Downright injustice,' Kishori muttered.

'Ah, I am not talking of that. I am afraid they have come to know of our secret club.'

Kishori burst out laughing. Kartik Babu went on, 'My friend, it is not a laughing matter. You don't know these British. They get all the news and have their spies everywhere.'

This was a good opportunity for Kishori to lead him on. He put on a grave expression and said, 'Well, you have guessed right. Otherwise why did that Englishman come to blows in the train that day?'

Kartik Babu replied, 'Ah, so there was really a fight then? And you thought that you could say anything to the man and get away with it?'

Kishori said, 'Sir, so many people are sacrificing their lives for the country and can't we endure even this much?'

Kartik Babu retorted, 'Well, you may give up your life or do whatever else you please but what I want to know is whether everyone will give the money?'

'For what?'

'For the soap. People easily talk about sacrificing their lives but giving money is difficult.'

Kishori guessed what was on Kartik Babu's mind. Then the idea struck him that if he could prevent him from coming to the next meeting, he could save the situation for himself. He said, 'Sir, you are a mature person. What shall I tell you—I don't want to discuss family affairs...'

Kartik Babu replied, 'Ah, I have understood. There is no hope of getting the money. That is what I was wondering about, how will these youngsters arrange for the money? But it was you who held out the hope to me.'

Kishori said, 'Even now I am not saying that nothing will materialize.'

'But that is what you are saying. After all, you and Jiban promised...'

Kishori said, 'Dada has gone to the west without arranging for the money and I don't have the courage to approach my father. We had an argument lately and he may insist that I leave the club.'

'Ah, it has come to that,' Kartik Babu exclaimed. 'Well, whoever among you wants to die may do so but I am giving all this up and I'll explain it to my brother.'

'Sir, what are you saying?'

'Look my boy, I didn't join the club to forfeit my life or my money. For sometime now my boss has been finding fault with me in the office. Now I know what the matter is. If I continue in this club, I'll lose my job. You are rich people—you have no problems. It is all right for you to work for the nation. It doesn't suit us. That is why I came to make enquiries. If I didn't ask you, you wouldn't tell me all this. Now, I can tell you frankly what I intend to do. I'll go and tell my brother everything. He has great faith in the club. Let me see if it holds after he hears all this. We are leaving the club.'

Kishori persisted, 'No, at least come to the meeting on Sunday. You have to let them know of your resignation.'

Kartik Babu was firm. 'No, I'd rather not go in that direction any more or else I'll get caught by the authorities and lose my job. I am giving my resignation to you.'

'But what about Ganesh Babu?'

'Ganesh Babu?' Kartik Babu exclaimed. 'My dear sir, the joint-family system still exists. The younger brother has no say while the elder brother is around, you understand? He won't come here, I am speaking on his behalf. If you want, I'll resign for both of us.'

Kartik Babu went away leaving behind a very amused Kishori. However, after a couple of days he read a report in the newspaper which made him angry. It was a first hand report—the reporter claimed that he was present in the train when the incident occurred but did not mention that he was not in the same compartment. He wrote:

Suddenly, without any provocation, an Englishman started beating up an innocent Bengali student, whose only fault was that he was sitting on a bench facing the Englishman. The writer of this report has heard from a reliable source that Englishmen hated all Bengalis because they wanted to compete with them in the intellectual sphere. This particular student had offended the Englishman by joining a nationalist club recently, with reference to which the British have lately passed the Gagging Act.

The news spread like wildfire all over the towns and villages but except for the people involved, nobody came to know who the hero of the episode was and in whose favour the report was published.

22

*I*t was nearly three o'clock but the president and the secretary hadn't shown up yet. The members who had assembled were getting restless and annoyed. As soon as Kishori Babu, the secretary entered, he had to face a volley of verbal charges from all sides. Jadav said, 'Hey, Kishori Babu, you have made it at last!' Krishna quipped, 'Oh, they are babus. They have their moods. Who can say anything to them?' Shyam countered. 'As though we have been brought here as thieves under arrest!' Hem said, 'At least you have come, but is the president still sleeping?'

'Dada has gone west,' Kishori announced.

Nabin was smoking his cheroot and watching the rings of smoke as he sulked silently. He now spoke up, 'West?'

Gopal joined him, 'Gone west, just like that? Very fine. He goes west, you go south and all of us, idle people wait here from ten to five.'

'Unity, determination, commitment,' muttered Nabin.

Kishori retorted angrily, 'Nobody has taken an oath of not going out anywhere because he has joined the club.'

Bihari said, 'That is all right but we are waiting here for him. He should have informed us in time that he was going west.'

'It is enough to inform the secretary,' Kishori cut in. 'He has done his duty. It so happened that I could not come early today.'

Somebody sitting behind Nabin spoke up, 'He was not just supposed to come, he was also supposed to bring something with him. Has he made any arrangements about that?'

Kishori was taken aback. Attacked from all sides on entering the room, he didn't have the chance to look around him properly.

Now he noticed Ganesh Chandra sitting behind Nabin. After talking to Kartik Babu the previous evening he was quite sure that the brothers wouldn't come for the meeting that day. Charu said, 'Kishorida, I haven't been able to bring the whole amount this time. I have brought fifty and will bring the remaining fifty next week.' Gopal commented, 'One person has absconded and the other has brought half the amount. What have you brought Kishori Babu?'

Kishori put his hand in his pocket and said, 'Of course I have brought it but Kartik Babu has not come.'

'But Ganesh Chandra has come,' Ganesh said.

'I deal with Kartik Babu,' Kishori said, trying to evade him.

'Does it mean that you don't trust me?' Ganesh asked.

'It is not a question of trust,' Kishori answered. '*Business is business.*'

Ganesh insisted, 'After all I'll do the actual work. My brother won't do anything.'

Nabin objected, 'Brother Kishori, when we are all bound as brothers you cannot treat it as a business dealing. This brotherhood has no meaning if we cannot trust each other and we need not keep it going.'

Jadav joined him, 'Kishori Babu, if you raise this issue now you will have to take the blame. If you cannot trust him, why did you *recommend* him to the club?'

Kishori said impatiently, 'All right, the fault is mine. If everybody is going to take me to task like this, I'll resign. You can look for another secretary.'

This upset Charu. 'Kishorida, how will the club survive if you resign? Don't take such a hasty step in anger. Think of our goal.'

Kishori continued, 'I am working so hard, spending money, making sacrifices, neglecting my studies, and incurring my father's displeasure. What am I doing all this for? For what purpose?'

Nabin said, 'For whatever purpose it may be, it is not to oblige us.'

'I am not saying that,' Kishori told him. 'I know I am unworthy—I should resign.'

Charu said, 'Nabin Babu, you are going too far. Please request him to stay on.'

Nabin was a pessimist by nature. He looked at the dark side of things first and was easily discouraged. This exchange aroused his cynicism. He felt that there was no point in keeping the club going. It was a sham, a phoney venture. 'I shall also resign,' he declared. 'What is the worth of sacrifice if it is looked upon as a burden. Kishori's statement shows that we do not know the meaning of true sacrifice, therefore we are not fit to make sacrifices for the country. When the office bearers of the club are not punctual, when they are not serious about the meetings, when they cannot keep their promise, and when they cannot tolerate just criticism, this club is a mere mockery. Let the club break up, we have no regrets about it, but we are sorry that our unworthiness is the cause of its dissolution...'

The discussion went on among the other members of the club but Kishori and Nabin had nothing more to say. The meeting ended on a note of dejection.

23

*K*ishori returned home very disturbed. He had managed to wriggle out of the situation that day but he would certainly be exposed when Jiban returned. That was his first concern. Secondly, however selfish Kishori may have been, the magnanimity of youth and the desire to work for the country was still alive in his heart. The strong current of his selfishness had not yet drowned his good nature completely, so he was genuinely remorseful about foolishly breaking up the club on which he had pinned such high hopes. In a few hours he seemed to have lost his previous carefree existence and was beginning to feel like an old man of hundred. On arriving home he lay down on the sofa. After a while he got up, opened his desk, picked up the dagger, played around with it, then put it back and took out the bottle of eau de cologne. Again he put it back, slammed the lid of the desk testily and lay down. A little later Hari entered the room with a lamp and seeing Kishori, exclaimed, 'O Dadababu, why didn't you call me? Shall I bring your dinner?'

'No,' Kishori snapped. 'Don't disturb me. Go away.'

The servant thought that the Babu had visited some friend and had more to drink than to eat. Seeing his nasty mood he slunk away without saying anything more. Kishori fixed his gaze on the lamp. He had visited the Kali temple once and the flickering flame of the lamp reminded him of the tongue of the goddess Kali, dripping with blood. He felt that he was drowning in that blood. He turned his head away from the lamp and then he saw nothing but darkness around him. Suddenly he heard footsteps and turning around saw Charu standing before him. Charu was also feeling miserable about the quarrel among the members of the club. Kishori felt a little relieved on seeing Charu—it was difficult for him to suffer the pangs of conscience in isolation.

Charu sat down on a chair near Kishori and said, 'Kishorida, was it right of you to lose your temper when the fault was Jibanda's?'

Kishori felt like confessing everything to Charu but having lied once, he did not have the courage to tell the truth. Instead, he said, 'Do you think one should listen to a friend being criticized and not defend him?'

Charu said, 'But truth should be respected above everything else. When Jibanda was guilty...'

Kishori interrupted him, 'How was he guilty when he had informed me?'

'But what about the money?'

'Money was not the problem. I could have given it. But let that be. Think of it, if someone criticizes you, should I remain silent?'

Charu was impressed with Kishori's proof of selfless friendship. He said, 'That is true, but why did you resign?'

'Do you think,' Kishori replied, 'that I am not unhappy about it. But what other alternative did I have in that situation?' It was not as though he was consciously misleading Charu; he was trying to convince him by the same argument with which he found a justification for his own conduct.

Charu said, 'Let bygones be bygones. Now let us explain things to Nabinda so that everything returns to normal.'

Kishori replied, 'I am willing to apologize or twist my ears or do anything you say but Nabin will not understand.'

Charu said, 'All right, let Jibanda come back. When he explains, Nabinda will understand.'

'*My dear boy, one can give reason but not understanding.*'

'But Nabinda does not seem to be such a difficult person,' Charu insisted.

Kishori sighed, 'You are a poet. You can only see the good in people.'

Charu smiled and said, 'That reminds me, Kishorida, I have composed some new poems.'

'Have you brought them?' Kishori asked. Charu pulled out some papers from his pocket. Kishori said, 'I'll read them tomorrow.' Charu wanted him to read them straightaway but was too shy to say so. He excused himself, saying that it was getting late, and took his leave.

Kishori's initial keenness of remorse had considerably subsided after talking to Charu and now the pangs of hunger had revived. He called out to Hari who responded promptly and went to bring his food. Kishori opened his desk and took out the bottle of eau de cologne when suddenly Charu returned to enquire why Snehalata had not received news of Mohan for quite some time. He was stunned to see Kishori holding the bottle to his lips. Kishori put it down at once but was too disconcerted to utter a word. Charu was also unable to ask him anything. He picked up a book from the table and muttering some excuse, made a hasty departure. By then Kishori had regained his composure. He called Charu back but he was gone. Kishori's mood was again spoilt.

24

*H*ow horrible! Kishori drinks. Not just any liquor but eau de cologne—pure spirit. Then he has really gone to the dogs. It is not proper to be friends with him. Charu had always thought drinking to be repugnant. He was really disgusted to see Kishori drinking and resolved that he would have nothing to do with him. But he was genuinely fond of Kishori. Kishori was older than him. Charu depended on him as women depend on men. He could not sleep at night, thinking of his resolution, and thought of writing a poem. He started the poem with a certain purpose but by the time he had finished, it turned out to be something different from what he had originally conceived. He wanted to compose a poem so strongly directed against drinking that young alchoholics, blinded by ignorance, would have their eyes opened. But when he got out of bed and opened the window, the clear, dewy moonlight of *Ashwin*[38] flooded the room, starting a new chain of associations in his mind. He wrote of a long-lost and vaguely remembered love whose shadow crossed his heart, made him restless and brought tears to his eyes. When the poem was finished he was very pleased but his happiness couldn't be complete unless he could read it out to someone. He had written:

> In the cool autumn moonlight
> Longingly gazes the night
> As if she has met the long-lost beloved
> Her smile is bathed in tears
> As the first breeze of spring brings a pang of sorrow
> In the midst of happiness.
> My heart cries at the wan smile of the night

The shadow of a lost memory floats up in my mind
Whose shadow is it, whose fleeting form?
Familiar, but indistinct?
My heart is eager to capture it
It eludes my grasp.
So close to me, so much my own
Will it not make me its refuge?
Will it draw near, only to retreat?
Making the bright moonlight tearful
And my heart cry out in despair?

Ordinarily, he would have rushed to Kishori's house early in the morning. But alas! Those days were over. Since he did not have any other listener, he read it out to Snehalata the next day. Although she was only twelve years old, she had read all the poems and novels in Bengali she could get hold of. Even if she did not understand them fully, she interpreted and enjoyed them in her own way. Likewise she found her own simple interpretation of Charu's poem. However, when after reading it aloud Charu asked her what she thought of it, she only looked at him with an expression of mute surprise and admiration. A poet thrives on appreciation. Charu thought that he had cast his pearls on barren soil and walked off disappointed. He began to miss Kishori acutely. Three days passed in this manner until Kishori's absence became unbearable for him. On the fourth day he worked out such an infallible argument in favour of visiting Kishori that any further hesitation was unnecessary. First, it was against the code of friendship to forsake a friend who had gone astray without guiding him to the right path. Second, Charu couldn't be certain whether Kishori was taking liquor or some other medicine. Third, it was his duty to find out what defence Kishori would offer for his behaviour. Fourth, and most importantly, he could not survive without seeing Kishori and had a powerful urge to go to him. Arriving at this decision based on unassailable arguments, he was preparing to leave for Kishori's house at once when Kishori himself turned up in his room.

Charu was sitting in a chair in the outer apartment of his house with a book in his hand, but his mind was wandering and he was staring vacantly at the wall before him. Kishori came in quietly, stood behind him and, placing his hands on Charu's shoulders, said in an affectionate tone, 'Hello, Charu, you have stopped coming to our house?' Charu got up, overjoyed. Kishori had himself come along to call him. Forgetting everything, be blurted out, 'I was about to go there just now.'

'Then come with me,' Kishori said, holding his hand. Their friendship was resumed the same evening in Kishori's study.

25

*C*haru looked quite like Jagat Babu; he was fair and there was a softness in his expression. He had a high forehead and his thick hair fell carelessly around his face. There was a negligent air about his attire too. He wore a plain dhoti and kurta and draped a shawl around his shoulders. He looked innocent; even the down on his upper lip hadn't yet taken the form of a moustache. Kishori presented a sharp contrast to him in his appearance. He dressed foppishly; wore a finely pleated stole over his jacket, a dhoti with a broad border, and a watch with a chain. His scanty hair was plastered so carefully around his head that a phrenologist could describe his attributes without even taking the trouble of touching his head. As we do not possess the subtle knowledge of phrenology we cannot give the readers a clear analysis of his nature. All we can say was that there was no lack of intelligence in his expression but there was a lack of generosity in his intellect—it seemed as though it was deficient in sensitivity.

Kishori had a wheatish complexion; his features were not perfect, but he looked handsome with his upper lip adorned with a thick moustache, a set of fine, white teeth, and a charming smile. His keen glance and his smile created the impression that he had a gentle nature. On hearing Charu's poem, Kishori remarked, 'It is beautiful. One would love to hear more of it. It is somewhat like Shelley's verse. I felt as if I was listening to Shelley.' Kishori had not read much of Shelley, but he had heard about him from Jiban and Nabin. Charu was thrilled with such praise. Kishori continued, 'Have you read Shelley's *Nightingale*? *Simply ethereal*. I never imagined before that anyone could write such *ideal* poetry in our language. It is excellent:

Whose shadow is it, whose form elusive? The more I try to grasp her
The further she flies from me.'

Charu said, 'Kishorida, I often have a feeling as though I know
someone who is very near me, yet out of my reach.'

Kishori said, 'This is *uncommon celebration*.' He had heard the
phrase 'unconscious cerebration' from Nabin the other day and was
keen to use it but now he could not remember the words correctly.
That did not matter, because Charu could not detect the error. He
said, 'Tell me why do I feel like this?'

Kishori replied, 'Genuine poets often have such feelings. You have
a striking similarity with Shelley. You even look like him. You are a
true child of nature.'

It was not as though Kishori was blatantly flattering Charu, but
as he listened to his poetry, he really began to look upon him as
Shelley. There was no mirror at hand so Charu could not confirm
the truth of Kishori's statement. He only expressed his pleasure with
a quiet smile. Then Kishori said, 'Charu, I am going to quarrel with
you. Why didn't you come all these days?' Charu could not give a
straightforward reply to this. He mumbled, 'I couldn't make it,
Kishorida.'

'What do you mean, you couldn't make it. You are trying to fool
me. You thought I was a drunkard, didn't you? Now, tell me the
truth.'

'No, not really, but why do you drink that stuff, Kishorida?'

'Very fine,' Kishori retorted, 'you think I have it everyday? If I have
a little sometimes, does it mean that I am a drunkard? Even the
scriptures say that wine can be taken as a medicine.'

'But you are not sick,' Charu commented.

'That's not fair,' Kishori said. 'How do you know that I am not
sick? I was dying of a headache at that time.'

'But if you do that you will get addicted to it,' Charu insisted.

'All right,' Kishori said, 'for the *sake of argument*, let us imagine
that I have a little everyday. I have got used to it. What is wrong
with that? After all, the British have it everyday. Do they neglect their
work for that reason or can we say that they are good for nothing?
It is just a prejudice, that is what it is.'

'Gradually your intake will increase,' Charu warned him. 'So many
people in our country have gone to the dogs like this.'

'That is my lookout,' Kishori shot back. 'It seems you have no trust in me. You think me to be totally *worthless*.'

Charu was cornered. 'No, no Kishorida, it is not that.'

Kishori said, 'I understand you perfectly. I am a confirmed drunkard and a contemptible wretch.'

'No, Kishorida,' Charu demurred.

Kishori got up, opened his desk, took out the bottle and said, 'I won't hide anything from you, Charu. See, I have it. When I feel out of sorts I have a little of it. Will you call me an alcoholic?'

Charu said, 'No, you are not an alcoholic but it is better not to have it.'

'What is wrong in having a little?' Kishori asked. 'Convince me first, then I won't touch it ever. All right, I am fixing up a little for you. Taste it yourself and tell me if it affects you adversely.'

Kishori poured a little eau de cologne in a glass tumbler on his desk, mixed it with water from a pitcher, and held it in front of Charu.

'No, Kishorida, please excuse me,' Charu said, scared.

Kishori said, 'Then I am an absolute drunkard and a blackguard because I have no prejudice about touching wine.'

'No, no, that is not true.'

'Oh yes,' Kishori repeated, 'I am a rascal, a good for nothing.'

'Who says that?'

'That is what you mean.'

'All right, I'll just taste it.' Charu put a drop on the tip of his tongue and set the glass down.

'Is this a homoeopathic medicine.' Kishori said scathingly, '*My dear friend*, have all of it. *I assure you*, you will not be ruined. At least have it to check how far I have declined.'

Eventually, Charu was compelled to drink but Kishori had given him so little that he could not make out its ill-effects—rather he felt somewhat elated afterwards. He felt that he could churn out a lot of poetry that day. He said, 'Kishorida, do you sometimes feel that there is a surge of moonlight flowing through your mind.'

'Don't I?' Kishori replied. 'But there is no pleasure in enjoying that moonlight alone. That is why I want your company.'

26

Charu said, 'Jibanda, don't be angry but actually it is because of you that this has happened. You should have informed the club that you were going west. Kishorida may have been at fault there but you could have left the money at least.'

Jiban got angry. 'I had given the money before going. I am surprised that Kishori didn't tell you that.'

Charu said, 'Yes, he was about to give the money—he did say something like that, but by then there was such a ruckus that nobody could be heard. Still, I am sure he mentioned it, or perhaps I misunderstood him. Ah, now I remember, he only objected to giving it to Ganesh Babu.'

Jiban asked, 'How is it that like you everybody misunderstood him? If he had clearly said that I had left the money, there wouldn't be any misunderstanding.'

Charu replied, 'You know, sometimes one doesn't know what to say. That is why you shouldn't be angry. Actually, Kishorida lost his temper while trying to *defend* you.'

Jiban said, '*Defend* me? Who asked him to do that when there was no need for it?'

This made Charu very angry. Jibanda was so ungrateful—the person for whose sake you steal calls you a thief! He said curtly, 'I wouldn't have done it in his place. I can't say why Kishorida did it. You can find out from him yourself.'

Jiban realized that it was no use discussing the matter with Charu. Concealing his suspicion he said, 'I am going to him just now. Please tell your father that Mohan is much better now. I'll come and see him myself, soon, perhaps in a day or two.'

Jiban went away with a feeling of hurt, annoyance, and misgiving. He had come just that morning, feeling happy to return after his long absence but by evening his mind was clouded with bitter thoughts. He had hoped that the club would be able to do something positive for the country. The thwarting of his youthful hopes and enthusiasm was painful for him.

Jiban did not have to go as far as Kishori's house. He met Kishori at the Beadon Street crossing. Kishori was engaged in a friendly conversation with another boy when Jiban suddenly accosted him and said in a grave voice that he had something urgent to tell him. Kishori's heart sank and his face turned pale as he silently followed Jiban to a secluded corner of the garden. He remained speechless when Jiban asked him whether he had spent the money, his face turned ashen, and his eyes were fixed on the ground. Seeing his miserable expression, Jiban's anger subsided and he asked him gently, 'Why didn't you tell me that you were in need of money? And if you spent it, why didn't you admit it before the members of the club? Instead you concealed the truth and misled everybody. You made me out to be a liar and dashed our plans and our aspirations to the ground.'

Kishori said in a feeble voice, 'Dada, I have realized my terrible blunder. What can I do now?'

Jiban replied, 'Why, you should confess the truth in the presence of all, what else?'

'Dada, please forgive me,' Kishori repeated. 'I'll never do this again.'

Jiban said, 'But you must rectify the wrong you have done. If you are honest, you will be pardoned and the club may start functioning again.'

Kishori's eyes filled with tears. He said, 'Dada, if I confess everything, people will hate me. I'll always be looked upon as a liar and a thief. Nobody will trust me. Please forgive me and forget what has happened. I promise I'll never repeat such behaviour.'

Jiban was touched by Kishori's anguish and was silent for a while. He realized that there was truth in Kishori's assertion. If he were exposed he would lose his prestige among his peers. There are very few people who can make a clean breast of their misdeeds. He began, 'Kishori I may forgive you but—'

Before he could complete the sentence, Kishori interrupted him, smiling, and extending his hand said, 'Jibanda, tell me honestly that you have pardoned me and will not disclose this to anybody.'

Jiban held his hand and said gloomily, 'I pardon you, Kishori, with the hope that this will prevent you from doing wrong in future...' Before he could finish the sentence, someone shouted from a distance, 'Hello, Jiban!'

Kishori and Jiban looked in that direction and saw Nabin coming. Kishori said hastily, 'Jibanda, I'll take leave of you now.' He did not want to face Nabin at that moment on any account, and beat a quick retreat.

After Kishori's departure, Jiban went up to Nabin and greeted him. Nabin said wryly, 'So, that's how you disappear?'

Jiban tried to explain, 'Yes, I had to go suddenly after hearing of Mohanda's illness. The club—'

Nabin cut him short, 'Unity, determination, efficiency! We can sermonize about them but we don't practise them, do we?'

Jiban was hurt by his taunt but didn't know what to say. It seemed they really considered him guilty. 'Dear Nabin,' he said gently, 'is there no pardon for a slip or two sometimes?'

Nabin replied bitterly, 'Everybody slips hundreds of times; it is not up to me to pardon them all. The fact is, we are not fit for the kind of work we had undertaken. We do not have faith in each other. We do not have dedication for truth and action. So we can get together to laugh and chat and spin fabulous yarns, but we cannot work. Then why do we keep up this empty show?'

Jiban argued with him for a while about this and pleaded with him to start the club again but he could not prevail upon Nabin to change his mind. Nabin was adamant and said that if they could not depend on Jiban, how could they depend on anybody else?

Jiban had forgiven Kishori wholeheartedly but Nabin was not so charitable. He categorically stated that Jiban had committed a grave wrong and was responsible for the break-up of the club. It would be sheer impudence on his part to work for the nation. Jiban was deeply hurt by these accusations. Even his forgiving nature could not help him get over the pain.

27

*W*hen Jiban returned home that day he found that Jagat Babu's wife was visiting his mother. She greeted him warmly, 'My dear, did you go on a trip? Are you well? Is Mohan all right?' Jiban returned her greeting and said, 'Yes, Mashima.'

Jiban's mother complained, 'What shall I tell you Didi! Our only possession was a watch and chain which was pawned. I wanted to redeem it but the boy didn't listen to me and went on a trip.' This was not altogether correct because Jiban's salary had been raised and he could have managed the travel expenses out of his own income, but he had to beg his mother for some money from her savings to contribute a hundred rupees to the club. Of course the mother was not aware of all this.

The Mistress clicked her tongue to express her sympathy with Jiban's mother. 'Alas,' she said, 'you have so much wealth and yet our boy has to endure such hardship. Won't the uncle give anything without going to court?'

Jiban's mother replied, 'If he did we would have no reason to worry.'

The Mistress remarked, 'If the wife is lucky, the husband prospers. You will get everything if that is my daughter's destiny.'

This was a hint that if Jiban married her daughter she would fight his case in the court. Jiban was already in a dejected mood. He was not pleased with the turn the conversation was taking. He was trying to think of an excuse to leave the room when suddenly a girl peeped into the room and seeing Jiban, withdrew quickly. Jiban, who was facing the door, caught a glimpse of the girl in the lamp-light and inferred that she was Jagat Babu's daughter and was hesitant to enter the room because of his presence. He might have lingered a little longer but after this he did not delay his departure and getting up promptly, said, 'Mashima, I'll leave now. I have some work.'

The Mistress smiled and said, 'You are welcome, son.'

Jiban's mother was annoyed. 'You always make work an excuse. Can't you spare some time for me?'

Jiban laughed and said, 'Even if I stay with Ma the whole day, it is not sufficient for her.' He quickly sprang up from the mat, thrust his feet in his shoes, and dragged them up to the veranda. When he was sure that he was safely out of the reach of his mother's call, he put on his shoes properly and went clattering down the stairs. Then he again started climbing up noiselessly because he had no desire to go out and wanted to be alone in his room. His room was next to his mother's and if she came to know that he was there it would be a nuisance. Luckily, he could enter his room by another door so he planned to give her the slip and go round the veranda to enter his room on the sly in the hope of enjoying undisturbed peace.

After Jiban's departure, the Mistress said to his mother, 'Well, we should now fix up a date. The girl is growing up. I can't keep her with me any more.'

Jiban's mother replied, 'Let me have a word with him. Once he gives his consent, there will be no delay in fixing the date.'

The Mistress said, 'You repeat the same thing every time. Why shouldn't he agree? I mentioned it in front of him just now and he did not raise any objection. If the parent agrees, the son will. I'll fix the date tomorrow and send word to you. Let us have the wedding in *Aghran*.'[39]

Jiban's mother couldn't counter the Mistress' firm stand for it would appear as though she was not willing. Driven into a corner, she said, 'It is fine. I'll talk to my son.' However, when Jiban came in for dinner she did not have the courage to broach the subject as he seemed to be in a grim mood. The next day the schools and colleges were to open so Jiban left soon after breakfast and she did not get a chance to talk about it. When he returned from school in the evening and sat down to eat, she drew him into a conversation and then said, 'Jiban, my boy, your mother-in-law wants to fix the date of the wedding.'

Not answering her directly. Jiban asked, 'Is she Jagat Babu's daughter? It seems the girl knows English well.'

Jiban's mother was pleased that Jiban raised the point himself without getting impatient. She said, 'Of course, she is well educated. You will like her. She will come up to your expectations.'

Jiban smiled. He had seen Snehalata last evening and remembered her well. His mother continued happily, 'Then let us settle it, my son. She is known to us, you don't have to see her formally but we must observe the custom. Bring me a gold sovereign, I'll go over one day and present it to her.'

'What a nice custom!' Jiban remarked in jest, 'The person who has to marry will not see the girl, someone else will do the needful.' There was perhaps an element of seriousness in his jest, perhaps he wanted to see once again the girl he had seen the previous evening.

Jiban's mother said, 'No, my son, it is inauspicious to see the girl before the wedding. There is no need for it since we know the family so well. You are my only son. Please see your bride at the auspicious time of *shubhadrishti*.[40] Don't invite misfortune by seeing her earlier.'

By this time Jiban had convinced himself that he had seen Jagat Babu's daughter the previous day and on an earlier occasion at Jagat Babu's house; so he did not want to let go of the chance to comply with his mother's request and prove his worth as a good son. He laughed and said, 'All right, I won't see her. You have approved of her; that should be enough.'

Jiban's mother was delighted. She said, 'You are a good boy. Hope you get a son like yourself. Ah, my son is always so mild. Only now and then he goes berserk and then he becomes difficult.' She might have continued in the same vein for some time longer but suddenly there was a noise downstairs. The maidservant called out that the betel leaves had arrived.[41] The servant rushed in, panting, and said, 'Mistress, people have brought betel leaves from Doctor Babu's house.' Normally betel leaves are sent from the groom's house but Jagat Babu's wife had realized that things would not move without her pushing. There is no harm in overruling conventions when the situation demands it. Hearing this Jiban sprang up and said, 'What is this, mother, you have made all these arrangements, without telling me about it. What if I turn the proposal down now?'

His mother exclaimed, 'Why, my boy, you didn't say anything when Charu's mother spoke to you. If you were unwilling, it would have been better for you to have told her so, frankly. How can you raise any objections now? Does anyone break off an engagement after receiving the betel leaves? Nobody will marry the girl and she will be considered unlucky. They have done so much for us. It is a sin to harbour such feelings. Don't make a fuss now.'

Jiban went away without saying anything. His mother was overjoyed. Within minutes the house was filled with the maids and servants from Jagat Babu's house. The wedding day was fixed in the coming month of Aghran.

28

The day Jiban returned from Roorkee, Jiban's mother sent some of the fruits and other things he had brought to Jagat Babu's wife. It was half past one in the afternoon. Jagat Babu and the children of the house had finished their lunch. The Mistress hadn't eaten yet. She had just bathed and was sitting on a rug in front of a mirror in the veranda. Kamli the maid was combing the wet, oily hair at the back of her head with a fine comb. The front part of her head was quite bald but her scalp was profusely oiled all over. She had a firm belief that if the top of the head and the nape of the neck were well-oiled, the body stayed cool and one never fell ill. She wanted Jagat Babu, Tagar, and Charu to spend at least an hour every day on an oil massage according to her suggestion but nobody found it convenient to do so. Jagat Babu and Charu were hard up for time, though the Mistress could not believe that if they spared an hour for it all of Jagat Babu's patients would die and Charu's studies would suffer a great loss. That was just an excuse on their part. Like father, like son. They just wanted to be like Englishmen. The Mistress had no hold on them regarding this matter, but Tagar, who could be prevailed upon was also not willing to submit to her. Although the Mistress threatened Tagar that if she did not oil herself under her supervision, she would be furious with her, Tagar gave her the slip and had an early bath. When she came to know of it, she gave vent to her anger in an outburst of ineffectual abuse and settled scores by using thrice the quantity of oil on her own self. Anyway, her maid was combing her hair while she was wiping the oil that remained on her face after her bath with a wet towel. After that she pulled out a container of *sindoor*[42] from a drawer and putting her finger into it, drew a big, round dot on her forehead. Then she dipped the edge of the comb in the sindoor and smeared a lot of it on her nearly bald head. Tagar was sitting next to her, looking into a small mirror, which had cost her one paisa. She was chewing a betel leaf and from time to time put her tongue out to examine how red it had become. Seeing her mother wearing sindoor she said, 'Ma, I'll wear it also.'

The mother replied, 'Little girls don't wear sindoor.'

'Why does Didi wear it then? I'll also wear it.'

The maid said, 'Silly girl, Didi is married.'

Tagar said, 'You keep quiet. Ma, I'll wear it.'

The Mistress got angry and cried, 'I haven't seen a girl like her. She is going to be married soon and yet she has no sense. Here, put it on.' And she put a dot on her forehead with her finger.

Tagar said, 'No, I want it on my head. Didi does it and she looks nice,' and she tried to snatch the box from her mother.

The Mistress shouted, 'I say, I'll kill you. Go away from here, you cheeky girl.'

The maid said, 'O, you'll be married soon and your wish will be fulfilled. See, there comes the maid from your in-laws.'

Tagar ran off. The maid Bhabi sauntered up with a basket, which she put down and touched the Mistress' feet. 'Dadababu has come with these presents,' she said. 'So my mistress has sent them to you and invited you to go over to their place soon.' The Mistress was planning to visit Jiban's mother to finalize the arrangements for the wedding. When she heard that Jiban had returned she said, 'Tell Jiban's mother that I'll come today itself.'

The maid said, 'My mistress has asked you to bring the girls too.'

Kamali said, 'How can that be? Can a girl go to her in-laws before marriage? She'll go there later, at the proper time, forever.'

Bhabi said, 'I have just conveyed what my mistress told me. After all, she is not marrying into an unknown household. It is like her own house. My mistress will be disappointed if you don't bring the girls. You can at least bring the elder daughter along, there is no harm in it.' The maid was particularly fond of the elder daughter; so when the Mistress agreed to this proposal she did not press the other request again.

The reader is aware that the Mistress had taken Snehalata with her to Jiban's house the same evening. Snehalata sat in their company for some time but not being able to take part in their conversation, she got up after a while and started wandering about. Eventually, she entered the adjoining room and started looking at the books on Jiban's table. There were no books in Bengali, so she picked up Lamb's *Tales from Shakespeare*, which she had read at home, and began to read it. It was getting dark and the letters were not clearly visible but she liked the book so much that she drew near the window and continued reading. When it became impossible to read any further, she put the book down and went back to Jiban's mother's room. Seeing Jiban there she again withdrew into the other room to continue reading. By then the servant had brought the lamp in, so sitting at the table she resumed her reading. She did not know when Jiban came silently into the room or how long he stood there, admiring this beautiful lyric in a living form. Suddenly, she lifted her bright, sparkling eyes and met his gaze. She got up, smiled at him shyly, and hurriedly left the room. That smile filled his heart with a pleasure he had never experienced before. He slowly walked up to the chair she had been occupying, sat down in it and picked up the book she was reading. He mumbled to himself:

> 'A thing of beauty is a joy for ever
> Its loveliness increases, it will never
> Pass into nothingness; but still will keep
> A bower quiet for us, and a sleep
> Full of sweet dreams; and health and quiet breathing.

Now the readers must have understood why Jiban agreed to his mother's proposal of marriage without raising any objections.

29

'*The* bridegroom is coming to the house. Blow the conch shells, sound the note of rejoicing.'

'O, Kamali, tell the band to play nicely.'

'Didi, where are the auspicious articles for the reception of the bridegroom?'

'I have taken everything: the basket, the *chiri*,[43] the lamp made with dhatura shells, the vessel for water, paddy and the durba grass. Let us go to the marriage pavilion.'

'Where is the barber? Here is the bottle of oil.'

'You must abuse properly to ward off the evil eye.'

The drums and the gong sounded loudly in the outer section of the house. After being received by the men, the bridegroom was brought inside, to the accompaniment of the sound of the band, the blowing of conch shells, ululation, and the noisy chatter of the women, and was made to stand under the banana plant. Seven married women went round him as per the ritual, after which he was received by beautifully dressed young girls while his middle-aged mother-in-law, her arms decked in bangles up to the elbow, completed the ceremony. Experts tell us that the purpose of this ritual is to cast a spell on the bridegroom. The discovery of magnet was made in Europe only a century ago but our familiarity with it is demonstrated in this ancient Indian ritual.

However, this ritual belonging to the golden age of the past does not always produce the desired results in modern times. The mother of the bride cannot depend entirely on this ritual to dominate the son-in-law, and has to take recourse to black magic for this purpose. In this case, every kind of spell was used according to the prevailing customs. The Mistress used a charmed container to hold the heart of the son-in-law captive for ever, pierced a banana stalk with a pin, and turned a key into a padlock to render him tongueless, and could not rest content until she had snapped a jute-stalk in two in front of his nose so as to make him noseless too.

Here, we must confess our inability to understand the significance of the last ritual, but the first and the second, specially the second one calls for our total approval and blessing. Two tongues together in one place are entirely redundant, so the sharp tongue of the better half should gradually become sharper in every way and triumph over the tongue of the lesser half. On this occasion, after turning the son-in-law mindless, speechless, and noseless, the mother-in-law gleefully placed a weaver's shuttle in his two hands, tied them up with thread and chanted:

'I have bought you with cowries
And tied you with a rope.
Now hold this shuttle in your hands
And bleat away, my son.'

The girls expressed their eagerness to hear the bleating of the bridegroom and the poor fellow was reduced to the state of a sheep even without producing a single sound. Suddenly, people were heard shouting, 'Make way, make way, it is time for shubhadrishti.'

So far the bride was sitting alone on a wooden stool in another room. Now four men carried her, stool and all, shouting, 'Make way, make way' and brought her to the wedding pavilion. A curtain was held before the bridegroom, the bride's stool was placed on the other side of the curtain, and the rituals associated with this ceremony were performed in which the question was raised, 'Who is greater, the bridegroom or the bride?'

Then the bearers of the bride took the stool seven times around the bridegroom, and placed it in front of him. The curtain was dropped. The priest warded off the evil eye and the bride's mother called out, 'Look, my son, look, my daughter, look properly and let the occasion be blessed.'

The bridegroom looked at the girl with longing. He had high expectations of gazing once again into the sweet and beautiful light of those eyes, but in a moment he was drowned in an all-pervasive darkness. His head started reeling, his body became numb, and he felt that he was lost in a great, black void.

Yet the marriage was not called off. After the shubhadrishti the bride and groom were brought to the spot where the bride was to be given away and the mantras were to be recited. Jiban went on repeating the lines of the scriptures after the priest like a mechanical toy. Then the couple was taken to the wedding chamber in the inner apartment.

It is well known how in our region, the custom of ragging the bridegroom in the wedding chamber gives immense pleasure to women. That day the groom is treated by the women as one of them. No reserve is maintained. Young women, related to the bride, cannot resist the temptation of having fun at the expense of the bridegroom: some take the opportunity to transgress the terms of the relationship temporarily, according to convenience, some do not consider it necessary to go so far but silently twist the ears of the bridegroom from behind and then, appearing before him with their faces half covered by their veils, shower him with choice and witty remarks. But that day the impish young women with their banter and pranks could not change the expression of profound disappointment and gloom which had come over Jiban after the wedding, and the festivities of the wedding chamber did not come off. The women were disconcerted by the unnaturally solemn countenance of the bridegroom. Their frustration was expressed in such remarks as, 'O dear, what a sullen bridegroom this is! He doesn't say a word,' 'Sister-in-law, give him a yam to eat, then he will talk,' 'A fine husband you have got, Tagar, he is reserving his speech for you' and so on. However, in spite of the disappointment, the ragging continued in the customary manner and the bridegroom was exposed to verbal and manual assaults on all sides. Not only that, Rama's mother, a neighbour, known for her wit and good voice, sang a song, teasing him and comparing him with the ragged-looking Shiva who came to wed the beautiful Parvati.

> Fie, what a bridegroom you have got!
> His eyes are half shut, he is dumb,
> His hair is knotted, his body smeared with ash.
> Our Uma is like an image carved in gold

A shining jewel fallen into dirt
O mother, how could you be so heartless!

The poet says:

Light shines only in darkness
And lightning in clouds
A blackbee adorns the lotus
The magic of beauty is set off by contrast.

Everybody was ragging the bridegroom. Snehalata had brought a betel leaf stuffed with mud to offer to Jiban but was hesitating out of shyness. One woman egged her on, 'Give it to him, there is no need to be shy. He is your sister's husband and also your husband's brother. You have every right to tease him.' Snehalata smiled, went up to him and giving him the betel leaf, said, 'Eat this, bridegroom.' Jiban looked at her. This was the first time he saw Snehalata on this occasion—the same gentle, sweet, and incomparably beautiful girl, like the image of a goddess. Jiban's dark mood suddenly brightened up. An indescribable feeling of amazement and delight overwhelmed him. Snehalata said again, 'Eat this, bridegroom.' Jiban took the betel leaf, lowered his head and absent-mindedly swallowed it, oblivious of what it contained. Everybody laughed at his stupidity. Even Tagar could not help giggling behind her veil. Jiban looked at Snehalata shamefacedly and she smiled. One of the women present gave Snehalata another suggestion for a practical joke. She went behind him and gently lifting the edge of his shawl pinned it to the bedsheet. Then she sprinkled some flowers and rosewater on his head and ran away. Much of the night was spent in frolicking. Then the Mistress came into the room and said, 'It is very late now—let the bride and the groom go to sleep.' The bridegroom stood up and the bedsheet which was pinned to his dress was lifted off the bed, much to the delight of the company. After this the couple was sent to bed with due ceremony, which included the customary eavesdropping. In the silence of the night, lying on the auspicious nuptial bed next to his newly wedded bride, Jiban suffered the pangs of unspeakable agony.

He began to feel in his innermost being how much he loved Snehalata. His heart and his soul belonged to her, yet in the eyes of the community she was another's wife. Instead of surrendering himself to her, he had to take on the responsibility of someone else. What an irony of fate!

Philosophers say that people cannot but be pleased to see the misfortune of others. This is not always true but one cannot be sure; perhaps some readers will laugh at Jiban's sorry plight and question his excessive reaction. How could Jiban be so much in love (they will ask) when he had seen Snehalata only a few times from a distance? It is something not easily explained, in fact we have also been wondering why it was so. It was not as though Jiban was enamoured of her appearance—her sweet face had fulfilled his longing for beauty, his imagination was stirred by it but Snehalata could not be regarded as a great beauty by any standards. Connoisseurs of beauty would show their surprise at Jiban's pedestrian taste. Snehalata's beauty lay in her gentle charm and a rather melancholy grace. Just as a flower curtained by a leaf does not attract attention so her sadness kept her safe from appreciative glances. Her tender appeal could not be grasped at once. Jiban had seen some very lovely girls in the neighbourhood, for instance Kalibabu's youngest daughter was universally held to be a stunning beauty but she didn't kindle his imagination as Snehalata did. It would not be right to say that Jiban was attracted by her virtues, for while Snehalata's form had invoked some ideal attributes in his imagination, he had no proof that she possessed these attributes. So we are forced to repeat our question: why did Jiban have such a passion for Snehalata?

It is true that magnet draws iron towards itself but there is no explanation as to why it does so. Man experiences a lack, an incompleteness in himself which he wants to round off by uniting with a kindred soul but everyone does not experience this fulfilment. When one sees in one's imagination another soul which could complement his own, one is drawn to it and longs to possess it. This is as true a law of nature as the one which is seen in the rotation of the earth, the falling of leaves, the sound of thunder, and the birth of living creatures. Who can say why this is so?

Man is in constant search of the other half of his incomplete self. Those who are fortunate get the real thing, although generally people mistake a piece of glass for a diamond. If a man's longing is fulfilled, he experiences the death-defying bliss of heaven and derives the strength to achieve a great goal in his life but in the absence of this fulfilment his life loses its meaning and purpose. Jibanchandra experienced this emptiness within his soul when he could not make Snehalata his own.

But one who loves truly and has faith in the sanctity of love can derive strength even in disappointment. He can overcome physical desire and experience the union of the soul. Thus Jiban's love, faced with disappointment, burnt with a brighter and purer light. He began to think, 'I couldn't marry her but does that mean that she is not mine? The stars in heaven are so far away from us, yet they give us sweetness and light. She is the queen of my heart, although I do not possess her in a worldly sense. Earthly love is sullied by impurity, desire, and pain, but this silent surrender, this pure devotion and worship is devoid of any taint. Then why should I be so miserable? I may not be her lover but I am her devotee; there may not be any physical relationship between us but she is my own.'

A human being is the aggregate of the body, the mind, and the soul; so even when love has an ethereal origin, one eventually desires to possess one's beloved physically and mentally. Jiban had also desired it but when he realized that this was not possible, his desires adopted another course. It is natural in a man to avoid pain, so when he finds that his aspirations cannot be fulfilled, he automatically lowers his expectations, and changes his attitude accordingly. A river is forced to change its course when it is faced with an obstruction, so love also changes into affection, friendship or devotion according to the situation. The more refined a person is and the more deeply he loves, the more his unrequited love takes him away from selfish desires towards a purer sphere. We cannot say whether he can adhere to the course which has been determined by his disappointment forever, but at least for the moment a higher realm is opened before his eyes. If he has good faith he may keep to this course all his life, in spite of numerous slips and difficulties and derive his strength from what he considers to be divine compassion. Those who do not have this faith feel truly wretched and persecuted by the whole world and can see nothing but evil around them. Overcome by disappointment and intense mental conflict, Jibanchandra prepared himself to sacrifice his desires.

The night changed into morning. The young girls came to the door on the pretext of observing the ritual of *shajjatulani*[44] and called out, 'O Krishna, the night is ended. Open the doors of the bower.' Jiban hurriedly left the bed. The girls barged into the room, lifted up the mosquito net, and settled down on and around the bed. Jiban asked, 'Can I go out?' One girl laughed and said, 'Will you be able to leave your Radha and go, O dark one?' Snehalata, who was sitting near Tagar on the bed, said, 'Chhotdi, our Jamaibabu is not dark, is he?'

Chhotdi was thinking of giving a witty reply when Bhabi, the maid from Jiban's house, came in with a letter and said, 'This letter came for Dadababu last evening. Ma forgot to give it to him on account of the confusion so she has sent me this morning and has asked me to find out when the bride and the groom will be sent back. It will be better if they return in the morning.'

Sneha said, 'Tell Jethima they will come in the evening. We won't let them go so early.'

The maid replied, 'O, your husband's brother has married your sister, that is why you are so concerned about him. What a pity Mohan Babu didn't come for the wedding.'

Hearing Mohan's name Snehalata looked down. Jiban, who was busy opening the letter, asked, 'Is she Mohanda's wife?' Bhabi said, 'O, how strange! Didn't you know this up to now?' Jiban gave a smile which was the expression of a secret joy in his heart. Snehalata was Mohan's wife, so now she was a close relative of Jiban's and he had the right to be devoted to her. Forgetting his earlier philosophy of self-sacrifice, Jiban now felt a deep satisfaction within himself. He was happy to have a claim on her, legitimized by their relationship.

Jiban stood in front of the window, opening the letter. Then he started reading it. His face turned ashen, his limbs trembled, and he could not restrain his tears as his eyes fell on Snehalata. Looking at the helpless, widowed girl he forgot the pain of his own disappointment in a moment, just as a dewdrop might lose itself in a vast ocean of sorrow. In great mental agony he said to himself, 'You are a widow, destined to suffer forever.' He was now ready to sacrifice his life, his mind, and his soul to relieve her suffering but it was beyond his power to do so. Needless to say, Jibanchandra had received the news of Mohan's death in the letter.

PART TWO

*D*ays and years pass by, the stream of events flows along silently and incessantly, transforming everything. Although we, the travellers on the barge of time, move continuously at a great speed on the surface of this current, we have the illusion that we are stationary and unchanging. We do not notice the gap between the present and the past or the constant turmoil all around us, until, at some particular moment a common occurrence, perhaps a very minor one, shakes us out of our slumber and we wake up alarmed and pained, and look around us and wonder where everything has vanished and how we have changed.

The readers will still remember the scene of Jagat Babu's daughter's wedding, the festivities of the wedding night, associated with so much joy and pain, as though it happened in front of them only a little while back. Time has, in the meanwhile, covered another ten years in its stride. The universe, which is eternal, is exulting about it. It has attained greater maturity in ten years by acquiring new knowledge and new experience, so its heart is full of bliss and its happiness knows no bounds. However, the unfortunate solar system, for whom this period of ten years is a very short span, is not capable of enjoying this happiness fully. Even at this present moment this earth is moving on its own path as before, with the same measure of joy and sorrow. The entire world of living creatures reflects these joys and sorrows. The same current of hope and despair, of pleasure and pain, of life and death which flowed ten years ago is flowing still. In this current, which is constantly changing and yet unchanged, during the flow of these ten years, the faint signs of solidarity which made their shadowy appearance on the Indian scene have become more prominent with the passing of the Ilbert Bill,[45] the triumph of Ripon, the founding of the National Congress[46] and the rise of nationalism.

From the perspective of Time, a thousand years are insignificant and from the perspective of a community a century is brief. However, in the life of an individual, ten years is a long period. In the midst of so many memories and forgetting, so many joys and sorrows, so much knowledge and so many delusions, people undergo a change. Yet, how many of them are aware of this change which is an outcome of the blending of the new and the old? Jagat Babu's world is no exception to this.

Charu is now about twenty-five years of age. He was married four years ago, but his young wife Amaravati died recently, and departed to an unknown world after kindling the fire of love in his young heart, leaving him in an agony of unfulfilled longing. Charu had never looked back at his past. He had imagined that his life would continue in a straight channel, moving from the past to the present and the old to the new. Suddenly, his illusion was broken by this tragedy. The broken strings of his heart could only produce the jarring notes of mourning. He realized with a shock that in one moment he had changed forever.

Only time could blunt the memory of this grief and heal his wounded heart with the balm of oblivion. Forgetting reduces the pain of memory, it does not destroy the memory itself, otherwise the world would not have been able to survive with the burden of old recollections; the sharp remembrance of loss and the pangs of desire would have haunted us forever. Then why do we disregard the importance of forgetting in this world? Memories can be enjoyed only when they are softened by oblivion. When the mind cannot endure the sharpness of pain, forgetting acts as a filter and leaves behind only what is sweet and pleasant. Only then do memories become mellow and our heart can receive divine grace. Only then can we get a hint of the nirvana of the Buddha. A grieved heart is consoled by the sympathy of a kindred soul which is akin to divine compassion. But sympathy, which does not touch the heart, even if it is expressed with sincerity sometimes disturbs the receiver more than consoling him. This is not the fault of sympathy but of the ignorance and imperfection of human nature. Jesus Christ's universal compassion did not touch the perverse hearts of the Jews who could not endure his boundless love.

Charu had many sympathizers. Everyone in his family shared his grief and this was amply demonstrated in their behaviour. Whenever Charu came to the inner apartment, his mother, sister and other relatives gave him their sympathy but behind this overt commiseration was the suggestion that he could get married to a good-looking girl, so in spite of their sincerity, their sympathy did not touch Charu. He only saw the heartlessness in their behaviour and felt that it was an insult to the memory of his dear wife. So he kept his grief locked up in his heart and tried to avoid their thoughtless kindness.

When Charu's wife was alive he did not visit Kishori often but now Kishori was his only support, his only friend. In other words, drinking was the only means to drown his sorrow, and forgetting the only remedy for his pain. Charu used to indulge in poetry as a teenager and he might have derived some solace from writing now but he had lost interest in it altogether.

It was nine o'clock in the morning. Charu had just got up from sleep and was sitting at a table in the outer room. He had taken to sleeping here at night. He could hear the street sounds from where he was sitting; the call of the hawkers and the vegetable sellers, the loud conversation of women returning from the market, the creaking sound of a bullock cart, the gardener singing off-key at his work. Facing his window was a small, two-storeyed house with an open terrace lit-up in the mild sunlight of the winter morning. A small boy was playing in the balcony with his sister. They were teaching their parrot to recite the name of Krishna. Suddenly, a fruit seller went past in the lane below, calling: 'Buy sweet lime, grapes, and pomegranates.' The little boy rushed to the terrace, stood in the sunlight and repeated the call of the fruit seller in his lisping voice. The sister followed him, laughing, and kissed him fondly, while he broke away from her impatiently and repeated, 'Buy tweet lime, glapes, and pomeglanates.'

Charu sighed deeply, watching the children at play in the mild sunshine of the tranquil morning. He too was like them at one time, pure and innocent and delighted with the world. Where had the happy days of his childhood vanished? Where had Amaravati gone? In her absence, who could redeem his gloomy and tainted heart from

THE UPROOTED VINE ✧ 139

the quagmire of sin? Lost in these sad thoughts, Charu placed his head on the table. When he raised it again he saw, instead of the happy children, a human skeleton hanging on the wall in front of him. His mood, already tinged with a tender melancholy, suddenly changed for the worse. This, he thought, was the culmination of human life. 'Was the world a wasteland?' he asked himself. 'Was there no substance in it? Was love and its memories only an illusion? Where was God then? Was there no meaning in life and was this skeleton the only reality?'

The despair that makes people lose faith in God's compassion is more terrible than death. Death destroys the body but despair destroys the soul. Charu's flow of dark thoughts was interrupted when he saw Tagar standing in front of him. Her eyes filled with tears at the sight of his bloodshot eyes, haggard face, and pained expression, she said, 'Dada, how long will you go on like this. You must get married.'

Not answering her question, Charu said, 'Why have you come here? Go into the house. Somebody may come here.'

Tagar replied, 'Ma is calling you. You don't respond to her so I have come to take you to her.'

Charu said, 'All right, I'll come after a while. You go now.'

Tagar said firmly, 'Dada, I am not going without you. If you don't listen to me, Ma will come here herself.'

Charu gave in and followed her reluctantly into the house.

The Mistress was busy chopping vegetables in the room adjoining the kitchen and scolding the maid for not bringing what she had wanted from the market. 'Why did you bring so little of the banana stalk,' she complained. 'And if you could not get the spinach I had asked for, couldn't you use your head and bring another green vegetable? How will the Babu have his rice without it? Kamali brought two seers of potatoes yesterday, but what you have brought today seems to be much less. And what will I do with these few drumsticks? Two paise? That's too much! You can't run a household if you spend money like that.'

Driven into a corner, the agitated maid tried to establish her honesty with Kamali's support. Kamali, who was cleaning the fish at some distance, tried, unsuccessfully, to appease both parties and the quarrel grew shriller every moment. Charu's arrival put an end to the confusion. The Mistress put her work aside and said, 'Charu, should you stay away from the inner apartment like this? How can I survive without seeing you?' She wiped her eyes with the corner of her sari. Charu was silent. Tagar said, 'Dada didn't want to come. I dragged him here by force.'

The Mistress said, 'Charu, how will you carry on like this at your age? Rakhal Babu's wife sent a proposal for her daughter today. There cannot be a prettier girl anywhere.'

Charu replied, 'Why do you repeat the same thing a hundred times? I have already told you that I am not getting married now.'

The Mistress continued to plead, 'Don't say that my son. You are a man, if one girl goes, you can get ten others. Will you give up your life for the one who has departed?'

Charu dismissed her. 'Let us not discuss that subject,' he said. 'I have to go to the hospital. I'd better go for my bath now.'

Charu left despite the tearful entreaties of his mother. Going up the staircase his eyes were drawn towards his bedroom which he had not entered since the death of his wife. On an impulse he stepped inside. Everything in the room was as it used to be before, everything was associated with the memory of his young wife. Her book was lying on the bed as though she had just gone out to fetch some betel and would pick it up in a moment to continue reading. Charu's heart seemed to burst. Overcome by misery he sank into the sofa near the window. He used to sit here with his wife every day, watching the beautiful garden. It was raining when they sat there together for the last time. There was thunder, lightning, incessant rain, and the dark clouds in the sky dimmed the light of the day making the garden look even more lovely. Charu was reciting the *Meghadoot*[47] to her, holding her hands in his. Suddenly, the thunder struck; the girl was alarmed and clung to him. This was their last embrace.

Now the rainy season was over and winter had arrived. The cold breeze blew, scattering dry leaves all around, ruffling the water of the pond, and casting an aura of gloom over the garden as though it was mourning the absence of the young girl. Charu leaned his head against the sofa and closed his eyes. When, after a long while he opened his eyes he saw Snehalata standing there with an expression of great sympathy and tenderness on her face. Nobody, it seemed to him, had ever looked at him like this. Suddenly, he felt as though peace had descended on his burning heart. He had a great desire to put his arms around her neck as he used to do in childhood and have a good cry. He let his tears flow unchecked and when the outburst was over he looked closely at Snehalata once again. He felt that he was looking at her after a long time, after a gap of ten years. His heart overflowed with unbounded compassion for her. He realized, as though for the first time, that Snehalata was a widow. As their eyes met again they were moved by an overwhelming sympathy for each other.

*T*here is a class of intelligent people who can comprehend any subject in a short time. They can quickly analyse complex arguments and assimilate them, but they cannot go very deep into anything. Charu belonged to this category. His intellect was sharp, but shallow. The principal strength of such people is that they are open to all kinds of views, so they do not adhere to any one kind of thinking blindly, but their weakness lies in their inability to have a steady goal in life. It is impossible for such restless people to acquire the strength and determination which is rooted in firm conviction and which can enable them to follow a steady path. If they come into contact with a more complex and domineering personality, their individuality is lost—they cannot determine which course to take. This is what happened to Charu. In the company of Kishori, his weak nature became weaker still. Had he associated with a superior individual instead of Kishori, his strong faith and devotion, conditioned by his dependent nature, would probably have made him take a totally different course.

The readers have known Charu as a bright, sixteen-year-old student of the Entrance Class, but after appearing in the LA examination he gave up studies. He began to think that the mission of his life was not to appear for examinations and that he should devote himself to writing poetry and develop his talent fully. When he left college, Jagat Babu was displeased at first, but when his poems began to appear frequently in monthly and weekly magazines and Jagat Babu's friends praised him as a prodigy, he started feeling proud of his son's achievement and did not oppose his decision. He had wealth—Charu didn't need to educate himself for a profession. It would be enough if he was able to establish himself in society, no matter how. But though Charu had talent, he was not a genius. He did not have the creative vision, the divine insight into universal truths and the magic touch which could turn everything in the world, from the most insignificant to the most profound, into pure gold; so in a short time his poetic inspiration dried up and his store was empty. Then his greatest pleasure lay in bringing out anthologies of the poems which had earlier been published in magazines, waiting continuously and greedily for the appreciative comments of reviewers and critics, and being referred to as Shakespeare by a perceptive person like Kishori. So after he stopped writing poetry, his intimacy with Kishori grew deeper day by day. Kishori was studying law, so Charu joined BA with the idea of pursuing law later, but gave up the project after a year, as he did not have the perseverance to prepare for examinations. Jagat Babu saw that Charu was doing nothing—he was neither studying nor writing poetry; so he advised him to take up medicine. At the age of twenty-three, a few days after his marriage, Charu took admission in the medical college and fortunately for him or for his college, his fees continued to be paid regularly.

Needless to say, Charu also passed through several religious phases during these ten years. From monotheism he shifted to scepticism and was quite obsessed with it until the advent of Madame Blavatsky on the scene which changed his point of view. Kishori, a staunch Hindu himself, became a theosophist in the hope of reviving the Hindu religion. Charu followed in his footsteps. The difference was that Kishori was a theosophist in name only, as his former religious beliefs were not influenced by theosophy. Charu was not a charlatan like Kishori and when he came into contact with a brilliant intellectual like Madame Blavatsky who was so learned and eloquent, he accepted her creed wholeheartedly and became an ardent member of her group. His life underwent a dramatic change at this point. He became interested in spirituality and after discussing such philosophical concepts as the nirvana of the Buddha, the moksha of the Hindus, the transmigration of the soul, and the controversy regarding the attributes of God, he finally accepted the theory of karma and an impersonal God, and coming under the influence of a guru, became a vegetarian. However, this European version of spirituality could not sustain his interest for long. He became sceptical about Madame Blavatsky's spiritual powers and about the existence of superior human beings in general. He did not become an atheist but began to feel the compassion and benediction of a personal God. This period coincided with his marriage but those happy days, when he was blessed with religious faith and love, did not last long and vanished with the sudden death of his wife. The light of his knowledge and faith was lost in the darkness of despair.

Evidently, Charu's religious fervour was not rooted in firm conviction. It could not become a part of his life and spread its branches into every aspect of his existence. His faith was not strong enough to withstand the storms of life or to guide him like the pole star in his darkest hours. Human beings have such a strong desire for fulfilment in their short and sad existence, and such an attraction for a perfect, just, and benevolent God that even in the depth of despair, a trivial incident is sufficient to revive their faith and give them the consolation they desire. The loving and compassionate gaze of Snehalata drew Charu out of his state of depression and pessimism. Once again, faith in the benevolence of God was aroused in his heart. His life was no longer burdensome and purposeless for him. In a moment he could clear the impasse and start a new phase of his life.

People were resting in their rooms in the inner apartment after their lunch. It was quiet all around. Snehalata had got a chance to sit undisturbed by herself in the veranda facing the garden. The sky was overcast. It was drizzling lightly and drops of rain were glistening like pearls on the plants growing in flowerpots on the parapet along the veranda. The rain-washed trees in the garden were swaying happily in the breeze. The dry leaves which had fallen on the surface of the pond were floating on the rippling water. The crows shook their wet feathers from time to time and gave out a shrill cry. Snehalata was watching the garden and humming to herself while holding a book in her hand.

Tagar came to the veranda and said, 'What are you doing, Didi? Are you reading? Ah, that's all you do the whole day.' She sat down on the bench near Snehalata who smiled faintly and shut the book.

The readers know that Sneha was two years older than Tagar, but

Tagar looked much older than her. Her forehead was nearly bald. The little hair that she still had was pulled tightly into a high knot and the wide parting was filled with vermilion. Her face was puffy; her plump, sluggish figure, covered with ornaments made her look like a middle-aged housewife. And Snehalata looked like a fourteen-year-old dream girl, with a fair complexion, a pretty face, and a slender body, like a flower growing on a creeper. Her face wore an expression of intelligence mingled with seriousness but there was no trace of worldly wiles in it. Her unspoilt, youthful beauty was like that of a half-opened blossom, still reminiscent of childhood. Tagar took the book from her hand and said, 'Oh, it is Dada's book. Don't read it now. Listen to me. Today is Saturday—let's go to the theatre.'

Snehalata said, 'Thakurpo is coming today. How can you go to the theatre?'

Tagar pursed her lips and said, 'How boring! He will come and chat with you and Dada, have his dinner and go to bed, while I'll have to stay up all night with the baby. It will be better to go to the theatre and spend a pleasant evening.'

Sneha smiled and said, 'We went to the theatre last week. Meshomoshai may not give us permission to go again.'

Tagar retorted, 'How will Baba know about it? You tell me whether you will come or not and leave the rest to me.'

Sneha had no desire to go out without informing Jagat Babu but it was not easy for her to turn down Tagar's earnest request. She was incapable of hurting anyone by a blunt refusal. She tried to extricate herself from the situation by saying, 'Let us not go today, it is raining.'

Tagar was annoyed, 'Even God would respond to so much pleading,' she said. 'If Ma didn't have to look after the baby, I would have gone with her and not asked you to come.'

Sneha asked, 'What are they showing today?'

Tagar said, 'The Marriage Tangle and Angel or Whore. Ah, how beautifully she sings. Sing that song for me please.'

Sneha said, 'I don't remember it. I have just heard it once.'

'You have the same excuse whenever you are asked to sing and here you are humming all the time. What were you singing when I came?'

'That is not a song from the theatre.'

'O, it is from Dada's book, I see. All right, you sing it now and teach it to me.'

Sneha had no option but to submit to Tagar's plea, so she began singing, somewhat reluctantly, fixing her gaze at the sky, but as the song progressed she lost her self-consciousness and sang with sweet abandon.

Alas, the garland could not be strung.
The whole day I gathered flowers
And came to the river bank
Thinking I'd string them
But I was lost in his thoughts,
The flowers dropped from my *aanchal*
And were swept off in the current.
The string remains in my lap.
The sound of the flute draws near
The boat comes floating in sight.
Smiling, he will ask for the garland,
What excuse shall I make?
He wanted it for his beloved
He said she would be happy
To wear a garland strung by me.
Alas, what am I to her?
Tears flow from my eyes
He is unaware of them,
He won't get the garland he asked for
And will return, disappointed.
Alas, I could not fulfil his desire
My life has been in vain.

It was Saturday, a holiday for Charu. As he came into the inner apartment, he heard the melody and stood transfixed at the entrance. Listening to his own verses so beautifully articulated and sung, he felt that his composition had become more meaningful. When Charu stepped into the veranda, Sneha blushed and stopped singing. Tagar laughed and said, 'Dada heard everything secretly. Now you are feeling shy in his presence. You used to sing together so often in the past.'

Charu said, 'Sneha, there is no reason for you to be shy. Please sing.'

Sneha blushed again. Charu repeated his request and Tagar joined him though she was not very appreciative of Sneha's singing. Just then the maid appeared and exclaimed, 'Didi, you are here! I have been looking for you all over the house. The baby is crying away and the Mistress is getting angry. Come quickly.'

'I am coming,' Tagar grumbled. 'One can't sit peacefully even for a moment.' She left the place in a huff.

32

*W*hen Tagar went away, Charu sat down at one end of the bench and requested Snehalata to sing again. She replied, 'I cannot,' and looked down. Charu said, 'I am asking you again and again and you won't sing?' Snehalata looked up at him and her face turned pale to see his ardent expression. She said miserably, 'I don't know what to sing and I can't.'

Charu said, 'You were singing so beautifully just now.'

Snehalata was quiet for a while and then blurted out, 'Charu, don't be angry. I can't sing. I would if I could—you don't have to press me so much.'

Charu noticed that Snehalata was really upset about not being able to comply with his request. He said, 'All right, let it be. Now listen to my new poem. I have come to read it out to you.' These days Charu had again started writing some poetry. He read:

> 'Who are you, the chastest on earth, virtue incarnate?
> A fresh white flower of the morning?
> Bereft of fine clothes, jewels and ornaments
> Matchless in your own beauty?
> The cruel world has shattered your haven;
> O lovely blossom, snapped from the stem
> Lying on the dusty ground, but with a smile on your lips
> Tears buried in your heart, compassion in your eyes.
> No one to call your own, you've made the world your home,
> Exalted are you in giving happiness to others!
> Whoever tramples on you is redeemed by your fragrance.
> O widow of Bengal, you are the glory of heaven!'

The rain was falling gently. Sneha heard Charu's sonorous voice reciting the lines in measured rhythm, mingled with the sound of the falling rain. With the utterance of every word Snehalata's heart melted as if she was hearing a declaration of love and experiencing the ethereal union of the souls. Never having faced such a rush of emotion before, she could not identify its cause—only her eyes filled with tears as she was overwhelmed with a strange happiness. Charu finished the poem and asked her whether she liked it. Snehalata was startled and two drops of tears which were arrested in her dreamy eyes suddenly rolled down. She looked down shyly and mumbled, 'It is beautiful.' Charu was moved by her tears. He thought, 'The poem has aroused in her an awareness of her helpless state.' He was silent for a few moments and then asked abruptly, 'Sneha, what are your views about widow remarriage?'

For a few weeks now Charu had been spending some time with Sneha every evening, talking about different subjects such as religion, politics, literature, and social practices, but he deliberately did not raise the topic of widow remarriage. Snehalata was taken aback by the question.

'How can one be married a second time after having been married once already?' she ventured.

'But what if the marriage is no marriage, when one is married in early childhood?'

Snehalata had not thought about the subject or formed any firm opinion about it. Like any other Hindu girl she had been unconsciously influenced by the commonly held opinions and had accepted an ideal image of widowhood. As she grew older she resolutely believed in the superiority of this ideal and its universal acceptability. Charu had himself eulogized the same ideal of a widow's chaste and selfless life in his poem, and it seemed to reflect his own thinking. She felt that her chosen path was smooth and commendable. She said, 'But is marriage the only goal of life? I believe there are many unmarried women in the West who devote their whole life to the service of others. We do not permit women to remain unmarried in our country, but widows...'

Charu cut her short. 'Yes, if all widows can happily dedicate their lives in the interest of others there is no problem, but it is not easy for everybody to ignore the instinctive attraction between the sexes and divert the course of their lives in another direction. In fact, for some people it is impossible to do so and it is not an unnatural desire either, because sexual union makes one a complete human being. However, just as the clear water of a stream is polluted by dirt, so pure love is often tainted by the frailty of human nature. That is why I say that if all those loving widows who cannot help loving someone, and whose life is meaningless without love and physical union, are permitted to marry, they can find fulfilment in their lives and can be useful in the world. Otherwise, their lonely and unhappy lives cannot bring happiness to others. How can the world gain anything from a person who is forever lamenting her own misery? Like a piece of wood she can only serve as fuel for the cremation fire. Is it not better for all those widows to marry who cannot derive pleasure from their widowed state permanently and who are compelled to pollute their love because of the harsh strictures of society and in the process bring more harm than good in the world?'

Snehalata had never reflected on the subject in this manner. There hadn't been any need for her to do so because she had never really experienced the emotion of love so far and did not feel deprived of its fulfilment. From time to time she did feel a void in her life, but in such moments she looked at Mohan's photograph and remembered his affectionate, caring nature. In childhood, she had not appreciated the value of that affection; now she wanted to preserve its memory and believed it to be love. Never until now did she think about love in this manner. She could not dismiss Charu's argument as irrelevant but she could not accept it totally on account of her conventional upbringing. Reluctantly, she said, 'Yes, that is true, but...'

Charu interrupted her, 'Why this hesitation? Just think of it. You may want to get married yourself sometime, may you not?'

Snehalata found the question disagreeable and quickly said, 'No, no, I won't like to marry.'

'No, imagine that you fall in love with someone. What then?'

Sneha said, 'What nonsense you talk! Does loving always mean wanting to get married?'

Charu realized that he could not convince her by talking against the conventions so he changed his approach. 'All right,' he said, 'I am not talking about widow remarriage. But if you were still unmarried, you would have to marry now.'

THE UPROOTED VINE ❧ 151

Sneha replied, 'In that case I would have married him and nobody else.'

Charu laughed and said, 'That's why women are called irrational. You know him now but if you were unmarried you wouldn't have known him.'

Their conversation ended abruptly as Tagar made her appearance on the scene and asked, 'What are you two talking about?'

Charu said, 'Tagar, you know it is Saturday. Jibanda will be coming soon.'

Tagar replied, 'Yes, I know that, but what were you discussing when I came? You stopped when I entered.'

Charu was irritated. 'We were talking about very important things but I won't tell you what they were and Sneha, you don't tell her either.' He got up and walked away.

Tagar was furious. 'Don't tell me,' she cried. 'I don't want to hear about it.' Pulling a long face she also followed Charu. Sneha called after her, 'Tagar, come, I'll tell you everything.' But Tagar did not turn back.

_S_ince Snehalata became a widow, Jagat Babu started paying more attention to her studies, because he knew that if she got interested in the pursuit of knowledge, her future life would not be entirely purposeless and unhappy. Snehalata was proficient in Bengali and could comprehend English fairly well too but it was not as though she had read a vast number of books. She had little leisure—almost her entire day was spent in housework. Besides, even when she had some time to herself she did not have access to a great many books and had to depend on others to provide her with reading material. Only when Jagat Babu got her a book or a magazine was she able to read it. Jagat Babu was not very liberal in this respect and did not allow her to read all kinds of books indiscriminately. He occasionally brought for her Bengali magazines, religious books, histories, and biographies, and once in a while a book of good poetry or fiction. Apart from these he sometimes read out to her books on natural sciences himself.

As a result of such carefully supervised reading, Snehalata's mental horizon had widened; her natural inclination towards religion had also developed. Having been placed in adverse circumstances since childhood, her sweet nature had taken recourse to a fortitude which turned into a firm reliance on God as she matured intellectually. She had such a deep faith in divine grace and compassion that if someone blamed God for her widowhood in her presence, she was not touched by such sympathy. She knew that God was just and benevolent and even if something unfortunate happened in the world, its ultimate consequence was bound to be good. Man, being imperfect by nature, was unable to comprehend divine ways and the good that came out of suffering. She believed that there was definitely a divine purpose in her being placed in such circumstances, otherwise it would not have been so. This faith gave her consolation even in those moments when she felt particularly oppressed. There was, in her speech, her expression, her demeanour, and her personality a sweetness and a contentment which was an outcome of her simple faith. So, surrendering herself to the will of the Almighty, adoring Jagat Babu, keeping herself engaged in housework and studies, and remembering Mohan from time to time, her days were spent quite peacefully in spite of the constant reproaches of the Mistress.

But that day she could not concentrate on her reading after Charu's departure. Her mind glowed with an unusual excitement. She had always adored Charu but this was the first time when she sensed Charu's genuine affection for her in his poem. She could not remember every line of the poem but some of the phrases echoed in her mind repeatedly:

'The chastest on earth, virtue incarnate
the fresh white flower of the morning?'

What a beautiful image! But whose was it? Who could be worthy of it? Certainly not Snehalata. 'The widow of Bengal! You are the glory of heaven!' Oh, this was an exaggeration. What qualities did she have? None at all. This was just an expression of Charu's feelings, his fantasy. Charu was a poet. His talent was genuine, the rest was false.

Although she realized fully that there was no resemblance between herself and the image in the poem and that she did not deserve such praise, she could not help deriving a strange pleasure from it because it was an expression of Charu's affection for her. The intense pleasure disturbed Snehalata's peace of mind. She used to look at Mohan's picture whenever she felt unhappy; now she thought of him in her excitement. She went into her room and took out his photograph. This had been taken ten years ago and had faded. Today, it looked more faded than it did before. Snehalata did not remember Mohan's face as she had seen it. This photograph helped her to create an image of Mohan in her mind. But even though she examined it very intently she could not call up the shadowy image of the past; instead it seemed to have a resemblance to Charu. When she closed her eyes, Charu's living image appeared before her and when she opened them again to look at the picture she felt that it was Charu's picture. Her reverie was broken by Hara's mother's call, 'Didi, where are you? Ma is calling you. She seems to be very angry. Come fast.' She felt as though she had woken up from a dream.

34

*I*t was Charu who had stopped talking when Tagar appeared but Tagar got angry with Snehalata. Snehalata had not shown any eagerness to accompany her to the theatre, so she was already in a bad mood. This incident added fuel to the fire. She went off to her mother and said, 'You know, Ma, Dada was talking about marriage with Konedidi.' The Mistress misunderstood her and said, 'So Charu is showing interest in marriage after all. Ah, the boy is so shy in front of us.' Tagar said, 'Oh no, he was not talking about his marriage but about widow marriage.' Tagar had been eavesdropping on Charu and Snehalata before entering the veranda. The Mistress fell from the skies. Widow marriage—how is that? The Mistress was aware of numerous faults in Snehalata. The principal fault was that Jagat Babu was fond of her. She was good-looking and studious, and a millstone around their necks, but she had never imagined that things could go so far.

The Mistress had just had a wash and was wiping her face with a towel. She flung the towel on the clotheshorse in a fit of anger and shouted, 'What did you say? Widow marriage? Does she want to seduce my son? Just call that witch here, I'll throw her out of the house right away.'

Tagar saw that things were going out of hand. Looking at her mother's reaction her own anger subsided. She said, 'Why do you get so excited? That is why I don't tell you anything. Dada may have talked about widow marriage but he was not proposing to Konedidi.'

The Mistress said, 'My son is a decent boy—as innocent as a baby. Why should he talk about marriage? I know, I know, this is the doing of that hussy.' With flaring nostrils and bloodshot eyes she shouted for her maid Kamali but there was no reply. Hara's mother, who was going upstairs, came to enquire what she wanted, for Kamali had gone to the market. The Mistress said, 'Hara's mother, just call that inauspicious, sly, sorceress right now.'

Hara's mother understood who the Mistress was referring to so fondly. She asked, 'Why Ma, what has happened?'

The Mistress replied, 'Whatever had to happen has happened. Call her now. Let that witch face me once.'

Hara's mother went out to call Snehalata. Tagar scolded her mother, 'Ma, will you stop now? I didn't say that Dada wanted to marry Konedidi so why are you getting so worked up? They were just discussing whether widow marriage was good or bad and you are throwing a tantrum. There is no telling what you hear and what you understand. From now on I'll never tell you anything.'

This did not reassure the Mistress totally but she calmed down a little. 'Charu is a grown-up boy,' she said. 'Why does she discuss these things in his presence. This is sheer depravity. If a girl is so shameless what can the poor boy do?'

Snehalata came into the room at this moment and her sight redoubled the fury of the Mistress. Ignoring Tagar's reproving looks, she screamed, 'Inauspicious wretch! After destroying three families you are now eyeing my precious son? You are trying to trap my innocent boy?'

Snehalata had never faced such an onslaught and could not understand what was being hinted at. She just trembled from head to foot on hearing this uncalled for accusation. The Mistress continued, 'Sly witch! Butter will not melt in your mouth! You act so dumb in front of us and then talk about marriage with someone who is like your elder brother! Get this clear, once and for all, that if you ever speak to Charu or have anything to do with him you will have to leave this house at once.'

Tagar said, 'Ma, this is not fair. Konedidi is not to blame. What can she do if Dada comes to her?'

The Mistress flared up, 'If she is not to blame, who is? Why should the boy go to her unless the witch seduces him? I haven't seen a more inauspicious girl. There is not a single person left in her own family and I can't get rid of her. She doesn't even die!'

Tagar realized that her mother was not going to be pacified easily now. She took Snehalata by the hand and led her away from there. After a while she came and sat alone with her mother and said, 'Ma, you really don't have any sense. You shouldn't have scolded Didi like that. If Dada comes to hear of it he'll be so angry. These days Dada comes inside the house and sits for a while, and it is all because of Didi. If you don't allow him to see her, he might not step into the house at all. Let us first get him married somehow, then you can do whatever you please.'

Tagar's advice worked. The Mistress said anxiously, 'My child, I forget myself sometimes. You do what you think is best. Tell Snehalata not to report all this to Charu.'

Tagar said, 'Of course, I'll do that, and you also tell Didi not to mind what you have said in anger. Let her continue to see Dada as before.' The Mistress agreed half-heartedly and said, 'All right, my child, I'll tell her that. But all this should not backfire ultimately.'

The moment Charu crossed the threshold of the inner apartment in the evening, he was accosted by Hara's mother who told him in a whisper, 'Dadababu, what did you tell Didi? The Mistress humiliated her so much. Fie, Babu, does one marry a sister?'

Charu understood at once what the matter was. This had happened because Tagar had given a distorted account of their conversation to the Mistress. In great agitation he rushed towards Sneha's room but changed his mind after going half way. Unfortunately, Tagar crossed his path at that moment; so he poured out his rage on her. After giving her a dressing down he went to his father in the outer apartment.

Jagat Babu was reclining on the sofa and smoking his hookah. Charu sat down on a stool near him. He had just returned from Kishori's house: his mind was alert and his heart was on fire, thinking of Snehalata's suffering. He raised the subject of the misery of child widows and began to present all the sound arguments in support of widow remarriage with great passion and fervour. Jagat Babu was impressed by his son's ability to argue his point, his sense of fairness and his tender, sympathetic nature, but he did not have the courage to act according to his proposal. There was a time when Jagat Babu had the highmindedness and the zeal to oppose the conventions of society, but now in his middle age he had lost his enthusiasm and could not even think about such things. His heart had been so tightly bound by traditions that he could not possibly break those shackles without injuring himself. Snehalata had been married to Mohan. She was like his possession left in Jagat Babu's custody. If he passed her on to somebody else, Mohan would claim her from the other world. He said, 'Charu, can one be married a second time?' Perhaps he had forgotten his own case.

Charu said, 'Of course, many people do, and besides, Snehalata's marriage was no marriage at all.'

Jagat Babu asked, 'What does Snehalata say? Does *she* want to get married?'

Charu replied, 'No, she doesn't say anything. I am saying it.'

Jagat Babu was relieved. He said, 'All right, let us drop the matter for the time being. We can consider it later.'

35

*A*fter being scolded by Charu, Tagar came to Snehalata and said tearfully, 'What have you reported to Dada about me?' When Snehalata denied it, Tagar said, 'You must have. He scolded me so much. Don't I have anything else to do except talk about you? Here I have been quarrelling with mother on your behalf. You are so ungrateful.'

Snehalata said, 'How could I say anything to Charu when we haven't even met each other?'

Tagar did not believe it. As she had no qualms about telling lies, she did not believe that other people spoke the truth. She said, 'If you didn't tell him, did someone come down from the sky to do it? Because of you I am not spared anywhere. Even at my in-laws' place I am harassed constantly. The other day my mother-in-law asked me to boil the milk. Is that my job, I ask you? All my life I have been occupied with reading and writing and am I going to grind spices and boil milk now? When I told my mother-in-law that, she said that no one was as good as you, the elder daughter-in-law. These are the kind of remarks I have to hear every day. Even when I come home I get no respite. My father and brother are no longer mine. It's all right—you rule here, I am off.'

Snehalata was brought up amidst insults and humiliation, so she was quite used to such comments. The Mistress scolded her every day on the pretext of supervising her daily chores. She was accustomed to it as to a working dress, but when she received some choice, hurtful rebuke, like a fancy garment, it hurt her immensely. On such occasions she felt that she should go away somewhere and not bother Jagat Babu's family any more. She was already smarting under the sharp words the Mistress had hurled at her, now Tagar's outburst shattered her altogether.

It was evening. The moon was up in the clear sky but its light was cool and pale, as though it was shedding tears at the sight of Snehalata's misery. Sitting in front of the open window in the moonlight, Snehalata was praying to God with all her heart. Presently, Hara's mother came into the room, saying, 'Didimoni, what are you doing?' Snehalata wiped away her tears quickly. The maid sat down comfortably on the floor near her and stretched her legs. She said, 'I have just got away for a moment after finishing all the work. Hope they don't call me again. I have cut and chopped everything for the cook. Now I am not going to move even if she calls. Please read out the Ramayana to me Didimoni.'

Before Hara's mother could finish what she was saying, Tagar came into the room. Standing near the window she said, 'Ah, what lovely moonlight! I can't open my windows because of the babies,' and sat down near Sneha. There was no sign of her having qarrelled with Snehalata only a short while ago—it was as though nothing had happened. She did not notice Sneha's gloomy expression for she was preoccupied with other thoughts. Suddenly, she said, 'You know, when Dada talked to me I smelt liquor on his breath. He seems to have got into the habit of drinking.' Snehalata was so upset to hear it that she forgot her own troubles. She could not think of how to stop Tagar from continuing on the same subject in front of Hara's mother, so she quickly asked, 'Has Thakurpo arrived?'

Tagar said, 'He has been here for a long time. He wants to take me back tomorrow.'

Hara's mother said, 'He loves Didi so much. He can't live without her even for a day. Why, she came here only the other day.'

Somebody called out, 'O Hara's mother, where are you? Come quickly.'

Hara's mother said peevishly, 'O, I am dead. See, they are calling me again. Won't let me rest even for a moment. Let me go and see what they want.'

The maid went away. Tagar said, 'O yes, he loves me all right. It only shows up when he has to give me my lessons. If I don't study, he sulks. If he finds me taking a nap in the afternoon, he says, "It's not good to be lazy." Do you call this love?'

Snehalata said, 'But he says this for your own good—that shows he loves you.'

Tagar said, 'I see it would have been better if he had married you. If I am not allowed to do what I want, it doesn't seem like love to me. Why, Khiro's husband doesn't say anything to Khiro. She does whatever she pleases. My husband grumbles when I chew tobacco. The other day he even threw away my tobacco pouch. Well, if I can't take it in his presence, I take it when he is away. What can he do about that?'

Snehalata said, 'Is it good to do things secretly?'

Tagar retorted, 'Why shouldn't I? You needn't do it if you don't want to.'

Snehalata saw that it was no use reasoning with her. Changing the subject, she said, 'All right, do what you like, but can I say something to you? Will you listen?' Tagar's curiosity was aroused and she said, 'Yes, I will.'

Snehalata said, 'First tell me if you will keep your promise.' Tagar repeated, 'Yes I will.'

Snehalata said, 'You said in front of the maid that Dada was smelling of liquor. Was that proper? Promise me you won't say this to anybody else.'

Greatly amused by Snehalata's solemn air, Tagar began to giggle. 'What is the harm in that?' she asked.

Snehalata said, 'Is it nice to give Charu a bad name unnecessarily? He doesn't really have liquor, does he?'

'Then how did I get the smell?'

'Maybe he had been handling some medicines in the lab. And even if he drank a little, is it proper to announce it in front of others? Isn't it better to make an effort to dissuade him from doing it?'

'I don't understand all these subtleties. I am not as clever as you are.'

'Forget about that. You promise that you won't tell anyone about it.'

Tagar said with a suppressed smile, 'All right, I won't.'

36

*T*agar had promised Sneha that she would not disclose the secret to anyone, but as soon as she met Jiban, she exclaimed, 'I have never seen such a fuss in my life.' Jiban asked her what she was talking about. She replied, 'Just listen to me. Dada was smelling of liquor. When I told Konedidi about it she could not bear it. She extracted a promise from me not to tell anyone and only then was she satisfied. As though Dada is closer to her than he is to me. She is much too concerned about him.'

Jiban asked, 'Really, has Charu taken to drinking?'

Tagar replied, 'After all he is a man, isn't he? Everyone is not a dried-up stick like you. What's the harm if he drinks? He has lost his wife—he needs some diversion.'

Jiban did not want to start a quarrel with her so he kept quiet. The next evening he found an opportunity to be alone with Charu and confronted him, 'What is this I hear, that you have taken to drinking?'

Charu was caught off-guard but he quickly collected himself and said with a laugh, 'Who told you that?'

'That's immaterial, you tell me if it is true or not?'

'I see that you are taking it very seriously. Having a peg or two in the company of friends is not called drinking.'

'That is how Kishori used to talk earlier. Now it seems he has got addicted to liquor. You are very cool about it but the matter is not so simple. There is nothing more pernicious than drink. It turns human beings into something worse than brutes. Besides, just think how hurt your parents will be to hear of this.'

'Anyway, how did you gather all this worthless information?'

'Tagar told me.'

Charu was surprised and said, 'How did she come to know about it?'

'She found you smelling of liquor.'

Charu got a little worried. If Tagar had got scent of it, there was every chance of his parents hearing about it too. He said anxiously, 'Jibanda, tell Tagar not to disclose it to anyone. Kishorida made me take a glass that day but I shall not go to his house again. Please tell Tagar—'

Jiban said, 'Boudidi has already told her that but I shall also forbid her if you say so.'

'Does Sneha also know about it?'

'Yes, she heard about it from Tagar and immediately made her promise to keep it a secret. See, you may not be concerned about yourself but other people are.'

Though Jiban counselled him properly at length, after his departure Charu did not remember what he said. It was only what Sneha had told Tagar that created a turmoil in his mind. He took that to heart. Charu did not go out that day. In the evening, he sat on the open terrace of the outer apartment. In the dream-like atmosphere, lit-up by the moon, the only thought that preoccupied his mind was Snehalata's concern about him and that she was pained to hear him being denigrated. Did she love him then? Living in close proximity to her since childhood, this thought had never occurred to him, but today this little incident aroused this question in his mind persistently. Although he was still uncertain regarding her feelings for him, he was now absolutely sure of one thing: whether she loved him or not, he loved her. Not from that day, not from that moment, but he had loved her all his life, from the very beginning. He remembered the day Sneha first came to this house; his grandmother had introduced her as his future bride much to his delight. He remembered how unhappy he used to feel if Sneha did not speak to him or felt too shy to play with him. He remembered when he was sick, Sneha would come and sit by his bed and how he fretted when she left his side. Within moments he clearly discovered the secret feeling he had nurtured for twenty-five years. He conjured up with fresh wonder and delight the gentle, affectionate Snehalata of the past in his imagination and it aroused a new upsurge of love in his heart. After a while he got up, for he found it impossible to sit alone with his heart overflowing with love. Snehalata was seated on a bench in her balcony and humming a song which Charu had composed in the memory of his dead wife.

> The one who goes away forgets all
> The one who is left behind weeps with longing.
> Gazes at the road and sings of the past
> Kindling hope from intense desire.
>> Alone on this earth
>> One tries to forget
> The love, full of agony, the eternal thirst of separation.

She was feeling Charu's pain in her own heart when Charu himself appeared before her. Generally, he never entered this part of the house after dusk. Seeing him Snehalata was simultaneously overcome with amazement and delight. When Charu sat down at one end of the bench she said, 'See, how lovely the moon is!' Charu said, 'Yes,' but it was not clear which moon he was alluding to because he was gazing, not at the moon in the sky but at Snehalata as though he saw the beauty of the whole world in that sweet face. Even if a hundred moons were shining in the sky, his infatuated gaze would not have turned in that direction. He gazed at Snehalata in silence while she sat looking down and wondering how to broach the subject with him. After hesitating for a long time she suddenly said, 'Charu, will you take it amiss if I say something?'

'No, tell me, what is it?'

Twisting the corner of her sari and still looking down, she said, 'Tell me the truth, Charu, have you been drinking?'

'Yes. I will not lie to you.'

Sneha's eyes filled with tears. She said, 'I wouldn't have believed it had you not told me yourself. Charu, why do you do it?'

Charu said, 'Is drinking a crime? Of course an excess of it is bad but a little drinking is harmless; it only lifts up your spirits.'

'But those who take to drinking go to the dogs,' Snehalata insisted.

Charu said, 'You are influenced by whatever you have heard. Everything is all right if it is done in moderation.'

'People won't understand that. Whoever hears about it will condemn you. And Meshomoshai will be so hurt.'

'Forget about what others say. They often condemn good deeds also. And how will Baba hear of it?'

'But if he does, he'll be upset. After all you have concealed it from him. It is not good to do things secretly. He is under the impression that you don't touch wine. Are you not deceiving him?'

Charu said, 'We do so many things in life which have to be done secretly. That kind of deception cannot be avoided.'

Two large tears fell from Snehalata's eyes. She said, 'Charu, I am pained to hear you say this. I don't know what other people do, but you—'

Charu said impulsively, 'Sneha, you don't have to say anything more. I won't do something which pains you. I won't drink any more.'

Snehalata's face lit up with an unbounded joy. Charu was not in doubt any more. He knew that Sneha loved him.

37

The Mistress had acted according to Tagar's suggestion, but that did not provide any relief to her mind. Earlier she used to fret when Charu did not come into the inner apartment. Now she considered it a disaster if he came that way and she made his life difficult with her persistent request to get married. Failing in her effort to bring him round, she finally gave vent to her frustration in front of Jagat Babu. Jagat Babu had returned home early that evening. He was in a good mood because one of his critically ill patients had shown signs of recovery. His food was laid out for him, the lamp was lit and Sneha was sitting there with a book in her hand. On seeing him she closed the book, stood up, and asked him with a smile, 'Meshomoshai, you have come early today. How is your patient?'

Jagat Babu patted her and said, 'He has recovered, Buri, and so have I. I was dying of anxiety all these days. No medicine seemed to work.' He stopped as the Mistress appeared in the doorway and said, 'Your food is getting cold. Won't you stop chatting, for God's sake!'

Jagat Babu said quickly, 'I won't eat today. I have already dined.'

The Mistress stepped into the room and said, 'Why shouldn't you have dined? Here you don't get mutton chops and roast meat as you do in that Muslim's house. But why don't you tell us beforehand instead of wasting food here every day.'

Jagat Babu scratched his head and said, 'When I leave, I think I'll dine at home but they don't let me come away without dinner. Anyway he has recovered now. From tomorrow—'

The Mistress said, 'All right then, don't eat. Why do you make up stories? Sneha, take the plate away. Give it to Tagar if she hasn't eaten.'

Sneha put her book away on the shelf and went out with the plate. The Mistress said, 'Your whole life has been spent in the service of others. I have never seen you bothering about your wife or your son. Even death does not come to me. Will you get your son married or not, I ask you.'

Jagat Babu could not fathom the reason behind her curt behaviour. He said sheepishly, 'He has lost his wife lately. He can marry some time later.'

The Mistress said sharply, 'You seem to have become senile. You can't see anything yourself. Don't blame me if there is a mishap at home.'

Jagat Babu said, 'Now, what mishap can there be at home?'

The Mistress replied, 'Why, there is a young woman around and your son isn't a child any more. Don't you understand this.'

An agitated Jagat Babu replied, 'Sneha is like his sister. They have grown up together since childhood. If Charu is so worthless as to look upon Sneha perversely then I'll disown him.' He forgot that he had himself been so eager to get Charu married to Sneha a few years ago. The Mistress was a little disheartened by his response. She had not spoken to him about it so far, fearing that he might put all the blame on Charu. She regretted having spoken to him so directly in a fit of temper. Softening her tone, she wiped her eyes with her sari and said, 'Have I said anything amiss that you are so angry? Tell me, who can I speak to about my worries except you? But if your feelings are hurt, I'll not speak again.'

Taken unawares by her change of tone Jagat Babu said, 'No my dear, I am not angry. I said this because I can never imagine Charu to be so depraved.'

The Mistress continued, 'You must remember that he is a young man. It is no use blaming him alone. And I haven't said that anything has gone amiss. All I am saying is that one should be careful and get him married soon.'

Jagat Babu said, 'Haven't you spoken to him about it?'

The Mistress replied, 'I have tried my best but your word will carry more weight than mine. He does not take me seriously.'

This is how their conversation ended. Snehalata was still in Tagar's room. Thinking that she might be able to study for a longer time with Jagat Babu that day, she somehow extricated herself from Tagar's company and coming to Jagat Babu, asked him, 'Meshomoshai, won't you teach me today?'

Jagat Babu said, 'No, let it be now, Sneha,' and left the room. From his unnaturally brusque tone and hurried departure, and the trans-fixed posture of the Mistress, Sneha guessed that he was greatly perturbed for some reason and perhaps she herself was the cause of this tension between them. She picked up the book from the shelf in a despondent mood and went into her room. Extinguishing the lamp burning in a corner of the room, she sat down near the window in the dark. The moon had not risen yet. As she gazed at the star-studded sky, her eyes filled with tears and an intense sadness de-scended on her. She began to hum softly to herself.

> No one has understood my heart!
> He sent me away with scorn and disdain
> When I went to offer my love and devotion.
> I cannot carry this burden any more
> O death, where are you?
> Give me shelter at your feet.
> You are my life, not death
> You are my haven, not a void
> You are the saviour of the wretched.
> Grant a home to the homeless one.
> Even you are denying me refuge,
> Even you are not responding to my call
> Do I not, a hapless soul,
> Deserve your pity?

38

Coming into the outer apartment, Jagat Babu reclined on the sofa and began to pull at his hookah. As the rings of smoke rose up in the air, thoughts began to crystallize in his head. Finally, when there was no strength left in the tobacco, he pulled the pipe out of his mouth and called out to the servant, who came in quietly to take away the bowl of the hookah for filling it afresh. Jagat Babu said to him, 'I don't want tobacco. Call Charu here.'

Taken aback by this unexpected order the servant replied, 'Yes, sir,' and turned round to look at him. Then he picked up the hookah and left the room. When Charu came in, Jagat Babu said, 'I have been appointed a delegate to the Madras Congress.[48] I won't be able to go but you can go in my place. I have suggested your name for it.' Charu agreed to the proposal happily. Jagat Babu said, 'But won't it affect your studies? This is your final year.'

Charu said, 'I'll go during the Christmas vacations. That will not affect my studies. Have you read the *Saturday Review*?'

Jagat Babu said, 'Yes, of course. They are feeling jealous that our society is also making progress. If that were not so, would the Congress have come into existence?'

Charu said, 'I feel that we should have a social congress also. I want to make the proposal this time. Undoubtedly we are now becoming conscious about social uplift and are also making some progress but it is so slow that if we don't speed it up, it will hardly make any impact on people. So, instead of getting angry about the comments of the British we should aim to reach a stage where they do not get a chance to criticize us any more. See, in spite of so many girls' schools having opened, how many of our women are properly educated? Although many of us have understood that widow remarriage is not contrary to the scriptures or law, how many of us have the courage to get a widow married? Anybody who has dared to do it has been excommunicated. There has been so much talk against child marriage, yet it has not been eradicated so far.'

Jagat Babu said, 'Charu, it is not possible for me to say whether child marriage and widow remarriage are proper for our society or not. I also used to think like you at one time but with age, all these social issues appear to be too complicated to me. I cannot say with any conviction that child marriage is evil or that widow remarriage is good. Instead of getting married again, if widows spend their lives selflessly as they did in the past, would it not be more beneficial for them as well as for society? And our society has not reached that stage in which child marriage can be condemned. If child marriage were totally prohibited now, I think it would cause more harm than good. First of all it will become difficult to get girls married. Many girls will remain unmarried throughout their lives.'

'If we all wait for the right occasion to take a step, it may never materialize. The greatest weakness of child marriage is the weakness of the progeny. Without a ban on child marriage the race cannot really improve, rather, it is better for women to stay unmarried even if the race becomes extinct.'

'Charu, you are young; all this enthusiasm suits you, but we in our old age are so eager to see our grandchildren that we cannot think along these lines. I have been wanting to tell you, Charu, that your mother is very unhappy because you are not getting married.'

Jagat Babu felt that there was no other way he could broach the subject. Charu was not prepared for it and for a moment he did not know how to react. Jagat Babu said, 'Not only your mother but even I want you to get married. Rakhal Banerji's daughter is a pretty girl.'

Charu tried to sidestep the issue and said, 'Baba, it is better not to think of marriage until the examinations are over.'

Jagat Babu replied, 'You need not worry about that. The girl can remain at her father's place until your exams. She is still very young.'

Charu was in a fix. For a Bengali boy it is easy to quarrel with the mother but not so easy to oppose the father. He said, after a pause, 'But so soon?'

Jagat Babu understood what he meant and said, 'Charu, there is no escape from suffering in this world but in spite of that we have to fulfil the duties of a householder. That is the law of the world which is of God's making. Charu, I have never asked you for anything, so please comply with this request of mine.'

Charu could not think of an answer to this. At a loss and overcome by confusion, he remained silent.

Jagat Babu declared, 'So, I'll tell your mother to finalize your marriage with Rakhal Banerji's daughter.' With these words he got up to go. Charu wanted to stop him and tell him that he wasn't getting married and there was no need to accept any proposal but he could not do it. Jagat Babu went away. Charu remained seated at the same place, his heart heavy with foreboding.

39

*C*haru did not sleep almost the whole of that night. How was he going to convey his unwillingness to Jagat Babu and prevent the wedding? The thought made his head spin and he felt he was losing his mind. Towards morning he fell asleep, totally exhausted. When he woke up, his mind was calm. He thought that there was no need to confront his father; it would be enough to convey his decision to his mother and stop the marriage. He went into the inner apartment to look for his mother but not finding her there he automatically moved towards Sneha's room. Sneha was not there and Charu stood wondering whether he should leave or wait for her. Just then Snehalata came in with a bunch of keys in her hand, her hair flowing loose and her face radiant. She smiled at Charu and said, 'Charu, there is good news for you. Your marriage has been fixed for the first week of *Magh*.'[49]

Her smile irritated Charu. He burst out in an unnaturally sharp tone, 'The good news is that I shall never get married.'

Sneha was surprised and said, 'What's that, Charu? You won't get married? You wanted to marry Rakhal Banerji's daughter, didn't you?'

Charu said, 'You believed that? You are cruel.'

Snehalata could not comprehend his meaning and said in a hurt voice, 'Charu, what is the matter with you? How have I been cruel and why are you angry?'

Charu said, 'Will you be happy if I tell you that you will be married to Haradhan Bhattacharya?'

Snehalata laughed and said, 'What is the comparison between you and me? I am a woman and a widow and Rakhal Babu's daughter is not Haradhan Bhattacharya either. You like her.'

Charu said, 'That's enough. Why do you torment me? I cannot tolerate you saying this to me. I thought you loved me.'

Sneha said, 'Why do you doubt it?'

Charu replied, 'Because you don't understand my feelings. Why don't you understand how much I love you and how pained I am if there is any talk of my marrying another person. Sneha, you are everything to me. I'll marry only you, otherwise I won't get married at all.'

Once the dam is broken, who can stop the current of the river? Having started once, Charu couldn't restrain himself till he had laid his heart bare. Snehalata was stunned into silence. Charu continued, 'Sneha, you are my whole world, my paradise. I'll sacrifice everything for your sake. If Baba doesn't consent to this marriage and disowns me, I'll accept it and I'll be happy with you even in a lowly hut. Just tell me whether you love me or not, whether you will marry me or not.'

Snehalata was silent. After a pause she said, 'Charu, have you gone mad? I am a widow and your sister.' As she said this, with her face lowered, her tears flowed silently. Charu would have continued pleading, but his words remained unsaid because he caught sight of Tagar standing in the veranda. Coming out of the room quickly he said, 'Tagar, where is Ma? I have come to see her.'

Tagar said, 'She is in the kitchen, but tell me what you want.' Charu went down the stairs without giving her a reply.

Tagar came up to Sneha and asked 'What was Dada saying to you?'

Sneha controlled her tears with an effort and said in a calm voice, 'Nothing in particular. I just told him that his marriage was fixed for the month of *Magh* and so—'

'So what?'

'So he said that he was not interested.'

'O, now I understand. So he has gone to tell Ma about it. Let me go and find out what he is saying.'

Tagar went away. Snehalata breathed a sigh of relief to be left alone.

40

Charu declared that he wouldn't get married. The Mistress begged, pleaded, scolded, bullied, and shed tears to bring her son round to her point of view, but it was all in vain. Charu was adamant and the battle between the mother and the son couldn't be resolved. After watching the scene for a while, Tagar came to Snehalata and said, 'Didi, Dada is determined not to get married. Ma is trying so hard to persuade him but he is not willing to listen to her. Why don't you talk to him about it?'

Snehalata was nonplussed. Charu's words were still ringing in her ears. She suspected that Tagar had also overheard them. She blushed and said falteringly, 'If he does not want to get married, will my saying have any effect?'

Tagar said, 'Everyone says that Dada is not getting married because of you. But how can that be allowed? Just think how shocked the old parents will be. They have brought you up like a daughter. Will you be able to bear their suffering?'

Snehalata could not take it any more. She wept and said, 'Tagar, what can I do? I do not want Charu to remain unmarried.'

Tagar said, 'I know that, but Dada is so unreasonable. Look, you can do one thing. You can go away from here for a few days till this whole thing is settled.'

Sneha asked, 'Where will I go? Do I have any place in this world?'

Tagar said, 'Why, you can go to your in-laws. It is only for a few days. You can come back after Dada is married.'

'My in-laws?' Sneha said with a shudder. 'Tagar, if my presence is causing so much inconvenience, I am ready to work as a maid to earn my living. It is better for me to die than go there.'

Tagar said, 'All right, then you persuade Dada to get married. See, he is coming. Talk to him nicely and don't tell him what I have said to you. I am going now.'

Tagar went away. Charu came and was distressed to find Sneha in tears. He asked her what the matter was. Not answering his query, Sneha said, 'Charu, Meshomoshai and Mashima are so unhappy that you don't want to get married. Please get married.'

Charu said, 'You are upset when others are unhappy, but you don't care about my suffering. Sneha, tell me truly, don't you love me at all?' His eyes filled with tears. Sneha did not answer him but her tears betrayed her feelings. Charu repeated his question once again and Sneha could not control herself any more. The force of her suppressed feelings overcame her inhibitions. She sobbed out, 'Charu, do I have to tell you afresh that I love you? I came to your house as a child. I have no family except yours. How can I not love all of you? But it is not possible for me to marry you. Your parents will disown you and the community will make you an outcast. What you desire at this moment will be the cause of your unhappiness for life. Do your duty with fortitude and faith in God. Don't be the cause of your parents' suffering and get married according to their wishes. God will certainly grant you peace and happiness. I know you will think me to be cruel but there is no other way out.'

Sneha's words pierced Charu's heart like sharp arrows. Tormented by pain and frustration he burst out angrily, 'Sneha, I don't want your sermon. I wanted to know your feelings. I know now that you do not love me so you cannot possibly accept my proposal. All right then, let it be so, but don't blame me if one day I turn into an inhuman beast.'

With these words Charu rushed out of the room.

41

*W*as it true that Sneha's fondness for Charu was not genuine love and so she did not consent to his proposal? Sneha's hesitation was overpowering in the absence of that passion which is preoccupied with the desire to possess the beloved, and is willing to stake the happiness of one's entire life on the satisfaction of that desire. The element of desire is not the same in everybody's love. In Sneha's case, even entertaining the possibility of marriage was unnatural, her life being without any hope or security or independence and her nature being so patient and mild. Moreover, her entire upbringing, her faith, education, and sentiments were opposed to this marriage. Everybody would unanimously condemn this marriage as sinful. In such a situation, her love, in spite of its depth was not an uncontrollable, hungry, all-consuming passion like Charu's. So she was content with very little of it. Her love was deep, but, in a sense, free of desire. It belonged to a higher plane. She loved him with all her heart and was grateful to receive a little brotherly affection from him. She would be happy to maintain the tie of a brother and a sister all her life. This was her ultimate aspiration. She did not expect anything more than that. But when she was confronted with Charu's burning, intense passion, when she heard him talk of his hopeless suffering, her heart was in a turmoil. Would his life be really destroyed if he could not marry her? This question tormented her heart and there was an intense conflict between her sense of propriety and the desire to sacrifice everything for the sake of her beloved.

There was no moon in the sky. The night was dark, but clear and free of clouds and fog. So the glow of the milky way and the peaceful light of the stars removed the dreadful aspect of the darkness and filled the night with a sweet luminosity. Snehalata was very fond of such nights when her soul was in tune with the music of the universe and the sorrow of her little life was drowned in a wonderful sense of calm. But tonight, the sweet light of the stars outside could not soothe her troubled soul. Her heart was numb with pain; her eyes were blinded by tears. She only looked at the row of dark trees at the edge of the garden which did not let in any light. The darkness there seemed to be dreadful, all-pervasive. Gradually it seemed to spread and engulf everything. Sneha shut her eyes with fear. When she opened them again, the darkness took on the aspect of a huge cremation ground from where countless fearful corpses rose up, and, surrounding her, began a macabre dance. Sneha had seen a picture of a cremation ground a few days ago which seemed to have come to life around her. Sneha was not timid by nature but this horrible scene seemed so real that she perspired all over on this winter night and her heart quaked with fear. Yet, she continued to gaze at the scene as though she was under a spell. Suddenly, there was a glow of light in the darkness which slowly became clear and then burst into flames. Sneha saw that it was a burning pyre with a corpse lying on it. She recognized herself as the corpse and shuddered. The corpse continued to burn and finally disappeared into the flames. Sneha's trance was broken. The darkness and the cremation ground had disappeared. The flame had burnt itself out. Only the moon had risen above the trees and cast a pale light on the scene. Sneha wiped her perspiring face with her sari. She heard the sound of slow, heavy footsteps. She turned around in alarm and saw Charu. Was it really Charu or was Sneha still dreaming? Now Charu's figure was distinctly visible in the bright moonlight. His gait was unsteady, his look agitated. His whole aspect was unnatural. Sneha shut her eyes with pain. Charu said in a strange, disjointed manner, 'Sneha, look at me. Look at what I'll be in future. You are responsible for my condition.' Sneha realized that Charu was drunk. In a hurt tone she said, 'Charu, you had promised not to touch liquor again.'

Charu replied, 'Then I had believed that you loved me, that you were mine and would rescue me from this hell.' Sneha's heart was numb with misery. Her beloved, who was dearer to her than her own life and happiness, and who she had looked upon as a god, was standing before her as an unnatural, inhuman and base creature, and she was the cause of his downfall! She could bring him back to normalcy if she so desired. Sneha's inhibitions dissolved in that instant and she lost her judgement. She sobbed out, 'Charu, I am yours forever. Please promise that you won't behave like this again. I cannot bear to see you in this state.'

Charu was overjoyed. In a moment, the entire universe assumed the form of Sneha before him. He caught her hand in his own trembling hand and said, 'Sneha, you are really mine. Say it again. Say it once again.'

Sneha was crying. Without saying a word she tried to free her hand from Charu's grip. The night was beautiful. The place was lonely. Sneha's sad face was lit-up in the pale light of the moon and looked sweet and alluring. Charu's heart filled with hope and delight. He could not restrain himself any more. He drew closer to Sneha—closer and closer still. Sneha tried to move away but before that Charu's lips had sealed her own.

42

*P*oets in the West have sung high praises of the first kiss. This may be true irrespective of time and place but not irrespective of situations. If the situation is unfavourable, even nectar can turn into poison. For those who have observed celibacy since childhood, who have been taught to consider it a sin to be touched by a man, this incident would be regarded as the first violation of a taboo and the first lapse from virtue. So, whatever may have been the outcome in another situation, the kiss, instead of pleasure caused great unhappiness to Snehalata. She was deeply hurt by Charu's behaviour. However, in Charu's presence her feeling remained suppressed and unrecognized along with other emotions. But as soon as Charu went away she was tormented by an intolerable feeling of guilt and along with this her old inhibitions and her hesitation regarding her marriage with Charu surfaced again.

Why was Charu, whom she looked upon as a god, so misguided and why had he fallen so low? Was it not because of her? When he had deteriorated to such an extent because of his love for an unfortunate person like her, could he ever prosper after marrying her? How could his happiness possibly last after being disowned by his family and condemned by society? And did Jagat Babu, who had brought her up and loved her more than a father, deserve this from Snehalata? How shameful! Why was she ever born if she could not bring happiness in anybody's life? Like a contagious disease, she merely destroyed the peace and happiness of whoever she came into contact with. Snehalata's heart was wrenched and tears began to flow out of her eyes.

The pale light of the moon and the morning star fell on her wan and tear-stained face and intensified her sad expression. The birds seemed to echo her miserable cry on this happy morning. Snehalata wept bitterly and with hands folded in prayer, called out fervently, 'O God, where are you? Please save me from this trouble. Let me suffer all the pain and misery myself and not be the cause of any trouble for them. O Merciful one, please listen to my prayer. Fulfil the lifelong desire of your unfortunate child to make them happy.' Weeping and praying like this, she entered her room and was urged by a strong impulse to begin a letter to Charu.

'Charu,' she wrote, 'I am burning with agony. I don't know what I am writing. If I write something amiss and hurt you, please forgive me. I am unfortunate. I bring a curse on whoever I love and whoever loves me. I lead them away from the right path. You are dearer to this helpless, unfortunate woman than her own life. You are everything to me. Being away from you for me is the same as being in hell. But—'

The letter remained incomplete. She wanted to write, 'But you will not find any happiness if you marry me' and so on. Suddenly she was startled and when she looked up she saw Charu standing in front of her. Her pen slipped from her fingers and fell on the floor. Charu picked up the half-written letter. Just then Tagar called from the veranda, 'Didi, I say, are you still asleep? The sun has come out,' and came into the room. Taking the letter with him, Charu made his exit through the other door.

43

*A*fter being thwarted by Charu, a change came over the Mistress. Her hysterics came to an end. She even stopped complaining to Tagar about her troubles. Suppressing her rage in her heart she became unusually calm, as before a storm, and began to silently muster within herself the necessary strength to face the powers hostile to her. After Charu's departure she came downstairs and saw that the nurse Khenti was in the courtyard with the baby in her lap. She had made the arrangements for making the paste for the *baris*,[50] and was waiting for the Mistress to grind the paste.

The Mistress sat down on the floor near the grinding stone but before getting down to work she directed her venom at the nurse and abused her soundly for not getting the ingredients in the right proportion and piling up a lot of cardamom skins unnecessarily. As she carried on her grinding, her tongue wagged without a pause. The nurse put the baby on the ground saying that she was going to put the quilts out in the sun and would be back soon. The baby played with her rattle, sometimes putting it in her mouth and sometimes striking it on the floor. Then she started crawling towards her grandmother. On the way she picked up one or two cardamom skins and put them in her mouth. When the Mistress saw what the baby was doing she began to scream, 'What a nuisance this is. I have no respite here. I can't take it any more. O Khenti where have you vanished, you slut.'

The nurse came running when she heard the noise and picking up the crying child, began to soothe it. Needless to say, the baby had already thrown the cardamom skins away and was in no danger of swallowing them. In the meanwhile Tagar's elder son came along, munching a piece of bread.[51] This infuriated the Mistress even more and she shouted, 'Can't you do without eating this rubbish? Go, Khenti, take away that piece of bread and wash the child with the water of the Ganga.[52] I have never seen such a troublesome child.'

Hearing this, the boy ran off, followed by the nurse who was happy to get away from the spot. When the Mistress had ground the paste, she made tiny balls with it and placed them on a stone in the courtyard to dry. Then she called Kamali and said, 'Have you made a switch with the hair I had given you? Bring it here.'

Some time back the Mistress had started making this switch but had left the work incomplete. She remembered it now, after all these days. Kamali said, 'O dear, when did you give it to me? You were doing it yourself, weren't you?'

The Mistress's nostrils flared. She said, 'This is what happens when you are given something to do. What a plight I am in. Go and bring it, I'll do it myself.'

Kamali did not argue any further but quickly brought the switch, some oil, water, and the remaining hair to complete it. The Mistress tied the switch to the wooden railing in the courtyard and started plaiting it. The progress was not quite satisfactory. Her hands moved slowly but her stream of thoughts was moving fast. She frowned, crinkled her nose, and knitted her eyebrows as she worked, and before she finished the job in hand she had already hit upon a plan. She had found an infallible weapon to win her battle.

After lunch she called her trusted maid Kamalini and held a secret council with her. Then the maid was sent to Kunja Babu's house. She returned in the evening and said, 'O dear, that old crone will not take the daughter-in-law back. She was on the warpath. As soon as I raised the subject she was ready to swallow me up. Anyway, I said what I had to. Then she actually tried to push me out of the house.'

The Mistress was somewhat discouraged at the news. However, her resolve was unshaken. She was determined to carry out her plan by any means. In the evening, she called Tagar aside and said, 'Tagar, you see what is going on. I don't see any way out of this except to send her away.'

Tagar said, 'I understand that but where will you send her?'

The Mistress replied, 'That is what I am wondering about. Which house can I send her to? She has swallowed everybody. Well, I'll send her to that witch of an aunt-in-law. Once she is there, they will not be able to throw her out. They will have to give her food twice a day even if they abuse her day and night.'

Tagar asked, 'But why will Didi go there? Can anybody willingly go to such a hell?'

The Mistress replied, 'She will have to go. Who will tell her that she is being taken to her in-laws? You take her with you to your house and when it is time for her to return, send the palanquin to her in-laws' house.'

Even Tagar was shocked at the proposal. She really felt sorry for Snehalata. It was like the fairy tale in which innocent persons were exiled to a forest. She said ruefully, 'But Ma, that won't be fair. Baba will be furious if you send her away like that.'

The Mistress said, 'Let him discover it first. I am not afraid of him. Am I not to see to the welfare of my son? Am I to keep a poisonous snake in my house and feed it on milk and rice? You take her away to your house tomorrow morning. Otherwise this house will be destroyed, as you can see.'

Tagar was reluctant to do this but she realized that she had no other alternative. Her brother would never get married if Sneha was not removed from the scene and it would lead to a big scandal.

She said, 'All right, I'll do it. But you must think of the consequences. Baba and Dada might do something terrible in a fury.'

The Mistress was adamant. Her decision was final. Let Baba and Dada get angry. Let the whole world go to hell. Tagar would have to take Snehalata to her house the next morning. Tagar was worried. How was she going to lure Snehalata away from here? The poor, trusting soul had no suspicion of their purpose. She had to be deceived and ensnared. Tagar felt so upset that she could not face Snehalata that day. However, the Mistress' order had to be carried out, even though it was disagreeable. Tagar worried about it all day and finally when she entered Snehalata's room it was very late in the night. Snehalata was not in her room. It seemed somebody was talking in the veranda. Tagar recognized Charu's voice and peeped out. What she saw made her speechless with shock. She slipped away quietly as she saw Charu coming towards the door.

Early in the morning the Mistress sent for the palanquin and pressed Tagar to leave. Tagar came to call Snehalata and once again saw Charu leaving the room. Last night's incident had made Tagar very angry. The sympathy she had felt for Snehalata had vanished altogether. The sight of Charu in the morning added fuel to the fire. Why was Dada going in and out of her room at all times of the day and night, she wanted to know. It was highly improper. When Snehalata did not reply, she continued in a sharp tone, 'God knows what you are thinking or doing. I don't like it. You are causing a lot of misery to yourself and everybody else.'

Snehalata felt as though Tagar was echoing her own thoughts. She shrank into herself like a sensitive creeper. Had Tagar found out everything then? Tagar said, 'Listen to me, it is for your own good. Get out of here for a few days. If you really love Dada, leave him alone for a while even if it is painful for you.'

Sneha had no time to think of herself. She felt that Tagar was saying the right thing. She mumbled, 'Yes, but where can I go?'

Tagar replied, 'Right now I am going to my in-laws' house. Come with me. Then we will decide where you can go.'

Sneha said, 'All right, I'll come with you. Let me take leave of Meshomoshai first.' She did not mention Charu. Tagar realized that Sneha's departure would be stalled if Jagat Babu came to know of it. She said, 'There is no need for that. You are going with me after all. What if he stops you from going? You will not be able to tell him everything openly. Just come away with me if you really want to go. Ma will tell him that you have gone with me. My palanquin is here. Come as you are. You can have a wash at my house.'

Tagar took Snehalata's hand and pulled her up from the floor. Snehalata was not able to say anything. She followed Tagar without a word and got into the palanquin. When the palanquin bearers left the house Snehalata could not control herself any more. She put her head on Tagar's lap and sobbed like a child. After a while, when she had calmed down, Tagar said, 'Didi, don't cry. In a few days Dada will be married. Then you can return home.'

Tagar's words pierced Snehalata's heart. But why did she feel so anguished when she had renounced him voluntarily? She sincerely wanted Charu to get married. She had prayed for it wholeheartedly. Then why did it trouble her so much? After all, self-sacrifice was lauded because it meant suffering. Tagar said, 'Real love means being happy in the happiness of the beloved. See, Suryamukhi got Kunda[53] married herself. Can't you stay away from Dada for a few days for his sake?'

Sneha asked, 'Where will I stay?'

'At your in-laws' home. Once you go there they will not be able to throw you out.'

Snehalata did not say anything further. In a fit of despair she thought, 'Let it be so. How can a wretched woman like me hope to have peace? When I have left his protection and rejected his ardent proposal, I should accept my fate. O God, please take care of my beloved for whose sake I am plunging into the fire?'

44

*H*aving seated Snehalata in her bedroom upstairs, Tagar came to the kitchen and said to her mother-in-law, 'Didi has come. She will go to her in-laws' house in the evening.' Here it must be pointed out that Tagar's relationship with her mother-in-law was different from such relationships in most Bengali families. Tagar had known Jiban's mother very well since her childhood and there was no reason for her to be shy with her after marriage. Moreover, Jiban's mother also did not insist on her being formal with her. Since Jiban was her only child, she liked to treat Tagar as the daughter she did not have. Hence, Tagar covered her head only partially in the presence of her mother-in-law and when she addressed her, her naturally loud voice was only slightly lowered.

Jiban's mother was surprised to hear that Snehalata was going to her in-laws' house. She asked, 'Has Kishori called her there? He seems to have become a little mature after his father's death.'

Kunja Babu had died about a year ago and Kishori was now the master of the house. Tagar shook her head.

'Then what is it?' the mother-in-law asked.

Tagar replied, 'Dada wants to marry her. So she cannot stay in our house. She'll have to go to her in-laws' house.'

Jiban's mother guessed what the matter was. Full of pity, she said, 'Then let her stay here. Going to their place is the same as jumping into the fire. Poor thing, she has no one to call her own.'

Tears came to Jiban's mother's eyes. Tagar said, 'How can that be? Can Dada not come here?' Jiban's mother did not dare to say anything further. Although she was the mistress of the house, a good-natured person has to accept defeat always. Instead of Tagar acting according to her wishes, she had to give in to Tagar and was afraid of her. When she came upstairs and saw Snehalata's pale, unhappy face, her heart broke and she could not hold back her tears.

A palanquin was called for Snehalata in the evening. Bursting into tears, Snehalata pleaded with Jiban's mother and said, 'Mashima, I won't be able to go alone. Please come with me and leave me there.'

There had been a misunderstanding between the members of the two families for a long time. It would be humiliating for Jiban's mother to go there uninvited. However, she could not turn down Snehalata's request. Her sorrow had melted her heart.

When the palanquin bearers, singing in rhythm, reached Kunja Babu's house and put the palanquin down in their courtyard, someone from the upper balcony shouted in a hoarse voice, 'Who has come? Whose palanquin is it?'

·In an instant that voice transported Snehalata to the scene ten years ago and she vividly remembered the torture she had undergone at her in-laws' house. She felt as though the same incident was being repeated all over again. Jiban's mother said, 'Didi, it's me' and holding the hand of the veiled Snehalata, took her upstairs. Sneha touched Jethima's feet and the old lady, who was telling her beads, asked, 'Who is that?'

Jiban's mother said, 'It is your daughter-in-law.'

Jethima screamed, 'Who is my daughter-in-law? Is she Mohan's wife? She has swallowed up everybody and now she has come here again? Get out of here at once. I told the maid who came yesterday that here she will get nothing but blows.'

Jiban's mother said, 'Don't say that, Didi. She has no parents. You are everything for her. If you don't accept her, where will she go?'

Jethima screamed again at the top of her voice, 'Those who are her own are not willing to keep her any longer I suppose!'

Jiban's mother said, 'Of course they are. Yet, the girl has grown up now. Is it proper for her to stay with others when her in-laws are around? Doesn't she understand that it lowers your image in society? When one grows up one comes to know who are one's own people and who are not. She has come here, willingly.'

Jethima shouted, 'So, she is my own! I don't want her. Tell her to get out.'

Jiban's mother persisted, 'Listen, Didi, one has to feed even the cats and dogs in one's house. Will you not feed your own daughter-in-law. Is such a thing possible?'

At this moment someone called out, 'Jethima, what is this uproar? Come here for a minute.'

Jethima said, 'Kishori, I am coming.'

Jiban's mother and Snehalata remained standing in the veranda. When Jethima entered Kishori's room, he asked, 'Who has come with Mejo Jethima?'

Jethima said, 'Who else? That wretched girl who has destroyed three families and devoured her own husband has come to stay here. At that time she had insisted on taking her husband away with her. I'll beat her up and throw her out.'

Kishori was surprised, 'Who has come to stay? Is it Bou? How did Jagat Babu send her?'

Jethima replied, 'She is a big girl now. People have started talking because they haven't sent her to her in-laws. That is why she has come. If they had to send her eventually, why did they keep her at all?'

'No, Jethima, it is good that Bou has come. Don't send her away. Let her stay here. Does one give up something that falls into one's hands? Jagat Babu could have gone to court to get her share of Dada's property. It is our good luck that she has come to us.'

'All right. But why didn't you tell me this earlier? The fellow wants to go to court and grab our property? I'll keep her here. I'll beat her with a broom every day and give her crumbs to eat.'

'Do what you like but don't let her go. I am going to my wife's house tonight to bring her back. You see to it that Bou doesn't go away.'

Kishori went away. Jethima returned to the veranda and told Jiban's mother, 'She is fortunate to have a good brother-in-law. Kishori said that we cannot throw out our Bou. Since we have enough for ourselves, we can provide for her also. So stay on, you pampered girl and don't you run off to Jagat Babu's house again.' And Sneha became a member of her in-laws' household.

45

W hen Jagat Babu returned home that night, he missed Snehalata and enquired where she was. He was told that she had gone with Tagar to her in-laws' house. Not seeing her again the next day he wanted to know whether she had come back. The Mistress told him that she had not. Jagat Babu was surprised and said, 'Haven't you sent anyone to fetch her? How long will she stay with Tagar's relatives?

The Mistress replied, 'Yes we sent for her but she was not there.'

Jagat babu said, 'Not there? Where has she gone then?'

The Mistress said, 'How do I know where she has gone?'

Jagat Babu got angry. 'You do not know? Then you must have turned her out yourself.'

The Mistress had become complacent after Snehalata's departure. So she turned up her nose, twisted her lips and said sneeringly, 'All right, I did it. If I threw her out who would have kept her? You are simply ungrateful to me. Tell me, how can that girl be kept at home? She has been educated, she wants to be modern, she wants to get married. How can she stay here any more? There is no scope for these things here. So I guess she has gone to find her own way out. You don't know her. I have always said that she is a very cunning girl.'

Hearing this, Jagat Babu's suspicion increased further. He said angrily, 'If you don't know where she is, I'll find her out myself and bring her back. I am going to Tagar's house just now.'

The Mistress realized that Snehalata's whereabouts could not be kept secret any more. She said, 'It is no use your going there. I believe she has gone from there to her in-laws' house.'

'Her in-laws!' For a moment Jagat Babu was stunned. It was unthinkable that Snehalata would willingly go to her in-laws' house without informing him. He suspected that the Mistress had sent her away on account of Charu. Rage made him tremble from head to foot. In a voice quivering with emotion, he said, 'She wouldn't go there of her own accord. This is your doing.'

Then the Mistress used her most effective weapon. She shed a couple of tears and said in a low voice, 'The more I care for others, the more you find fault with me. And why shouldn't that be? It is all in my destiny.' She struck her forehead with her hand and sobbed, 'You say that I threw her out. But she did not even tell me that she was going, otherwise I would have prevented her from doing so. An Englishwoman comes to her in-laws' house regularly, so she can conveniently become a Christian. Don't you understand?'

Jagat Babu said impatiently, 'I am not asking you about any convenience or inconvenience. I want to know the reason for her leaving. Why did she go away?'

The Mistress said, 'This is indeed a problem! I told you that she left without informing me. Yet you keep repeating the same question: "Why did she go away". As though I know the answer.'

Jagat Babu exclaimed, 'She didn't tell you? Can it really be true?'

The Mistress retorted, 'Am I telling a lie then? Why don't you check with the servants and everybody else? Even Tagar, who came to say goodbye, did not tell me that Sneha was going with her. Perhaps she did not know of it. It seems Sneha just got into the palanquin with her.'

Jagat Babu was aware that the Mistress did not hesitate to lie if the situation demanded it. However, he could not fathom what she would gain by telling such a lie about Sneha. Then another question arose in his mind. Sneha had departed suddenly without informing him or the Mistress. Could Charu have misbehaved with her? Perhaps she could not confide this secret to anyone and was afraid that the incident might be repeated. That may have compelled her to leave Jagat Babu's protection. This seemed a plausible explanation because the Mistress did not mention Charu's inordinate interest in Snehalata. Jagat Babu came to the outer apartment in a state of great agitation and asked Charu, 'Charu, I hear that Sneha has gone to her in-laws' house. Did she tell you about it?'

Charu had also looked for Sneha and had been told that she had gone with Tagar, but when he heard this from Jagat Babu he turned pale with astonishment. He said in a pained voice, 'She has gone to her in-laws' house? But she didn't tell me about it.'

Jagat Babu asked, 'Did you say anything which might have caused her pain?'

Charu repeated, 'Could I say anything which might cause her pain?'

Jagat Babu said, 'Is that such an impossibility?'

Charu looked down. He remembered the incident of the night. Since then Snehalata's behaviour had undergone a change. He recalled her unnatural timidity, her sad and shocked countenance, her hesitant, inaudible, monosyllabic replies to his persistent questions and the incomplete, desperate letter of the following morning. Earlier he had interpreted all these things differently but now he realized his error. It alarmed him and he was at a loss for words. Without waiting for his reply, Jagat Babu said, 'What could the matter be? I am going to investigate it properly and if you are at fault, I'll disown you.'

Jagat Babu went straight to Kishori's house. Kishori was nonplussed to hear that he had come to fetch Snehalata. He had been very pleased to have got Snehalata in his grip. He went to the inner apartment but returned without seeing Snehalata. He told Jagat Babu that Boudidi had decided to stay on there and not return. Jagat Babu heard this with bated breath. Controlling himself with great difficulty he said, 'Let her not return with me but I would like to see her once.' Kishori replied, 'I said that to her earlier but she was not willing to see you.'

Jagat Babu was speechless. He felt he could not breathe anymore. Forgetting to say farewell to Kishori, he quickly left the house.

In the meanwhile the Mistress was getting very anxious. If Jagat Babu went directly to Kunja Babu's house and brought that wretched Sneha back, all her scheming would be of no avail. But when she saw Jagat Babu return alone in a dejected mood, she hid her astonishment and asked in a cheerful tone, 'What happened, my dear?'

Jagat Babu said miserably, 'I could not meet her.'

The Mistress understood that Kishori had not allowed them to meet, and had availed of the opportunity to insult Jagat Babu. She said, 'You have no common sense whatsoever. You go to people's house to be insulted. They have long been our enemies. Why should they not insult you if they get a chance to do so.'

Jagat Babu said miserably, 'It is not their fault. Sneha herself refused to see me.' This surprised the Mistress, for she could not believe it to be possible. There must have been a misunderstanding and Jagat Babu was suffering unnecessarily. However, she exulted like a beast who had caught its prey and said, 'Why should she want to see you? Then she would have to return to this house and she won't be able to remarry. See, what I said has turned out to be true.'

Jagat Babu could not endure the Mistress's sarcasm. He went out without a word and paced restlessly up and down alone in the outer room. Like a soul in despair he began to think, 'Sneha did not come and see me. This is the return I get for raising her. Is it true that one cannot trust anyone in this world? Is it true that women are like vipers and are born only to mislead men? Are they not capable of any higher emotions and ideals?'

His gentle and compassionate nature was submerged in a wave of pain. Hard cynicism swallowed up his spontaneous trust in humanity. He cried out in despair, 'O God, is there any suffering greater than this? Did destiny have this in store for me? I have become like a heartless rock and this is the result of my loving my daughter! O Merciful One, save me from this misery!'

46

Charu began to wonder whether Snehalata had left because she was offended by his behaviour. The incident of that night, and Snehalata's subsequent attitude and behaviour began to create a turmoil in his mind. He read her incomplete letter a number of times and was convinced that Sneha had left their house because she was angry with him.

Charu felt as though he was struck by a thunderbolt. He thought miserably, 'What have I done? I loved her more than my life. Was that a sin? I was willing to give up my parents and all my wealth for her sake. Was that the offence for which she left me? If this was so, why did she consent to the marriage? I had kissed her joyfully, thinking she was my own. If that was an offence, could it not be pardoned? Had she loved me, could she have treated me like this? Did she behave so callously because I placed my heart at her feet? Did she spurn my love because it was sincere?'

Utterly humiliated Charu began to regret having loved Sneha. However, along with this feeling of remorse, he also had an intense desire to see her, fall at her feet and beg for her forgiveness. He wanted to bring her back, to fill up the void that had appeared in his life after her departure.

He was very angry with himself for his own weakness. It would have been a great relief if he could tear his chest apart, like Hiranyakashyapu,[54] and destroy his love. But he was powerless in the face of this monstrous love of his. Like a helpless child he struggled in vain with his turbulent emotions.

In the evening he went to Kishori's house but was told that Kishori had gone out and would return after a couple of days. Charu returned home burning with desire and frustration. Sneha had become inaccessible to him now and he could not see her even for a moment. Eventually he decided to send her a letter. He wanted to pour out his heart in the letter but fearing that it might fall into another person's hands he controlled himself and wrote:

Sneha, why did you go away from here? Baba is very unhappy because of that and so are all of us. We want to know the reason for your departure. Please write to me and tell me when I can come and meet you. Please forgive me if I have done anything wrong. If a brother errs, shouldn't the sister pardon him? If you come back I'll know that you have pardoned me. I am eagerly waiting for your letter. Charu.

Charu posted the letter and waited anxiously for the reply. A couple of days passed; each hour seemed like a decade to him but no reply came. On the third day Charu went to Kishori's house again in the evening. Kishori was sitting on a chair in the veranda. In front of him was a table with all the paraphernalia of drinking. He greeted Charu with a 'Hello', shook his hand, made him sit on a chair near his own, and handing him a full glass said, 'What is the matter, friend? You have come after a long time. You don't come this side at all. Come! let us drink. You look very dejected. Is it a love affair?'

Taking a sip, Charu said, 'All my time is taken up in studies. There is no time for other things.'

Kishori shook his head like a soothsayer and said, 'People fall in love even while studying.'

Charu said with a smile, 'It is all right then if I have. Are you going to attend the Congress?'

'No, I don't go in for all that humbug. Are you going?'

'Yes, I am thinking of going. If you come along we shall have company. I came to your house the day before yesterday but you were away.'

'How long can one stay alone at home? You don't come here these days. Besides, one gets fed up of hearing all that good counsel at home. It was bad enough listening to one person's lectures, now another one has joined her. One can tolerate anything but not the preaching of women.'

'I want to meet Sneha once. I had written her a letter. I wonder if she received it.'

'O yes, she did. Letters do not miscarry in the British regime.'
Needless to say, this was a blatant lie. Sneha's letter had not reached her at all. Kishori had intercepted it. Charu, relieved at Kishori's affirmation, said, 'I didn't get her reply.'

'I don't know about that.'

'Kishorida, please tell Sneha I want to meet her.'

'Don't worry, I'll go and call her here. There is no one else in the house.' He got up and playing the same trick, returned in a few minutes and said, 'I don't know what the matter is. Boudidi does not want to meet you at all. I tried to persuade her as much as I could, but I couldn't force her to come.'

Charu felt the whole world spinning around him.

47

*C*haru could not imagine, even in a dream, that Sneha could be so cruel. He was deeply hurt and tried to tell himself that if she did not love him, he should not love her either. Why should he be hurt by her indifference?

> Shall I, wasting in despair
> Die because a woman's fair?
> If she be not fair for me
> What care I how fair she be.[55]

However, this train of thought did not relieve him of his misery. Snehalata's indifference continued to rankle him. He wanted to destroy his unrequited love with anger and hatred but it was like Raktabeej.[56] Every attempt to kill it—every drop of blood which fell on the ground would cause a new demon to rise up and wound his heart with redoubled strength. After a couple of days Charu wrote another letter to Snehalata:

> Sneha, is it true that you have become estranged from us? Even when we go to see you, you are not available. I thought you loved me, that is why I declared my love to you. If that was an offence, you could have pardoned me. There was no need to be so cold. Anyhow, I am again asking for your forgiveness. Please forget what has passed. If you reply to my letter I'll take it that you have forgiven me. I am not going to trouble you again with a proposal of marriage. Please come back. I promise I will not see you if you don't want me to. Please trust me. I may have misbehaved with you but I have never lied to you and never will. Charu.

After posting this letter, Charu again waited expectantly for a reply.

He still had faith in Sneha but he felt that the whole sequence of events was a mystery which he could not resolve. He thought that his letter would clear up Sneha's misunderstanding, and realizing the depth of his love she would certainly forgive him.

But all his hopes proved to be false. Days passed without bringing a reply to his letter. Greatly disheartened, he once again appeared at Kishori's house. Kishori welcomed him with a smile and said, 'What is the matter, friend? You are simply withering away. You may not admit it but I can see that you are in a pretty bad shape.'

Charu said, 'Dada, the world goes on like that. Some people are in good shape and others are not. Some laugh and others cry. You may laugh at me as much as you want to.'

Kishori said, 'O, fie, why should I laugh at your misery. But my friend, I warn you, if you are touched by that fire, you will be destroyed.'

Charu said drily, '*Many thanks for your kind sympathy.* However, I do not need it for *it is better to have loved and lost than never to have loved at all.*'[57]

'Oh, you are superhuman, your case is different. We are ordinary mortals, so the mere mention of that fire terrifies us.'

'But what you say does not match with what you do.'

'Ha, ha, my friend, you are a poet but you are so raw. That boy Cupid cannot be bound like that. If you try to do that he will run away. Then the seductive smile and passionate gaze will disappear. Then you will sit with bleary eyes and a glum face. But there will be no fear of losing your life.'

'So, you are quite safe then?'

'Absolutely. Take my advice and get married. Then all your suffering will be over.'

'Who does not want nectar, but where can one get it?'

'If you are not getting it, you have taken the wrong road. Remember this my friend. *A woman is like your shadow. Follow her and she will fly from you. Fly from her and she will follow you.*'

Charu felt that Kishori was right. He seemed to echo his own thoughts. He said, 'All right, Dada, when the time comes, I'll follow your advice. I wrote to her some days back but I haven't received a reply yet.'

Kishori sat silent for a few moments with his head lowered. Then he said, 'You are my friend. I have always loved you. I should be frank with you.'

Kishori paused. Charu understood that he wanted to say something about Sneha and he waited for it with bated breath. Kishori said solemnly, 'Brother, never trust a woman, no matter how innocent she may look. Remember, the more harmless she appears to be, the less she should be trusted.'

Then he took out a letter from his desk and giving it to Charu said, 'See this.' It was the second letter Charu had written to Sneha. Bristling with indignation, Charu said, 'What is this, Kishorida, you opened her letter?'

Kishori said, 'I opened her letter! Bou wanted to send it to Jagat Babu after reading it. Brother, women are like vipers. I have clearly understood that she led you on the path of temptation. Now that she has got you in her grasp she wants to prove her innocence.'

Charu was stunned as though he was struck by a thunderbolt.

48

Charu opened his eyes and saw all the members of his family sitting near his bedside. Seeing him, the Mistress said, 'O God, you are great,' and burst into tears. Jagat Babu was feeling his pulse. He examined his chest and head and said cheerfully, 'There is no fear now. Don't cry, all of you, be quiet.' Tagar wiped her eyes and asked softly, 'Dada, do you recognize me?'

Amazed at all this, Charu asked what the matter was. The Mistress was overjoyed and said, 'My child, we had no hope that you would speak properly or recognize us again. You have been in bed for three days now. Kishori brought you home in a carriage early that morning. Since then you have been unconscious.'

Charu again repeated, as though in a dream, 'What happened?' Jagat Babu rose from his seat and said, 'Much has happened. But let that be. Don't make him talk now. I'll go and inform Dr Sanders about his condition.' When he left the room, Tagar said, 'Dada don't you remember anything? You arrived here dead drunk, and you have been delirious all these days. Baba said that you had delirium tremens. Only last night you had proper sleep so you are better today.'

Then Charu remembered what had happened. He also remembered what he had heard about Snehalata from Kishori. But was all that really true or was it his delusion? He asked, 'Where is Sneha? Didn't she come to see me?'

Tagar said, 'Dada, you have forgotten everything. She is at her in-laws' house. She doesn't live here any more.'

Charu realized that what he remembered was not a dream and Sneha had really been cruel to him. His heart was again wrenched with pain. So Sneha was really prepared to send his letter to Jagat

Babu? Charu closed his eyes. The Mistress got a fright—what was happening to her son? She promised to offer sweets worth five rupees to God if he were saved. When Charu opened his eyes again, she pleaded, 'Charu, my child, please get married. With what trouble I have borne you and brought you up. Please listen to me.'

The Mistress thought that Charu had gone crazy over Snehalata and only marriage could cure him of the obsession. She continued, 'Has she cast a spell on you? She just left the house without a word and you want to give up your life for her? Aren't you a man? Get married, my child. If you want a grown-up girl, I'll find one for you.'

Tears started rolling from Charu's eyes. The Mistress cried, 'My son, I can't bear your tears. Say that you'll get married.'

Charu placed his hand on his chest, closed his eyes, and thought, 'I want to forget her, and her cruel betrayal, but how shall I do it? Will this suffering end if I find someone else? I must uproot her from my heart anyhow, even if I have to drown her memory in new events and new ties. All I want is peace—a release from this pain. It has to be either oblivion or death.'

The Mistress said, 'My precious, why are you silent? Say that you will get married.'

Charu mustered all the strength he had and said, 'Yes, I will.' The Mistress was overjoyed and said, 'The coming month of Paush[58] is not an auspicious one. My good boy, just give your consent and I'll arrange everything within this month.'

Charu let out a sigh and mumbled, 'All right.' The Mistress's emotions overflowed in tears. She held Charu's hand and said, 'Blessed is the woman who has such a son.' Charu did not hear her words. He had withdrawn deep within himself and was thinking, 'Peace, release, oblivion or death.'

49

*E*veryone wants to be happy in this world, right up to the end. Death comes uninvited, to people who are unaware, in the midst of happiness. It does not answer the call of an agonized soul. Snehalata was alive, though separated from those who were the source of her joy in life. And why should they remember her? In return for their genuine love she had come away without telling them or seeing them. Could such behaviour be pardoned? Certainly not in this life.

Snehalata's days passed in torment and despair. No one came to see her, nor had she received a single written word from them. Even the maids and servants of the house seemed to have forgotten her. She could not endure this suffering in silence any more. Eventually, swallowing her pride and shame she approached Kishori and said, 'Thakurpo, I haven't had any news of them for a long time. I'll go and see them today.'

Kishori was having his lunch in the hall of the inner apartment with his wife Kamala seated before him. Raising his head with an air of annoyance he said, 'I am fighting a case against Jibanda. How can I send you to his in-laws' house? That would be an insult for me.'

Sneha's eyes filled with tears. She controlled herself with an effort and said, 'Meshomoshai and Mashima are like my parents. I cannot stop visiting them because you are fighting Jiban Thakurpo in court. I haven't heard from them for a long time. I must go and see them.'

Kishori replied, 'You are being childish. Let this case be decided, then you can go. If you want to get news of them I will make the enquiries.' Saying this, he quickly got up to wash his hands. He had to dodge this request somehow.

Snehalata said in a tearful voice, 'Thakurpo, let me go just for a day or two. I won't go again after that.'

Kishori said, 'Whether you go for one day or ten days, it is the same. It is an insult to me.'

Kamala was a straightforward person and could not tolerate any unfairness, so in spite of being a Bengali wife, she spoke up. She said, 'Then how did you endure the insult all these years when Didi stayed with them? They are her parents, you cannot expect her to stop seeing them?'

Kishori scolded her, 'Go away, don't preach to me. What do you know of these matters?' Taking a betel leaf he quickly walked away. Snehalata realized that she was a helpless captive now.

But no one is absolutely helpless in this world. Even in the darkness of a cloudy night, there are flashes of lightning. Even a straw can offer support to a drowning person. Snehalata had been an orphan since childhood. She was destined to suffer. Yet, in the course of her life someone or the other had appeared like the polestar and lit-up the darkness. Here too she was not without a friend. Kamala was her polestar, her beloved companion. When Kishori went away, Kamala said sympathetically, 'Didi, don't cry. You will go there, let him say what he likes. I'll try to bring him round at night.' These affectionate words made Sneha smile gratefully in spite of her pain.

The next morning Snehalata was arranging the betel leaves when Kamala came in with her baby in her arms and stood near her with a downcast expression. Sneha did not have the courage to ask her any further questions. Her eyes filled with tears. Kamala also did not have the heart to say anything and stood there without a word. The baby called out to Sneha and tried to scramble out of Kamala's arms. Kamala placed him on the floor and sat down near Snehalata. The baby crawled up to Snehalata and putting his arms around her neck from behind, asked for a cardamom. Snehalata put a few cardamom seeds in his hand. He put them in his mouth greedily but seeing her unhappy expression, he took the seeds out of his mouth and put them in Snehalata's. She wiped her eyes, smiled, and kissed him. Then the baby settled down happily in her lap. Snehalata thought, 'Why do I increase my pain by getting attached to this child? All the people I have loved so far have become estranged from me. I am not destined to enjoy the pleasure of loving and making other people my own.' She hugged the child to her bosom and her tears overflowed. Kamala drew near her, pulled the betel tray towards herself and began to arrange the leaves. She said, 'Didi, the baby loves you more than me. You are his mother.'

Kamala's loving words of consolation touched Sneha's heart. She could not afford to ignore anyone's sympathy or affection. She had received so little love in her life that she valued it more than anything else. Just then Kishori appeared on the scene and said, 'Boudidi, I have come to give you some news. Have you heard that Charu is getting married again this Sunday?'

Sneha's tears stopped and she felt that her blood had frozen. But why was it so? This is what she had wanted; for this she had left her happy home and plunged into the boundless sea. Now her wish had been fulfilled. Charu had forgotten her. He would get married and be happy. Then why should she mourn? This was a day of rejoicing for her.

50

There is a saying among the women of our country that there is no sorrow greater than hope and there is no relief greater than despair. It seems like a paradox but a careful analysis shows that it contains the essence of the Hindu philosophy of action without the desire for fulfilment. In fact, hope breeds desire and desire leads to restlessness and disquiet. Hence, if one gives up hope one can be at peace, and peace is the only happiness in this world. *Blessed are those that never expected for they shall not be disappointed.*

Snehalata realized that there was no hope left for her. Her connection with that household had ended forever and that Jagat Babu would not come to her rescue even if her heart was bursting with sorrow. Sorrow was going to be her constant companion and her only possession. The hope of seeing them again was only a fantasy. She had no right to it. So she began to adjust to her situation. She derived strength from her disappointment. Putting all her faith in God and adopting Kamala's children as her own, she regained her composure.

It was not as though she had no desire to see Jagat Babu or Charu any more. But she knew that it was like a child's longing for the moon. So she did not indulge in it any more. Further, even in the midst of her suffering, she experienced a secret satisfaction that she had been able to bring peace to Jagat Babu's household and make Charu happy by her self-restraint. She tried to rejoice that Charu had got married, and was able to drown the keenness of her agony in his joy. However, when she had achieved a degree of tranquillity through habitual restraint and derived comfort from her dedication to duty and faith in God, her peace of mind was shattered by a new turn of events.

A restlessness came over Snehalata. Her mind was occupied with troubled thoughts. Now and again her eyes filled with tears. When Kamala made sympathetic enquiries, Snehalata stopped short of giving a reply. Sometimes she asked strange questions such as whether suicide was really a great sin. After all, Rajput women were glorified for jumping into the fire to preserve their chastity. So whether suicide could be regarded as a sin depended on the situation, she thought.

Kamala had just delivered a baby and was now confined to the labour room. Snehalata often sat with Kamala's two children near the entrance of that room and talked to her in a dejected tone. Kamala was also depressed for various reasons and Snehalata's sadness deepened her own. She thought that Snehalata was sad because she was pining for her family. Her impression was strengthened when she saw Snehalata consciously maintaining a distance from Kishori. Whenever Kishori came into view, she quietly slipped away. When he asked her a question, she frowned and did not reply. Kishori often sent for her when he came inside for a meal or to see Kamala but Snehalata always sent word that she could not come. Kamala thought that Snehalata was greatly offended by Kishori's refusal to send her to Jagat Babu's house. In order to compensate for Kishori's cruelty, Kamala tried to comfort Snehalata in various ways and quarrelled with Kishori over trifling matters.

It was a silent night. Everyone in the house was asleep. The baby who had been fretting for his mother had cried himself to sleep. Snehalata left him with the maid and entered her bedroom. Kamala's elder daughter was fast asleep on Snehalata's bed under the mosquito net. Snehalata looked at her sleeping face, then moved away and opened the window, as she was wont to do every night, to look at the sky. It was a beautiful, star-studded night. She was reminded of the past, and an unfulfilled longing seemed to lift her up to the stars. She started humming a prayer.

> There is an eternal thirst in my heart
> Can it be quenched with drops of mundane love?
> I want fame, wealth, friendship,
> The more I get the more I crave
> It is merely a false hope.
> Nothing brings peace
> I am deluded by desire,

The mirage of unfulfilled dreams
And attachment which spells disaster
O Beloved Lord, the Ocean of Love, my heart longs for you
But drowned in ignorance I fail to understand,
Come, O Lord, come into my heart
Merge with my soul
Fill up the void
Quench my unslaked thirst.

After a while, Sneha closed the window and turned around. She was about to shut the door and go to bed when she suddenly recoiled as though an insect had touched her. Kishori was standing in the darkness in the room. She quickly tried to get out of the door but Kishori blocked her way and said, 'Where are you going? Am I a toad or a snake that you avoid me like this? What harm have I done you? Boudidi, listen to me. Let me tell you how much I love you.'

Snehalata said, 'Go away, Thakurpo. If you don't, I will...'

Kishori laughed and said, 'What will you do, Boudidi?'

Burning with rage from head to foot, Sneha said, 'I shall scream.'

Kishori said, 'How will that hurt me? Only you will get a bad name. Boudidi, this house, this property and wealth is all yours.'

Sneha said in a trembling voice, 'I can't hear this. Go away, I say.'

Kishori continued, 'Boudidi, you can't go anywhere. Whatever I possess is yours. You are the queen of my heart. Don't drive me away. I'll stay at your feet.'

Kishori bent down to touch her feet. She quickly stepped aside and, weeping with helpless rage, said, 'I don't want your protection any more. Even if I have to beg for a living, I won't see your face.'

Quick as lightning she unfastened the bolt of the door which connected her room with the nursery and slipped out. Since this door was always closed she had not thought of it earlier. Greatly disappointed, Kishori muttered under his breath, 'All right, I'll see where you can go.'

Snehalata thought, 'No matter where I go, I won't stay here any more.' That night she lay awake in the children's bed. The first thing she did next morning was to write a letter to Jiban's mother and send it to her through her maid.

51

It was morning. A fire was burning in an earthenware vessel in the labour room. The midwife was fomenting the baby who had been massaged with oil. Kamala was lying on her bed nearby. Outside the room, Snehalata was sitting on the floor with the youngest child in her lap. Her face was drawn and anxious but Kamala was so troubled herself that she could not refrain from expressing her own worries in spite of Snehalata's dejected mood. She said, 'Didi, he started coming into the house in the daytime and I thought he had changed for the better, but I hear he has stopped coming home at night. I don't think God will bless him with good sense in my lifetime. The money is nearly finished and some of the property has been mortgaged. If he spent the money on some good venture it would have been fine but he never spends a penny on such things. He has borrowed all the money that belonged to Jethima and when she asks for it he flatly refuses to give it back. The other day she wanted to buy a present for her niece but he didn't give her any money. Finally I gave it to her from what I had with me. Now she wants some money for her religious observances but he turns a deaf ear to her. I am sick of her nagging. I don't have any money in hand to give her. Whatever I had I have given away. I don't want to live any more, Didi.'

Snehalata may have been very unhappy herself but she could not help sympathizing with Kamala in her misery. She said, 'Try to reason with him a little. Will he not appreciate where his own interest lies?'

Kamala said, 'I have told him so many times, that is why he does not come near me. If a person is not sensible himself, no one else can prevail upon him.'

At that moment Jethima walked up with a rosary in her hand. Taking long strides she stopped about four feet away from the door and said, 'Everyone has become like the sahibs. No conventions are observed. Did you have the soup? O nurse, is this called fomentation? Look at the state of the fire! I have seen how fomentation was done in my time with a blazing fire and the mother sat so close to it that she got blisters! These days nobody does these things properly.'

Kamala was unwell and could not endure Jethima's words. She mumbled softly, 'It was the golden age and people could even pass the fire-test. Can it apply to the present times?'

Some of her words reached Jethima's ears and she retorted, 'One cannot argue with modern girls. I am very sorry about it. But why am I not getting the money that is due to me? Am I a beggar?'

Kamala said, 'Hasn't he given it to you yet? I shall remind him again.'

Although Jethima was complaining about her nephew to his wife, she could not tolerate the idea of Kamala speaking to Kishori on her behalf. She said with biting sarcasm, 'It is your father's money, isn't it? Kishori has become like this since his marriage. Before that I used to be his favourite. All these daughters of inauspicious women are witches.'

Kamala said, 'You can say what you like to me but do not abuse my parents.'

Jethima made a face and said, 'Just listen to that. Am I going to be intimidated by you? I shall abuse not only your parents but fourteen generations of your ancestors. Let us see what you can do about it.'

Kamala wept and said, 'One does not even die. I can't bear it any more.'

Jethima worked herself up into a fury. 'You dare abuse me?' she shrieked. 'You want me to die? You can die yourself along with your ancestors. I'll get my boy married again.'

Jethima started cracking her knuckles in her agitation. Snehalata could not endure it any more and said tearfully, 'Jethima, she didn't say that to you. She was talking about herself.'

Jethima shrieked again, 'Get out of here, you witch. You have corrupted her. She was a good girl before you came. She didn't utter a sound even if she was slapped seven times. She meant me.'

Sneha said, 'No, Jethima, she did not. And whenever she sees Thakurpo, she reminds him to return your money to you. What can she do if he does not listen to her?'

Jethima said, 'Oh, you are trying to plead on her behalf and turning her against my boy. My son does not return my money, these women do! What cheek! You have come and created trouble in the family. Will you leave the house or do I have to leave it? Wait and see what happens now.'

Cursing Snehalata's ancestors heartily, Jethima came to the threshold of the outer apartment and began to bang her head on the floor, calling out loudly, 'O Kishori, come and see what the daughter of the cursed woman has done to me.'

The servants of the house collected around Jethima.

52

$\mathcal{T}$he moment Kishori returned home he found himself in the midst of a commotion, but it did not displease him. The entire morning he had been in consultation with his lawyer and had just learnt that if a woman became a widow while her father-in-law was alive, she had no right to claim any part of his property. In fact, she had no claim to any maintenance either.[59] Kishori had wanted to keep Snehalata in the house for this reason but now she had become a burden for him and he was in a hurry to get rid of her. There was no point in keeping her and increasing the household expenses. So he expressed his full agreement with Jethima's proposal that Snehalata, who was becoming a nuisance in the house, should be asked to leave immediately. Jethima's heart swelled up with pride, beyond all proportions.

After lunch, Kishori came inside and saw Snehalata and Jiban's mother sitting on a mat outside Kamala's room. Kamala was engaged in a conversation with them while she sat on her bed inside the room, nursing the baby. Jiban's mother had come to their house that day as she could not ignore Snehalata's request. Seeing Kishori, Snehalata got up on some pretext and so did not notice Kishori's fierce glance directed at her bowed head. When Kishori came near, Kamala pulled her sari over her head. Jiban's mother said, 'Are you well, my son?' Kishori greeted her with folded hands. Jiban's mother said, 'Bouma is looking very weak. What does the doctor say?'

Kishori replied, 'What can doctors say? She is ill throughout the year. How can the doctor help her; he cannot change her constitution. After all, there is no neglect as far as the treatment is concerned.'

Jiban's mother said, 'Treatment alone is not sufficient. The girl is unhappy. You don't take care of her so her health is not improving.'

Kishori retorted, 'Jethima, you are becoming sentimental now. Does one carry on a courtship with one's wife forever?' Turning to Kamala, he said, 'Why have you started a quarrel again? It is not possible to survive here on account of your quarrels; that is why I don't come into the house.'

Kamala spoke up softly from behind her veil, 'Whose fault is it? You don't return Jethima's money and she fights with us about it.'

Kishori said, 'If the old lady says anything to you, should you answer her back? What has Boudi said to her that has upset her so much?'

Kamala said, 'One doesn't have to say anything to Jethima. She scolds the whole day for no reason.'

Kishori replied, 'This never happened earlier. It has all started since Boudi came to stay here.'

Kamala got angry and said, 'What are you saying? Have you ever heard Didi say anything to anyone? If there were no quarrels earlier, it was because I had some money with me and whenever Jethima asked for it, I could give it to her. Now I can't and so there are quarrels. It is not Didi's fault.'

Kishori declared, 'Whoever may be at fault, these quarrels never end. We cannot abandon Jethima so it is better for Boudi to go away.'

Kamala said, 'She is made to work all day like a maid for the little food she gets and then you talk like this? It is Didi's bad luck that she has come to stay in your house. Why didn't you let her go when she wanted to and why should she go now? She has as much right to stay here as we do. She has her own share in the property; you cannot chase her out like a cat or a dog.'

Kishori replied coolly, 'I guess Boudi has been saying all this to you. She thinks she can intimidate me. Fine then, let her try to claim her share if she can.'

Kamala said, 'Why should she say all this? I am saying it because it is true. You didn't let her go to Jagat Babu's house earlier, you should be ashamed to send her there now. In any case you should give her the maintenance. Don't you feel bad about forsaking a member of the family?'

Jiban's mother remarked, 'Why only maintenance, my child. She has a right to Mohan's entire share.'

Kishori shot back, 'Has she engaged you as a lawyer? I can't keep her here any more, I tell you.'

Jethima, who was coming in that direction, overheard a part of the conversation and started shouting, 'What is the matter? The woman wants her share now? Throw her out at once.'

Kishori softened his tone and said, 'I have no desire to send away a member of the family but what can I do? She wants to stake a claim to her share. Let her do it if she wants to but that will end her connection with the family.'

Having made this declaration, Kishori prepared to leave. Kamala realized with anguish that Snehalata might really be forced to leave the house. She pleaded, 'O, listen please. Don't say such things. Where will Didi go?'

Ignoring her altogether and turning to Jethima, Kishori said, 'Tell Bou that I am sending for the palanquin. She can go wherever she wants to. She can't stay here any more.'

Jethima answered, 'There is no fear of that. I shall turn her out this minute. She wants to go to court to claim her share? Isn't she ashamed to show us her blackened face?'

Snehalata had come down and overheard the talk. When Jethima left the scene she came forward and said to Jiban's mother, 'Take me with you, Jethima. You have servants in your house. I shall also be like one of them. I had called you to say that I can't endure it here any more.'

Jiban's mother knew that Tagar would not be happy if Snehalata was given shelter in their house but being a kind-hearted person she didn't allow that thought to trouble her and said, 'All right, I'll take you with me.' Snehalata's heart melted with gratitude and drops of tears fell from her eyes. Kamala also said tearfully, 'Go, Didi, this is not a place for good people. Pray that I can also leave this place after you have gone.'

From that night Kamala started getting fainting fits.

53

One hears that marriage is the most popular, desirable, and praiseworthy institution and the highest goal of life, at least for the people of Bengal. One can not say, however, that it is the happiest thing, because life does not end with marriage and people have to carry on with their prosaic lives after marriage. Novelists have the freedom to end their narratives with marriage and build up fantasies of continuing happiness. It was not for any other reason, but to gratify the readers that we had drawn the curtain over Jiban's married life. This may have kindled the wrath of our fair reader whose curiosity had been aroused but not pacified. Let her be appeased now, for we are raising the curtain once again. However, she is warned beforehand that the writer should not be accused of not providing her with any novelty. We believe that if she controls her anger and looks at the scene around her (her own household excepted) calmly she would not have to wait very long to satisfy her curiosity, because, as far as we know, the lives of young Bengali men become dull and commonplace after marriage and their daily routine is limited to eating, moving around, and other such humdrum activities. There is hardly any variety in the lifestyle of these young married people. As long as they are unmarried, there is a little spark in their lives and like an empty earthenware vessel they make a noise and show a little independence. Their minds are filled with ideas about reforming society and religion, and they are full of high hopes and pleasant dreams, sometimes to an excess. But when they step out and face the cold breeze of marriage, all their enthusiasm disappears, and nothing can make them return to their previous state. However, those who have an iron constitution are an exception to this rule. Society cannot control them or grind them into the desired shape. The more it tries to pressurize them, the more they resist it, slip out of its grip, and assert their own identity.

Unfortunately, in our country, the number of such iron vessels is very limited; so it is very difficult to find a hero for a novel. At least our Jiban Chandra does not belong to that category. Like other ordinary Bengali young men, the shackles of marriage have made him very listless and dull so there is nothing interesting to report about him. He is surviving as a practising lawyer. He goes to court every day to earn his bread and butter and when he returns home in the evening he is always faced with some problem or the other. Today, the eldest boy got fever after getting drenched in the rain, yesterday the little girl had covered herself with soot and was given a beating by her mother, the day before that the baby had fallen down and hurt its head. Tagar, having been pulled up by her mother-in-law about it, was very angry and was ready to leave for her parents' house. She could not be pacified by the tearful pleading of the old lady. Arriving suddenly in the midst of this scene Jiban found himself in a fix. This sequence was repeated everyday. If Jiban questioned Tagar about it, Tagar put the blame squarely on his mother: she had pampered the children and was responsible for spoiling their future, she had made Tagar's children drift from her and to cap it all, she was always scolding Tagar. If Tagar ever asked her to mind the children for a while she came out with all her complaints. She was there to pamper the children and Tagar was there to take care of them and be scolded in the bargain!

If Jiban listened to all this in silence, the matter would be settled peacefully for the day but if he spoke up on behalf of his mother the consequences were disastrous. There would be a quarrel, Tagar would leave the room in a temper or start crying, and Jiban would go into the outer room and bury himself in his books. Books were his only comfort now. The high ambitions and fantasies of his past life were like a distant dream for him, though they had not totally vanished from his inner world. Even now he sometimes thought that if he had the money he would take his family to England and fulfil his ambition through his children. However, all these dreams did not assume the form of reality in his mind as they had done earlier. He was not as optimistic as he used to be. Experience had taught him that one's hopes were never fully realized. The life of a householder was beset with disappointments.

Nevertheless, while experience guides a man's intellect, it does not change his inherent nature completely. The reason is that intellect is not everything in the life of a human being. There is another independent entity, which is the heart, whose influence is not insignificant. Jiban's suffering and disappointment had not changed his essential nature. His intellect made him pessimistic but there was still hope and trust in the innermost depths of his heart. In other words, his cynicism was acquired but his faith was natural. He declared that a blind power governed the world, and compassion, generosity, and kindness were alien to it. However, in spite of these assertions, he worked for the Congress as enthusiastically as he used to work for his secret club when he was young. Jiban earned well but he was not wealthy. He did not have enough money to go to England himself, but he was never short of money if he had to help out poor students or his friend Nabin who was now in England.

Since the arrival of Snehalata in his house, his scepticism had also diminished. His previous passion for Snehalata had now taken the form of a calm friendship. When he conversed with her, he found a new rationale in her simple faith. The pessimism which was slowly eating into the core of his heart like a worm was gradually being wiped out by Snehalata's affectionate and reassuring words, and his heart was again becoming normal. We quote an extract from his letter to Nabin, written after Snehalata's arrival. It will enable the readers to understand and gauge his present state of mind.

'No, brother, you have left me behind. Sometime back I used to think that nobody could be as pessimistic and cynical as I am. Now I realize that India is a land of sunshine. No darkness can settle here permanently. Staying in a cold and gloomy country like England your mind has become so frost-bound and materialistic that it is difficult for you to return to your normal self again.

'Just think, could the world have survived if it were really based on some chance or accident? When we accept this world as real, do we also not accept that it is there for a purpose? In other words do we not accept that it is based on truth and that there is an intimate connection between the creation and the Creator? Otherwise, what is the status of the world or creation?

'Perhaps you think that the deception we encounter in life, the dichotomy we face every day between our desire and reality (for instance we desire what is good and it turns out to be bad, we want to do something beneficial and it turns out to be harmful), this enigma which we cannot comprehend with our intellect and which we call blind fate or destiny is a proof of the universe being moved by an irrational force. However, if you think seriously, you will realize the existence of a great, rational power underlying it which manipulates the individual will according to its own logic and controls it merely as its instrument.

'We see a similarity of purpose between the life of an insect in the external world and the functioning of the vast solar system. Likewise, even the universe of the mind is moved by a conscious purpose. There cannot be any doubt about it. This purpose is beyond our comprehension so we think of it as an enigma or delusion. We fail to perceive the connection between one event and another. When the events of our life go contrary to our will or expectations, it is because they are a part of the supreme purpose of the Universal Will. We are only fragments of the universe. The harmony and well-being of the entire universe depends on the movement of these small fragments. Conversely, our well-being also depends on the well-being of the entire universe. The Mover knows the direction the universe has to take. We fall into error when we judge things with our limited vision. My being, my will or action is controlled by that omnipotent, omnipresent Being. Knowing this one should have full faith in His purpose. Only with an attitude of total self-surrender can we reach our destination safely. Once we realize this truth, we can never be overpowered by dejection. But if, like you, we look at everything through coloured glasses, truth may appear to us as falsehood, life may appear to be disorderly, purposeless, and a vacuum. Then, all worldly commitments and even the ties of affection become weak, our knowledge turns into ignorance, and our existence turns into non-existence.

'What you have written about love makes me think that you have lost touch with your real self. Your loss of faith in love has made you lose faith in the whole world because our life depends on love. Everything in this world may be false but love is not. It is the bond between the Creator and his creation. It is the force of attraction in the inanimate world and love in the world of living beings. In fact, what we call ties of blood are ties of love; otherwise; what connection do people have with one another? Everyone is born as a separate being but it is love which makes a distinction between what belongs to us and what does not. Love gives human beings their humanity, their life. Just as food is necessary for the nourishment of the body, love is necessary for the nourishment of the soul.

'I admit that a human being can never be totally selfless. He has to depend on others to some extent. If you are not there someone else will take your place. In your absence, your share of food would go to somebody else. Therefore, a struggle for survival in this world is inevitable. But the body is not all in all. Human beings are unique. Just as they cannot maintain their bodies without being selfish, they cannot maintain their spirit without loving another or without sacrificing themselves for another. The more humane a person is, the deeper and more expansive is his love, and the more loving is his nature, the more happy he feels about making sacrifices for others.

'You will ask: can people be truly happy by sacrificing themselves? Do they not expect anything in return? The answer is no. Love does not have expectations as we see in the case of the Buddha, Christ, and Chaitanya. Did they ask for anything in return for love? Do we have any expectations when we have a spontaneous compassion for sufferers or when we have reverence for the great. And love which has expectations is not entirely selfish either. I know the happiness of loving and I wish the person I love the same kind of happiness. There is a selfless desire in this kind of exchange. In fact, in giving and receiving love one experiences the same kind of happiness. The nature of love is such that the more one is capable of giving, the more one can receive, and God is the ideal lover. He receives universal love and is immersed in that love. Hence the desire to love and unite with the loved one are higher feelings. It is true that 'Blessed are they that expect nothing', but it is not true that expectation or desire is necessarily bad or that it is an aberration. Otherwise, we would have no desire to unite with God when we love Him.

'Actually, this desire arises out of a feeling of incompleteness and the wish to be complete. Human beings are finite but they aspire to move towards infinity. When we see that divine spark in somebody, we love that person and want to be united with him. Attraction is mutual; so the person who does not respond to love is either a liberated soul or a rock, incapable of feeling.

'Hence, desire and expectations are not without meaning. They are necessary for our survival and the continuation of the universe. Thus, nothing in this world is based on error. Seen in the right perspective, everything is founded on truth. The Congress is so important because it has awakened a great love in us. It has bound together in a tie of love not only the different communities in India, but different regions, the victor and the vanquished. In creating this sense of unity lies the glory and the triumph of Congress. Our social and political progress is but secondary to this great endeavour.'

54

One can evade everything but not fate. Fate dogs our footsteps. If a fortunate person holds a fistful of ashes, those ashes turn into gold, while an unfortunate person gets nothing, whatever his desire may be. Snehalata's misery was not relieved even after she left Kishori's house. Although Jiban and his mother were considerate towards her, she was an eyesore for Tagar and her fate remained unchanged.

Yet, Snehalata made light of this suffering which was insignificant in comparison to what she had faced in Kishori's house. She was so grateful for the affection she got from Jiban and his mother that she could easily ignore the pinpricks from Tagar. But could she forget her friends in these new surroundings? Were the deep sighs that frequently escaped from her caused by her longing to see Kamala and her children or for some other reason?

It was not as though Tagar was totally dissatisfied with Snehalata's presence in her house, but she was not totally satisfied with it either. How could she be? She could not be expected to rejoice that her mother-in-law was fond of Snehalata and that her husband respected her and liked to converse with her. However, Snehalata's presence was convenient for Tagar. She did not have to attend to the household or the children any longer. Sneha worked like a maid all day and Tagar could spend her time in idleness. She could visit her mother whenever she pleased and she could rebuke Snehalata if anything was out of order. This was very convenient for a lazy and comfort-loving person like Tagar. Moreover, she did not have to face any criticism from Jiban for neglecting her children. In fact, he was now quite mild with Tagar in every respect and she had the satisfaction of exercising a hold on him and scolding him whenever she had the opportunity to do so.

The fact was that Tagar was neither Suryamukhi nor Kundanandini[60] who would lay down her life for the love of her husband. She was happy if she could control her husband and rebuke him freely. Their household was now functioning smoothly. She was quite sure of Jiban's nature and had no reason to distrust him. She knew that his affection for Snehalata was merely compassion for an unfortunate soul, and therefore harmless. In fact, it had given Tagar an advantage over Jiban as she could tease him about her. She did not disclose the news of Snehalata's arrival at her house to Jagat Babu for fear that he might call her back to him. Whenever Snehalata mentioned him, Tagar replied in a manner which suggested that she could never hope to be reconciled with him. She reminded Snehalata again and again in a tone of reproach that Charu was on the point of losing his life on account of her and that no one in that house wanted to hear Snehalata's name any more.

Snehalata sometimes expressed her desire to go and see Kamala but Tagar put it off on some pretext or the other. She was afraid that her children would be neglected if Snehalata went away even for a day. This led to a great commotion one day, when Kamala's maid came crying and declared that Kamala was on her deathbed and wanted to see Snehalata urgently. Snehalata went straight to Jiban's mother in a state of agitation and said, 'Ma, I must go, Kamala is very ill...' Jiban's mother gave her permission and Sneha sent the maid for a palanquin.

In the meanwhile, the news reached Tagar's ears. She was furious when she heard that Snehalata was going away without asking her. She had just finished an early lunch and was doing her hair with the idea of visiting her parents. When she heard the news from her elder son she stopped immediately and flinging her plait on her back, rushed to Snehalata and said, 'I am not well and have to go home. Don't go today, Didi, you can think of going tomorrow.'

Sneha replied, 'Kamala is very ill and I must go today.'

Tagar was not to be deterred so easily for she had planned to go to the theatre that evening from her father's house. She said, 'Kamala has been ill for a long time. People suffering from chronic ailments do not die in a day. Ma is not well and I can't stay here today.'

Meanwhile, the maid came and announced that the palanquin had arrived for Snehalata. Sneha said, 'Tagar, Kamala's condition is serious. No one can say what will happen. If you go home, Ma can look after the children.'

Tagar replied, 'Then you have a talk with her, I am leaving.' Saying this, she quickly rushed downstairs with her plait hanging down her back and her half-done hair falling on her forehead and got into the palanquin which had been summoned for Snehalata. The maid stood speechless with astonishment. Snehalata was annoyed and reported the matter to Jiban's mother. Jiban's mother agreed to take care of the children for the day. Snehalata sent for another palanquin and left for Kishori's house.

Kamala was lying in a delirious condition in the sick chamber. Tears were flowing from her half-closed eyes and she was mumbling, 'Didi, have you come yet?' The maids were crying quietly as they attended on her. Jethima was standing at a distance and shouting, 'Why hasn't the doctor arrived yet? Who has gone to fetch him?'

Snehalata quietly entered the room and stood near Kamala's bed with a trembling heart and tears in her eyes. Kamala opened her eyes and the painful expression on her emaciated face turned into a tranquil one. She said, 'Is that you, Didi? You have come after such a long time.' Snehalata sat on the edge of her bed and took Kamala's cold hands into her own. Kamala looked at her helplessly and whispered, 'Didi, I am leaving. Please forgive him. He has troubled you so much.' She fell silent and her eyes became glazed. Sneha said tearfully, 'O my sister, where are you going? Take me with you.'

Kamala did not reply, her lips were motionless and her vacant eyes looked upwards. In a moment the stream of her life which had flowed steadily for twenty years came to a standstill. It seemed that she had warded off death all this while, only to see Snehalata once again.

*T*agar returned home the next day and found the house in a chaos. Her youngest son had brought on a fever after fretting for his mother the whole night. Jiban was furious and after a long time Tagar had to put up with his reproach which made her angry with Snehalata. If she had stayed back this would not have happened. When Sneha returned that day with a heart heavy with sorrow, Tagar turned away from her without speaking. On returning home in the evening and not seeing Snehalata with the sick child, Jiban asked Tagar, 'Has Boudidi not returned yet?'

Tagar muttered sullenly, 'She has returned.'

'Where is she?'

'You look for her yourself. She will come fast enough if she hears that you have arrived. Otherwise she does not care whether people are sick or well.'

Tagar wanted to get even with Jiban who had scolded her in the morning. Jiban was annoyed and said, 'What kind of a person are you? She looks after the children the whole day. She is so fond of you and does so much for your children. Perhaps she is sitting by herself because she is sad. Don't you realize how pained she would be to hear these words from you.'

Tagar said sullenly, 'She is the only person in the world who is so unhappy. Nobody else has any problems.'

Jiban said, 'I don't know in what state you would have been if you had suffered like her.'

Tagar said, 'Why do you grudge me the happiness which God has granted me? That will not give her what I have. People suffer because of their karma. She is suffering because of her own actions. Wasn't she happy before? If she courted trouble, what can be done about it?

'Don't frown and grind your teeth like that. I can tolerate everything else. Only God knows what Boudidi did in her previous birth, but if her actions in this life are responsible for her destiny, she certainly deserves to be more happy than you or me.'

'Is that so? Won't she have to suffer for making Dada crazy about her?'

'Was it Boudidi's fault that he wanted to get married to her?'

'What nonsense you talk? Can a man approach a woman without getting any encouragement from her? I know everything that happened. You think your Boudidi is a paragon of virtue, you are mistaken.'

'Tell me what you mean.'

'So you really want to know what happened? I was too ashamed to tell you earlier. I saw Dada kissing her with my own eyes. What more do you want to know?'

Jiban was astonished to hear this. He said, after a pause, 'Does anyone else in your family know about it?'

'If they did, it would be a disaster. Ma threw Didi out only because of her suspicion. No, I did not tell anyone. You are the first person I have disclosed it to. Yet, you say that I do not sympathize with Didi and I grind my teeth!'

56

*H*uman beings are very short-sighted. They are incomplete and their intellect is inadequate. Their actions are prompted by the desire to gain something but often the result is contrary to their expectations and all their effort is in vain. This is what we learn from experience and it confirms the idea of divine justice. It proves that our intelligence cannot fathom the purpose underlying the universe. This is why sages tell us to work without the expectation of success.

Tagar thought that after her disclosure to Jiban, Snehalata would be vanquished and Jiban would cease to respect her. But his reaction was to the contrary. He was furious with Charu and thought him to be a scoundrel not to have married Sneha after going that far. Snehalata had to suffer and wander from pillar to post due to Charu's weakness and selfishness. Jiban's heart was already brimming over with respect and sympathy for Snehalata. Now his desire to take care of Snehalata and make her happy became even more intense.

Not having met Snehalata for some time Jiban said to Tagar, 'Boudidi seems to keep to herself these days. Why don't you call her and talk to her. It may help her to forget her sorrow.'

Tagar replied, 'I don't know what sorrow you are talking about. People survive even after they have lost their husbands and sons. What is she mourning for?'

'Boudidi does not have a husband or a son, so she cannot be compared with such people.'

Tagar said sarcastically, 'O my! don't develop blisters on your skin for her sake.'

Jiban retorted, 'If I were sensitive about what you say, my whole body would have been full of blisters.'

Tagar said, 'Indeed! Then don't listen to me.' Turning to her eldest son she said, 'Jatin, my boy, call your Jethima here.'

The boy went away. Jiban realized that it would be unwise to quarrel with Tagar on account of Snehalata, for Snehalata would have to suffer the consequences. He smiled and said, 'O, you are angry again? Look, I have not had the pleasure of pampering you for sometime. Now, shall I fall at your lovely feet or shall I adorn them with the anklets the goldsmith delivered today?'

Tagar beamed with pleasure and said, 'Is that so? Why didn't you give them to me earlier?'

Jiban replied, 'I left them on the table in the outer room. Send someone to fetch them.'

In the meanwhile, Jatin appeared on the scene, holding Snehalata by the hand and Tagar sent him to get the anklets. Jiban asked Sneha to sit down and she sat on one edge of the large mattress on the floor on which Jiban and Tagar were seated. Jiban asked, 'Boudidi do you know that I have finally won the case?'

Tagar said, 'Everybody knows about it and so does Didi.'

Sneha said, 'Yes, Thakurpo, I have heard about it, but it seems that after all the accounts have been settled, Kishori Thakurpo will be left without a penny.'

Tagar said, 'Serves him right. He should have given us our share earlier like a gentleman. Here, Jatin has brought the anklets. Let me have a look at them.'

Smiling with pleasure, Tagar got up, took the anklets from Jatin and marched off to show them to her mother-in-law. Sneha said, 'If Kishori Thakurpo loses everything, what will happen to his children?'

'When I get my claim,' Jiban reassured her, 'I shall certainly make some arrangement for their maintenance.'

Sneha's face brightened as she said, 'Thakurpo, you have such a kind heart.'

Jiban looked embarrassed and tried to change the subject. 'Boudidi, who looks after the children now?' he asked.

Sneha replied, 'They have gone to their maternal uncle's house. They are very unhappy after their mother's death. Those who are needed in this world, depart, but unfortunate people like me get left behind to increase the misery on the earth.' She heaved a long sigh and said to herself, 'God, only you know why you are keeping me alive.'

Jiban said to her, 'You are here to relieve other people's suffering, Boudidi. You suffer but bring happiness to others. Why do you say that your life has no value?'

'I would have been happy if I knew that I had made someone happy. What greater happiness can anyone expect to have?'

'You women are goddesses, we men are monsters. You deserve to be worshipped but we disregard you at every step. You sacrifice so much for our comfort but we only kick you in return. Our race is in such a sorry state because of our sinful behaviour and yet we are proud of it.'

Snehalata exclaimed with surprise, 'What are you saying? Are we to be worshipped or you, who are our gods? We are not your equals with respect to either knowledge or feelings. Really, I often wonder why men love women at all for they are totally devoid of any worth. Perhaps it is their greatness and their generosity that make them love us. Their compassion for us is like the compassion that the great have for the lowly and the strong have for the weak and helpless.'

Jiban smiled and said, 'I see that you can blow up a bubble and raise it to the sky. Education develops one's knowledge and intellect, so at present men and women cannot be compared. Since ancient times up to the present, women have not enjoyed equal opportunities for education with men. And in whom do you really find evidence of natural superiority or the superiority of the heart? Can men's nature be compared to women's sympathetic and selfless nature?'

Sneha could not help smiling and said, 'If you talk in this vein it sounds like a mockery. Where did you learn that women's nature is superior to that of men? Women are at the root of all the misery and trouble in this world. They quarrel day and night over petty, selfish interests. If women could be like men, there would be no problem. In comparison to men, we don't even seem to be human. I am amused whenever there is an argument about which sex is superior. If men were not superior, neither Jesus Christ nor the Buddha would have been a man.'

Jiban said, 'You are mistaken. Most of the time men, not women are at the root of evil deeds. However, men are crafty: they withdraw after inciting women, who get all the blame. Besides, when a good thing gets spoilt, we feel worse. Sour curd can be eaten, but when milk turns sour, it cannot be consumed. When there is an ink stain on a white-washed wall, it is noticed immediately. We condemn women for small lapses but men go unpunished for actions which are a thousand times worse. This is why women get a bad reputation easily. Buddha and Christ cannot be compared with ordinary people. They fall in the category of superhuman beings. Yet, it is my belief that in the inner apartments of every home we can come across many little instances of sacrifices like theirs. Jesus Christ was crucified for his compassion in a large context; you women shower your love and affection within your small families and receive ingratitude and insults in return. You give up your lives for us in silence and we are not able to recognize your love and your greatness.'

Snehalata protested, 'This is not true, Thakurpo. Women do not recognize the depth of men's emotions. Love may be everything for us but it does not go as deep. We are not as large-hearted as men are, so our love is also narrow in its scope. We are easily distressed with a little suffering and you think that it shows the superiority of our hearts! We do not deserve even to stand near your feet.'

Sneha heaved a long sigh. She remembered Charu's helpless tears. The memory of the pain she had given Charu was a source of great mental agony for her. Jiban was also reminded of Charu and his callousness towards Snehalata. Unable to control himself he smiled sarcastically and said, 'Near our feet? Who are we? People like me and Charu? I do not deny that there are some heroic men in this world but it would be an insult to them if you place us in their category.'

Sneha was hurt by his sarcasm and said, 'Thakurpo, I haven't told you who my hero is. And if I think highly of some people, there is no need to make fun of it.'

'Who does not like to be praised? But if you can influence Tagar with your views, I will be spared.'

Sneha smiled, but continued in a solemn tone, 'Honestly Thakurpo, I don't know why you jest about it. It is Tagar's misfortune that she does not understand you. It proves that women cannot fathom the depth of men's hearts.'

'So it seems you have understood me! To tell you the truth, it makes me unhappy that I cannot love Tagar as she loves me. It seems all your ideal men are alike in this respect. The person for whom you have staked your life and your happiness in spite of being deceived by him—'

Snehalata could not maintain her composure any longer. She realized who Jiban was alluding to and forgetting herself for a moment, cried out, 'Nobody has deceived me, Thakurpo. If there has been any deception, I am responsible for it myself. He was willing to give up everything to marry me. There is nothing that he did not do for me. In return for that boundless love, I left him without telling him. Nobody could be as ungrateful as I am. He was about to lose his life for my sake. May the merciful God forgive me but I do not have the courage to ask a human being for his forgiveness.'

Sneha's voice was choked with emotion, and tears fell silently from her eyes. Tagar entered the room and saw that Jiban's compassionate gaze was fixed on her tearful face and his heart seemed to melt with pity for her. Unable to endure it, Tagar cried out, 'You don't even die. Here again you are trying to seduce with your tears? Carry on then, I am going to my father's house.'

She marched out of the room in a fit of anger.

S nehalata had been living in Jiban's house for the last two or three
months but Jagat Babu did not know about this. How could he?
Neither the Mistress nor Tagar were in favour of allowing the information to reach his ears. However, even in the most orderly house-
holds there is disruption from time to time, so despite the wishes
of the women in the house Jagat Babu did come to hear of this
eventually.

The other day, he was resting after lunch in his private chamber
on the second floor of the house. Contrary to its dignified name—
'khas mahal'—it consisted of just one room divided into two small
sections. The outer one was his charitable dispensary. Each of its walls
had eight large wooden shelves holding medicine bottles. The inner
room, which was his study, was lined with cupboards and shelves full
of books on science and medicine. Apart from these, there was a
sofa, a table and two chairs in the room. The table was piled with
books. Though this floor was a part of the inner section of the house,
the Mistress seldom set foot here. She said that the sight of the
dispensary made her sick. Actually climbing up so many stairs to
come to the second floor regularly was too much of an effort for her.
When Snehalata was around, she often sat here reading her books or
chatting with Jagat Babu. It was nearly two years since she had left
this house. In her absence this room had become a desolate place.

It was a still and silent hour. The sound of a distant siren reverberated like the breath of the quiet afternoon, drowning the call of
the birds. The cooing of two pigeons, perched on a column in the
balcony, created a dream-like ambience, appropriate for a pleasant
reverie.

But time does not permit such undisturbed peace to continue for long. So the clock on Jagat Babu's table ticked away rhythmically as though giving a warning: 'This will not last, the dream will be over.' One does not know whether Jagat Babu could hear this warning. He was quietly smoking his hookah and gazing at the sun-drenched winter scene—the houses, the trees, the sky, and the distant chimney—framed by the open doorway. The smoke was rising like a column from the chimney. It rose, uncoiled itself into finer and finer particles of vapour, and gradually dispersed in the atmosphere. The smoke from the pipe of Jagat Babu's hookah also rose up without a pause but Jagat Babu's gaze was fixed, not on himself, but at the column of smoke outside. Needless to say, he was looking at the smoke but his mind was elsewhere. He was thinking of Snehalata. One's mind always reverts to a subject which is painful. The pungency of the smoke never bothered Jagat Babu, but Snehalata had really caused him much pain. It is the rule of the world that what can give you the greatest happiness can also bring the most suffering.

Whenever Jagat Babu sat alone in his study he remembered Snehalata; her tender, sweet and sensitive face, her sincere devotion along with her departure without any explanation, her disregard of his earnest request to meet her, her meanness and dishonesty. All these memories disturbed his mind. He could not reconcile the contradiction between these two contrasting impressions. The more he thought about it, the more it puzzled him. Eventually, he felt as though he was immersed in a vast sea and a wail of sorrow arose from the depth of his innermost being. His eyes grew misty and his heart ached. He removed the pipe from his lips and sat as though half-dead, with his cheek resting on his hand and his eyes staring vacantly into space. A little while later, when the clock struck two, he started up, glanced all around and, raising his hand, wiped his eyes quickly. A few moments later Jiban entered the room and greeted him respectfully. Jagat Babu acknowledged his greeting and said, 'How are you, Jiban? You have not been here for a long time. Is everybody all right?'

'Yes, sir, I was rather busy with my case.'

'Justice will be done, eventually. How many shares of the property will there be?'

'After the division, the shares will not be very large. Initially there will be three shares. However, some people may or may not get any part of it.'

'The shares will be yours, Kishori's, and Mohan's, I guess.'

'No, Jethima's, Kishori's, and mine.'

'But why should Mohan not get a share? After all, his widow, who is his heir, is alive.'

'According to our law if the son dies before his father, his widow does not have a claim to his property and is reduced to a state of destitution. She has no right to food or clothing either.'

'I don't understand your law. The wife has no standing then. How dreadful! Something ought to be done about it.'

'Well sir, we haven't come into the world to fight injustice, have we? After all, this law does not have any adverse effect on Hindu society, does it?'

Jagat Babu scratched his head and said, 'I have been wondering why there is this injustice in our country. The Hindu law is quite liberal towards women after all. Look at England. To this day, British women haven't had any right to *streedhan*.[61] Till very recently all the possessions of the wife belonged to her husband. In our country a woman has absolute right to her streedhan.'

Jiban frowned and said, 'What is streedhan? Just a little money or jewellery which a woman gets at the time of her marriage, that is all. Considering the extent to which our women are dependent on others, the law had to make this provision for them, otherwise it would lose its sanctity. You may call it the liberality of the Hindu community but I don't. And as for British women, I would say that they do not have any need for streedhan of this kind. They are not dependent on the charity of others as our women are. If they marry, they can enjoy their husband's wealth and those who are entirely without resources are well equipped by their education to earn their living.'

'How is that? I have heard that in England the law of primogeniture is operative.'

'That is applicable only to those who possess an entailed property, that is, those who belong to the aristocracy and hold a hereditary title. But that is not the common law of the land. Unless the father leaves a will, depriving any of his children of the inheritance, his sons as well as his daughters have a claim to his property. And in cases where the eldest son is the chief heir, the daughter inherits a portion like the other sons. In this respect there is no law as unjust as ours. From this, one can infer how much we respect and care for our women.'

'My son, this may hurt your sentiments about women but I do not see any unfairness on the part of our law in this matter. The law is framed according to the requirements of a society. It is not the custom of our society to let girls remain unmarried. They have to be married and they prosper on account of their husbands' wealth. Now, if in addition to this they also get a share of their father's property, what would the future of men be? If you talk of injustice, I would say that your suggestion is also unfair.'

'You would not say this if you examine the matter more seriously. If a daughter has a claim to her father's property, while a sister will have to be given her share, the wife will also bring her share into her husband's family. So it will amount to the same in the long run. There will be no injustice to any party.'

Twisting his moustache thoughtfully, Jagat Babu remarked, 'I think you are right.'

Jiban continued, 'Once again, it is my firm conviction that if the foundation of our society rests on such a law, not only will the condition of our women improve but India as a nation will rise in the world. The debate that has currently started in our society regarding women's education and independence and the abolition of child marriage signifies that we have begun to realize to some extent that the welfare and progress of the nation is contingent on the improvement of the condition of women. However, no one seems to have paid attention to the fact that the unfairness of the law is a hindrance to our progress. I am sure all upright people, whether they favour or oppose social reform, would agree about this wholeheartedly.'

'How can that be? I don't understand.'

'Those who are against social reform are not inimical to the welfare of society or wish to persecute women. The fact that they support child marriage and are opposed to higher education of women and widow remarriage only shows that they believe that the welfare of society lies in this.'

'That is true.'

'But they can see that despite their will, marriage has become a difficult proposition in these changing times. Those who have daughters are tormented by the anxiety of getting them married. Now, if the law grants women a right to their fathers' property, would they be so troubled about the marriage of their daughters? The status of women would be considerably enhanced in men's eyes and so it would be much easier to get girls married. Not only that, the parents would not have to worry so much about their daughters' future, as they would be treated with respect by their husbands' families. In case a girl became a widow, she would not be ill-treated by her brother, sister-in-law, and other relatives. There would be much less unhappiness in society.'

Jagat Babu nodded his head in silence.

Jiban said, 'And those who are in favour of women's education and believe that the abolition of child marriage is necessary for the advancement of our country, can, on serious consideration, arrive at the conclusion that the progress of real education would be easy if women can stand on their own by their birthright, and the fruits of social reform would be fully realized. There is an unfavourable opinion about women's education and the abolition of child marriage because of the problem of arranging the marriage of girls. If women are educated, they will have their independent views about marriage, which their parents will not be able to ignore, and give them away to any undeserving fellow they can conveniently get hold of. As a consequence, many women in our society may have to remain single all their lives, as they do in England. So far, in our society, marriage is the only support for women, the husband's relatives are their kinsmen and his home is their proper shelter. If a father dies without making any provisions for his unmarried daughter, owing to our traditions or for any other reason, she is reduced to begging in the streets. In such a case, our traditions instead of benefiting society are likely to lead to more misery. Therefore, it is the duty of those who stand for justice and social welfare to rectify this anomaly. I have decided to raise this issue at the social conference. Let us see what others have to say.'

'Jiban, you are right. Previously I also used to think that women's education is beneficial for society but now I tend to agree with you that educating women is of no use. It only increases the malaise in society. What we used to have earlier was fine.'

Jiban smiled and said, 'I see that you have misunderstood me. I did not say that women's education is bad, because my conviction is otherwise. What I mean is—'

'But, my dear chap, what is the necessity for women to get education? Their glory lies in love and kindness. They should remain satisfied with that. Too much of reading is likely to pervert their nature.'

'There is no doubt that the glory of women lies in the supremacy of their hearts, but doesn't the heart become expansive as a result of proper education and intellectual exercise? Doesn't the emergence of women like Miss Nightingale, Miss Carpenter, and Miss Manning show the good consequence of the spread of higher education in the community?'

'Let's not talk of England. Can the kind of education that is effective for them be effective for us too? One must consider the place, the time, and the people. I have observed that as a result of education the women of our country have started manifesting masculine tendencies. What is the good of women becoming like men?'

'This argument is commonly forwarded against women's education these days. However, I fail to understand how people arrive at such an irrational conclusion.'

'Women are involving themselves in social action through organizations and conferences like men! How absurd it is! One is disgusted to hear of all the ridicule they have brought upon themselves because of their behaviour.'

Jiban's patience could hold no longer. He said heatedly, 'How can the greatness of our countrymen find expression, unless they ridicule what is good? True enough. When women sit at home and quarrel and gossip about others, their tender feelings are suitably expressed but when they launch Sakhi Samitis[62] and work for widows and orphans, they go against their feminine nature and hurt the sensibilities of nice people with their masculine hardness. I believe this kind of hardness is not proper for men either, is it?'

'Why this anger, my dear?'

'Excuse me, I cannot tolerate this line of reasoning. A few of our women have got together to do good work, but instead of helping and encouraging them, our countrymen are all too ready to find fault with them and condemn their work. Pandita Ramabai[63] has founded a widows' home and do you know that she is being supported by the people of America? Even then we say that people of no other country are as compassionate as we are. O God, will this country ever prosper?'

'My dear Jiban, why are you so agitated? Here are ten rupees as my contribution to Sakhi Samiti. That should satisfy you. But there's one thing I want to ask: 'Will these widows' homes inculcate the ideal widowhood of the past?'

'The past never returns. Life does not remain the same forever. What we call progressive today, we might call retrograde tomorrow. So if you want to see the ideal widowhood of the past in present times, you will probably be disappointed. Yet that does not mean that such homes are not beneficial. See how many helpless women find shelter in these homes, stay on the path of righteousness, and lead a good life.'

'Friend, one cannot say that such helpless women do not find any shelter in our country. Even those who have no one to call their own are given their meals by their extended families.'

'Accompanied by much ill treatment. And some women are so unfortunate that they do not find any shelter at all.'

'Now, you are exaggerating, surely.'

'Why, take the instance of Boudidi. Even small plants have shelter but she has none. She is driven away wherever she goes, though you seldom come across a person who is as gentle and patient as she is. When she has to endure such ill treatment, one can imagine how much more miserable would be the plight of widows who are intolerant, sensitive, and dependent on others. If the Hindu community permitted the setting up of ashrams where widows voluntarily engage themselves in serving others, their suffering would be much reduced, don't you agree?'

Jagat Babu was astounded to hear Sneha's name being mentioned. After a pause he said, 'Have you met her recently?'

'Have I? Don't you know that she has been staying with us for the last three months?'

'How would I know? I have written to her so many times but not received a single reply from her. When I went to see her, I had to return disappointed.'

Jagat Babu's eyes again filled up with tears. The memory of that tragedy in his life was heart-rending. Jiban was taken by surprise and exclaimed, 'How is that? I was under the impression that you did not reply to her letters. All these days you did not even enquire about her well-being! Now I see that Kishori is entirely responsible for this misunderstanding.'

Jagat Babu asked, 'Why did she leave her in-law's place and come to your house?'

'There is a limit to what one can endure! Besides, initially Kishori had thought that Boudidi would get a share of the family property. But later when...'

Jagat Babu did not hear the rest. Jiban's words echoed in his ears: 'There is a limit to what one can endure.' This meant that Sneha had been compelled to leave his home in great distress. This confirmed his suspicion. Interrupting Jiban he said, 'Tell me, was it true that Charu had wronged her?'

Jiban remained silent. Jagat Babu was no longer in doubt. He trembled with anger and sympathy. He said, 'Jiban, go at once and send Snehalata here. Her sight will relieve my pain. I have some urgent work here so I cannot fetch her myself.'

Jiban believed that Snehalata would be genuinely happy if she could come to Jagat Babu's place; so he was overjoyed on hearing Jagat Babu's words and set off for home immediately.

58

Charu had imagined that his life would have no meaning without Snehalata and he would never taste happiness again. However, after his marriage he was full of a new joy. It was not as though he had forgotten Snehalata but her memory made him shiver as the memory of a fit of madness after regaining normalcy or the memory of a bad dream after waking up. What a disaster was he courting then? Had he married Sneha, he would be a homeless, penniless outcaste, an object of universal ridicule. His life would be a despicable one, a veritable living death. And to think that he was making this sacrifice and undergoing such torment for the sake of that treacherous, heartless woman! She would have failed to appreciate the enormity of his sacrifice and would probably have told him even before a couple of days had passed, 'I was so happy before. Why did you marry me?'

Charu was profoundly disturbed by such fantasies, so whenever he remembered the tragic events related to Snehalata, he heaved a sigh of relief that he had been saved from that calamity. He cursed Snehalata in his heart and showered his love on his wife. Along with this transformation in his feelings, his thinking also underwent a change. He was now a confirmed Hindu and got very agitated when he heard about social reform. Now he worked hard for the welfare of the nation by writing articles in defence of Hindu conventions. The main thrust of his arguments was that widow remarriage was a despicable practice and anyone who supported it should be excommunicated forthwith. Although most of his essays were returned to him by the publishers with thanks, he did not mind it because his wife Priyatama read them repeatedly and praised his powerful style and his commitment to religion. So Charu's labour was amply rewarded.

That afternoon there was an argument between the husband and the wife about Snehalata who was frequently a subject of their conversation. Charu had told his wife many stories about Snehalata, though not the whole truth. He had told her all that he safely could, that is, after leaving out his own share of the blame. Lately Priyatama had come upon Snehalata's old letter in Charu's desk, when she was looking for one of his old poems. So there was a lively exchange between the couple about this letter. Priyatama was trying to prove on the basis of the text of the letter that Sneha loved Charu still and such love could not be wiped out so easily. Charu did not agree with her but there seemed little chance of his winning the argument. Priyatama was reading the letter over and over again, expounding and commenting on it. Finally she said, 'I am not going to listen to you. She certainly loves you.'

Failing to convince her, Charu said, 'As you say, my queen. Will you put the letter away now or will you talk about it the whole day?'

Priyatama put the letter in his pocket and said, 'Here is your letter since you don't want anyone else to see it. Anyway, I do want to see her very much. I believe she has come to Boudidi's house. I'll go there one of these days.'

'What is the point in seeing her?'

'I shall see what she looks like, for you were drowned in her love.'

'I was drowned indeed. What nonsense!'

'All right, she was drowned then. I want to know what she would think of you if she saw you now.'

'What would she think? I am telling you she didn't love me.'

'Didn't she? You men do not understand a woman's heart.'

'Why did she leave me if she loved me?'

'Can there not be some other reason for it?' Priya had heard from Tagar how she and her mother had conspired to send her away. She said, 'No matter what you say, I know she loved you.'

Charu laughed and pulling her hair, said, 'All right, I agree with you. Won't you feel jealous to see her?'

'Why should I be jealous? I would have been jealous if you loved her still, but it isn't so. Rather, I feel sorry for her.'

'Why?'

'Why? You have got married comfortably, while she, poor thing, may still be suffering for your sake.'

Charu was a little surprised at her generosity. It is doubtful whether in her place he would have been as charitable. He looked at her appreciatively and said, 'Tell me, has she confessed her feelings to you?'

Priya replied. 'Doesn't this letter reveal her feelings? I know she loves you though you are so callous.'

Charu put his arm around her shoulder and said, 'It seems you have become her bosom friend. I accept whatever you say. Now forget her and sing a song for me.'

'No I won't.'

At that moment the maid called out to Charu, 'Dadababu, the Master has sent for you.'

59

*J*agat Babu was pacing restlessly in his study. Charu's heart sank when he saw the dark, brooding expression and the angry frown on his face. Once before, he had seen him in this terrible mood, though he didn't remember when it was. Jagat Babu motioned to him to take a chair and took another himself. Then he fixed his gaze on Charu and said in a voice of thunder, 'Charu, you lied to me. You drove Sneha away from this house.'

Charu wondered why his father was raising this question after such a long time. What could the matter be? He looked at him, speechless with astonishment. Jagat Babu repeated, 'Have I lived so long to see your despicable, immoral conduct? God, why have you punished me with a son who is a disgrace to the family? Scoundrel, you tormented a helpless innocent creature like her—'

Jagat Babu's voice choked with pain and he could not speak further. Unable to tolerate such false and unfair allegations, Charu became vocal. He said, 'I did not lead her astray, nor did I torment her. My fault was that I loved her.'

Jagat Babu said sharply, 'You loved her? It was because of you that she was driven out into the streets like a beggar. You ought to be ashamed of yourself.'

'She left of her own accord, not because of me. I was even prepared to marry her.'

Jagat Babu flared up from head to foot. Trembling with rage, he said, 'Be silent. Why didn't you go and hang yourself instead? You were prepared to marry her—a person you had looked upon as a sister! Only you are capable of making such a vile, sinful proposal. It is a sin even to hear about it.'

Charu fell silent. Jagat Babu drew a long breath and said, 'Have you understood now why she was compelled to leave this house and jump into the fire? If you have realized your fault, you should make amends for it and if you don't, I'll try to redress her wrongs.'

Charu replied, 'I am not unwilling to make amends if I committed a wrong unknowingly. I am ready to do anything to help her or make her happy. Tell me what I should do.'

Jagat Babu said, 'Nothing much. I am bequeathing half of my wealth and property to her. You sign the papers as a witness.'

Charu felt as though the sky had fallen on him. Even if he had wronged her in some way, it did not call for such a compensation. He took some time to regain his composure and then said, 'But how will all that wealth benefit her? It is enough for a single woman to get a monthly allowance. Parting with so much wealth will be a great loss to us.'

'So this is the love you were boasting about! You were ready to sacrifice everything for her and now you are so reluctant to part with the wealth which she would probably return to you in future.'

'She can give it to Jiban also.'

'Let her give it to whoever she pleases. Half of my wealth is hers.'

Jagat Babu took out a sheet of paper to write his statement. His pen moved swiftly, transferring his estate, his house and his wealth, and stabbing Charu's heart like a sharp knife. Charu had to endure this pain silently and helplessly, like a wounded snake. When the document was ready, Jagat Babu said to him, 'Listen to this and then sign it.'

Charu could not restrain himself any more. He had listened to all the accusations silently so far but a wave of hot rage swept over him and he said angrily. 'I will listen to you, but you listen to me first. You think that I am totally to blame and she was not at fault at all?'

'Keep quiet, you reprobate. Don't accuse her falsely out of greed. I disown you. I have given her half my estate so far. Now I shall give her everything.'

'If you want to give it, go ahead but you ought to know that she is no saint and I am not a devil either.'

'Hold your tongue. Even if the gods proclaimed her a sinner with a hundred tongues, I will not believe it.'

'Don't believe the gods but you will believe her own statement, won't you? See this letter, written to me by Sneha herself.'

Charu pulled out Sneha's letter, unfolded it, and dropped it on Jagat Babu's table. Jagat Babu turned pale like a corpse and shivered from head to foot. He had neither the desire nor the strength to read the letter, but he had to hide his weakness and determine what the truth was. For a while he sat motionless, holding his head in his hands. Then he gazed at the letter as though he was under a spell. Finally, he picked it up, turned it this way and that and put it down again. When he saw Charu getting impatient he pulled himself together and glanced at the letter cursorily though he could not read it till the end or comprehend its meaning. Only a few phrases stood out and captured his attention: 'My heart is burning with pain... you are dearer to this unfortunate creature than her life... you are everything to me—separation from you is like being in hell...'

Was it true then that Snehalata had declared her love to Charu and led him astray? Alas, how fickle and shallow human beings are! Just a few moments earlier, Jagat Babu had expressed his full confidence in Snehalata's innocence. However, this momentary doubt upset him so much that he cried out, 'No, no this is false. That chaste, self-denying widow would not declare her love for another man. This is a lie, a forged letter. She could never write like this.'

Somebody echoed his words from behind, 'It is not a lie. That sinful woman had indeed written the letter. It is all her fault.'

Startled, Jagat Babu turned around and saw Snehalata. She looked stunned, petrified like a corpse, her face ashen. Before Jagat Babu could get up from his chair, she collapsed on the floor like an uprooted creeper.

60

*W*as it an illusion or reality? Was it true that Snehalata was moving towards the realm of happiness and light? Would her lonely, empty, barren life become truly blessed with that ever-desired, life-giving glance—or was all that merely a mirage, a fantasy? Filled with apprehension and hope, Snehalata approached Jagat Babu's room on the second floor with trembling steps. Her limbs seemed to be charged with a current of delight and the sweet, familiar music of past memories echoed in her ears. At first, she could not recognize Charu's voice but it seemed to welcome her lovingly, inviting her to unite with him. In a moment Snehalata forgot her doubts and anxiety and was overcome with joy, the kind of joy which the individual soul experiences when it is dissolved in the divine soul, the kind of joy that sages aspire for but cannot achieve even after years of penance and which ordinary householders seldom experience even after accumulating great wealth. All her sadness vanished and she was immersed in an ocean of calm happiness, as she stood motionless like a picture.

This moment was followed by another. Charu's voice was heard no more. She was jolted out of her happy trance by Jagat Babu's angry voice, like a person who wakes up with a pounding heart from a beautiful dream by the sound of thunder. Her attention was directed towards Jagat Babu's words.

What was happening? To whom was Jagat Babu giving his wealth? Who was Charu blaming? Snehalata's head started spinning. When Charu said, 'Don't believe the gods but you will believe her own statement, won't you? See this letter written to me by Sneha herself,' everything became clear to her. She had suffered much in life but there is a limit to one's endurance. She had the same feeling as Caesar who yielded to the fatal blow of the enemy, saying '*et tu Brute*' and she lost her composure. Her heart was aflame and she suffered intolerable agony. The fire was destructive but it did not produce light but rather darkness, dense with smoke. Its dark flames pierced her head and heart, spread in all directions and engulfed her totally. Once again she had the vision of profound darkness she had seen before she was turned out of Jagat Babu's house. However, this time she did not see the spirits of the cremation ground, only the huge, dark figure of a woman stood blocking her view. It was the terrible figure of the goddess Kali who had appeared before her to show her compassion to her. But where was her lolling tongue, her garland of heads, her sharp dagger? Her huge body gradually became smaller and smaller and took the form of a black stone image. Snehalata remembered how she had seen it in childhood, in one of her troubled dreams. That day her face had a sneer; now there were tears of pity in her eyes as she beckoned to Snehalata to approach her. Snehalata obeyed her, as though in a spell, and murmured in a heart-rending tone, 'Mother, I cannot bear this pain any longer. Give me poison, give me death.'

The goddess replied, 'Not poison but nectar, not death but life. This will be the end of all your suffering. Open your mouth.'

As soon as Snehalata quenched her thirst by drinking the nectar offered to her and bowed her head in reverence and gratitude, the sorceress laughed aloud and vanished. Snapping out of her momentary spell of insanity, Snehalata found that she was standing alone in the room, facing the medicine shelves, with an empty bottle in her hand. Her head was reeling and her limbs were becoming numb. She put the bottle of poison away quickly and as she moved towards the inner chamber she heard Jagat Babu saying, 'It is a lie, a forged letter. She could never write like this.'

Snehalata remembered the incident of the past and called out, 'It is not a lie. That sinful woman had indeed written this letter. It is all her fault.'

Saying these words, Snehalata fell down unconscious. Jagat Babu came up to her, stroked her head affectionately and said, 'Get up my child. Everybody commits errors in such circumstances. There is no need to be ashamed about it. Get up. You are the Lakshmi[64] of my house. You are my Snehalata, my child. Don't ever leave this old man again.'

Snehalata was silent. Suddenly, her body started trembling, her eyes turned upwards and her face darkened. Jagat Babu felt her pulse anxiously but it had stopped. He realized that she had swallowed poison and there was no hope of her recovery. He cried out miserably, 'My child, did you come here only to bid me goodbye? Was that your plan? Could such a gentle creature be so cruel?'

Snehalata breathed her last, with her eyes fixed on his tearful face. Charu stood transfixed.

EPILOGUE

Snehalata is no more. Yet the world is carrying on happily as usual. So many Snehalatas die every day, still the world remains ever-smiling. Jagat Babu had resolved not to love anyone as much as he loved Sneha, but now Charu has a son and a daughter and he loves his grand-daughter in the same manner. To him Subala's smile seems to resemble Snehalata's. With Subala in his lap, his heart is filled with joy and once again he becomes the Jagat Babu of yesteryears. Yet, he has changed entirely in one respect. He can no longer tolerate any discussion on social reform. He is a proper conservative Hindu now. He believes that had Snehalata not been educated, she would have accepted her fate happily and not brought about her own downfall and death. He is convinced that it was shame and remorse which drove her to commit suicide. Hence, Jagat Babu is now wholeheartedly engaged in arresting the changing course of time.

AN APPEAL

Snehalata was written nearly eighteen years ago. After it appeared serially for two or three years in the journal *Bharati* it was published for the first time as a book in the year 1892. Still, if we examine the attitudes, the thinking and practices expressed through different facets of contemporary Bengali society, it is the same old picture of the days gone by. The novel presents an earlier version of the trends which continue in modern times, and the readers can see the connection between the present and the past, the close resemblance between the present-day conditions and their earlier manifestations. In short, if the new readers of *Snehalata*, on reading this book can perceive the continuing expression of the social attitudes, conventions and practices, the author's effort would be sufficiently rewarded.

MARCH 1911

NOTES

1. p. vii   The year of her birth cannot be stated with certainty. Sen and Bhattacharya (*Swarnakumari Debir Sankalita Prabandha*, Kolkata, Bikalpa Prakashan, 1998) mention it as 1855 or thereabouts, Tharu and Lalita (*Women Writing in India*, Delhi, Oxford University Press, 1991) have settled for 1856, and Das (*A History of Indian Literature*, Vol. VIII, Delhi, Sahitya Akademi, 1991) for 1857.

2. p. vii   The dates of the publication of her works have been computed from the Bengali calendar and therefore only approximate to the dates of the Christian calendar.

3. p. viii   *Naba Kahini* (short stories, 1877), *Chhinna Mukul* (novel, 1879), *Basanta Utsava* (opera, 1879), *Gatha* (tragic narrative poems, 1880), *Malati* (novel, 1881), *Prithibi* (scientific and informative essays about the earth, 1882), *Mewar Raj* (historical novel, 1889), *Bidroha* (historical novel, 1889), *Snehalata ba Palita* (novel, 1892), *Bibaha Utsava* (play, 1892), *Phuler Mala* (novel, 1894), *Kabita o Gaan* (poems, 1895), *Kahake* (novel, 1899), *Hooglir Imambara* (historical novel, 1901), *Kautuk Natya* (comedy, 1901), *Deb Kautuk* (poetic play, 1905), *Kone Badal* (comedy, 1906), *Pak Chakra* (comedy, 1912), *Raj Kanya* (novel, 1913), *Bichitra* (novel, n.d.), *Swapnabani* (novel, n.d.), *Milan Ratri* (novel, n.d.), *Bibidha Katha* (short stories, n.d.), *Dibya Kamal* (play, n.d.), *Juganta* (verse play, n.d.), and *Nibedita* (play, n.d.).

4. p. viii Rabindranath Tagore was against the publication of *An Unfinished Song*. According to him, Swarnakumari Debi's writings lacked authenicity as she had little expereince of the outside world (Chitra Deb: *Thakurbarir Andarmahal*, Kolkata, Ananda publishers, 1998 rpt. pp. 51–4). The unfairness of Tagore's judgement will be evident to the readers of *The Uprooted Vine*.

5. p. viii Pashupati Sasmal, *Swarnakumari O Bangla Sahitya*, Visva Bharati: Visva Bharati Research Publications, 1971, pp. 252–3.

6. p. xiv Rajul Sogani, *The Hindu Widow in Indian Literature* (New Delhi: Oxford, 2002) pp. 181–8.

DEDICATION

7. p. xv Swarnakumari Debi's name for her friend Girindra Mohini Debi, a Bengali poetess.

8. p. xv This seemingly obscure line refers to the names the friends gave to each other: *Viraha* (separation) and *Milan* (union).

9. p. xv *Sneha* means love in Bengali.

THE UPROOTED VINE: PART ONE

10. p. 4 Bou or Boudidi means brother's wife.

11. p. 5 Husband's sister.

12. p. 7 Kone means the bride-to-be.

13. p. 12 Mashima means mother's sister.

14. p. 12 Meshomoshai means uncle (mother's sister's husband)

15. p. 13 Lilavati was the daughter of the mathematician Bhaskaracharya.

16. p. 14 A term of endearment for a little girl, meaning old woman.

17. p. 14 Shashti or Durga who looks after the welfare of children, is worshipped by women in Bengal. She stands flanked by her children.

18. p. 14 A sweet made with semolina and milk.

19. p. 15 Deep-fried bread, popular in Bengal.

20. p. 15 A Bengali sweet.

21. p. 26 In English, in the original Bengali version.

22. p. 28 A black stone found in the river Gandaki and worshipped by Hindus as a representation of Vishnu.

23. p. 40 The italicized expressions are in English in the original.

24. p. 49 The Indian month corresponding to February–March.

25. p. 52 Husband's brother.

26. p. 54 *Phulsajja* (lit. bed of flowers) is the ceremony of the wedding night and *boubhat* (lit. feast for the bride) is the wedding reception at the house of the bridegroom.

27. p. 57 See Chapter 9. Kishori uses the word 'juxtaposition' to mean perplexity. It is a malapropism.

28. p. 62 The Indian month corresponding to March–April.

29. p. 63 The Indian month corresponding to April–May.

30. p. 63 Jamaibabu means sister's husband.

31. p. 64 A curved blade fixed on a wooden block, used in Bengali kitchens for cutting fish and vegetables.

32. p. 68 The day of Jamai Shashthi, the sixth day of the waxing moon in Jyaishta (May–June), is observed in honouring a son-in-law.

33. p. 69 Gifts sent to the house of the son-in-law.

34. p. 72 The eleventh day of a lunar fortnight, a day of fasting and prayers for many Hindus, especially widows in Bengal.

35. p. 76 Ishwarchandra Vidyasagar (1820–1891), educationist and social reformer.

36. p. 99 Sweets made of puffed rice.

37. p. 102 In English in the original.

38. p. 111 The Indian month corresponding to September–October.

39. p. 121 The Indian month corresponding to November–December.

40. p. 122 A ritual in which the bride and the groom see each other for the first time at the wedding.

41. p. 122 Signifying the announcement of the engagement.

42. p. 124 Women wear sindoor or vermilion powder in the parting of their hair to indicate their married status. They also place a vermilion dot on their forehead or between their eyebrows.

43. p. 127 The mound of rice paste considered auspicious and used in the marriage ritual.

44. p. 132 Young girls wake up the couple the morning after the wedding and do not let the bridegroom leave the chamber until he gives them money.

THE UPROOTED VINE: PART TWO

45. p. 138 The Ilbert Bill passed in 1883 during the viceroyalty of Lord Ripon amended the Criminal Procedure Code and specified that only European judges could try European offenders for serious misdemeanours.
46. p. 138 The Indian National Congress was founded in 1885.
47. p. 140 *Meghadoot* (The Cloud Messenger), a long love poem by Kalidasa.
48. p. 170 The Congress session was held in Madras in 1887.
49. p. 173 The Indian month corresponding to January–February.
50. p. 182 Small balls made of ground pulses, which are dried in the sun and used in various curries.
51. p. 183 Bread was taboo for conservative Hindus as the bakeries were run by non-Hindus.
52. p. 183 The water of the Ganga served to purify anyone who had broken a taboo by partaking of forbidden food.
53. p. 185 Suryamukhi and Kunda are characters in Bankim Chandra Chatterjee's novel *Vishavriksha*. Suryamukhi's husband Nagendranath falls in love with a young widow Kunda. When Suryamukhi finds the situation unbearable, she gives her consent to Nagendranath's marriage with Kunda, quietly leaves home, and becomes a wanderer.
54. p. 194 In the well-known story of Prahlad, who was tortured for his faith in God by his father Hiranyakashyapu, Vishnu took the form of a man-lion, tore apart Hiranyakashyapu's chest with his claws, and killed him.
55. p. 197 Lines from *The Lover's Resolution* by George Wither (1588–1667).
56. p. 197 The general who fought on behalf of the demons Shumbha and Nishumbha who were killed by the goddess Durga symbolizing a race which cannot be exterminated.
57. p. 198 Italicized sentences are in English in the original Bengali version.